Dealing with Privilege

Dealing with Privilege

Cannabis, Cocaine, and the Economic Foundations of Suburban Drug Culture

David Crawford

LEXINGTON BOOKS
Lanham • Boulder • New York • London

Published by Lexington Books
An imprint of The Rowman & Littlefield Publishing Group, Inc.
4501 Forbes Boulevard, Suite 200, Lanham, Maryland 20706
www.rowman.com

6 Tinworth Street, London SE11 5AL

Chapter 2 is reprinted with permission. Crawford, Dave. "Suburban Drug Dealing: A Case Study in Ambivalent Economics." In The Economics of Ecology, Exchange, and Adaptation: Anthropological Explorations, edited by Donald C. Wood, 197–219. Emerald Insight, 2016.

The featured epigraph is reprinted with permission. Epigraph from "The Cerebral Savage: On the Work of Claude Levi-Strauss" which was published in *Encounter*, Vol. 28, No. 4 (April 1967): 25-32 by Clifford Geertz.

British Library Cataloguing in Publication Information Available

Library of Congress Cataloging-in-Publication Data Available
ISBN: 978-1-4985-9816-3 (cloth)
ISBN: 978-1-4985-9817-0 (electronic)

"All ethnography is part philosophy,
and a good deal of the rest is confession."
—Clifford Geertz (1967:25)

Contents

Acknowledgments

This book owes its existence to the many people who spoke with me about their bad behavior, and especially the select group who let me ask direct questions about it and tape their answers. I cannot thank any of you by name, but I am deeply grateful.

As for other help, Laura Whitman read an atrocious early draft and provided a sensible reframe of the project. If the book is readable now, much credit goes to her red pen. John Ibson, Sonya Huber, Terry Ann Jones, and Emily Orlando provided helpful feedback on sections of this revised approach. Alistair Highet, Anita Deeg-Carlin, Ramon Guardans, and Bob Epstein read subsequent whole drafts and contributed further structural improvements, and the inspiration to keep working. The anonymous peer review solicited by the press was positive and provocative, so a thank you is due here too.

Kristin Dalli assisted with many technical details that are beyond my capacity, and I deeply appreciate of the College of Arts and Sciences Publication Fund at Fairfield University for help with the professional index. I also received assistance, advice, and inspiration of various sorts from Scott Lacy, Michelle Phillips, Daniel Keller, Rose Rodrigues, Paul Silverstein, Dan Jones, Rachelle Brunn-Bevel, Melissa Hannequin, Clare McElaney, Dennis Keenan, and Mike Andreychik. As always, Hillary Haldane kept me positive when I was inclined otherwise, and our kids Lu and Calum filled our lives with love and laughter. I only wish that Gisela Gil-Egui and José Labrador could have been here to see this book finished; we miss them every day.

The errors, ambiguities, and omissions that remain are mine, and were beyond the power of my friends and colleagues to fix.

Introduction

This is a book about drug dealing in the American suburbs. It draws mainly on taped, formal interviews with nine dealers, and less formal input from their friends, family, and others who knew them.[1] Most of the people in this book retired a long time ago.[2] None of them ever spent any serious time in jail, and none of them experienced any violence related to their drug business, with, as we will see, one notable exception.[3] All of the dealers sold marijuana, most sold cocaine, and some dealt in hallucinogens and other substances. The two drugs that end up being the most important for our story are cannabis (because it is ubiquitous in the U.S. suburbs) and cocaine (because it was immensely popular in the 1980s, when most of these dealers were working). While many psychoactive substances have entertained Americans over the last forty years, and new ones emerge all the time, marijuana and cocaine are the most important drugs for exploring the cultural and economic origins of drug dealing in the suburbs.

While this is not a memoir, my interest in the topic is personal.[4] I made my first drug deal in 1979, freshman year of high school, in unlovely Garden Grove, California. It seemed commonplace, on one level, and thrilling on another. Now, four decades later, as a mostly sober father of two teenagers, I am trying to make sense of what happened. The answer, I think, is that my generation is responsible for consolidating a suburban drug culture that is still with us.[5]

Looking back, one striking thing is the risk. The penalties for drug sales were draconian in those bad old days, absolutely terrifying. You could go to real prison for small amounts of dope, even now-legal substances like pot.[6] Starting in 1961, "Simple possession of any amount of marijuana [would draw] a minimum 1–10 years in prison, with no parole until a year had been served. . . . Sale of marijuana [would be] punished by a mandatory five . . . years to life, with no possibility of parole until three years had been served."[7] We did not seem to care. I don't think we noticed. One reason is that young people—and young men in particular—lack the ability to accurately assess risk, or even perceive it.[8] I suppose I was no exception to this rule. But obliviousness cannot be the whole answer.

In fact, there was not as much risk as it might seem. Despite the prison population beginning its stratospheric rise in the 1970s,[9] nobody I knew ever ended up in the slammer, or even came very close. Nor did the people in this book, most of whom I did not know thirty or forty years ago. As is clear from sociological and criminological studies, when it comes to drug prosecutions there are two Americas: one for the poor (and urban, often black or brown) and another for white, educated kids of at least modest means.[10] In our spectacular naughtiness we middle-class boys somehow grasped this reality.[11] We had "white privilege" and "class privilege," though we did not know the terms. Eventually America would imprison a higher percentage of its population than almost anywhere else in the world, almost entirely from drug crimes. But this never registered as a crisis among dealers in the white suburbs, and for some pretty obvious reasons. I began this book because I was interested in the economics of drug dealing,[12] but the story turns on the operation of privilege in America. This is the inevitable backdrop to a project like this. Privilege indemnifies stupidity, luckily for me.[13]

Even more remarkable than the risk is the fact that I very much *wanted* to make that first deal long before I actually did.[14] It was a deliberate choice, a move to establish a specific type of masculine identity. As a young man, I aspired to sell drugs, which necessarily means that there was a drug culture in place already, that it was understood to relate to masculinity, and was available for my aspirations. I didn't invent it. I just wanted to be part of what was already going on. Now, to claim that there was a drug culture in Southern California in the 1970s is hardly controversial, but what does that mean?[15] In this book I use the term *culture* for the taken-for-granted norms and values associated with illegal drugs, the understood techniques and appropriate language to ingesting them, the way that embodying these norms and values works as a social tool, a way to render oneself legible as a member of a group. That's what I wanted when I was fifteen. And even though chemical reactions happen in individual brains, understanding the sensations generated is both learned and shared, and is therefore cultural.[16]

For me, at that time, America seemed at war with itself and I needed a side to be on. Nixon had dissolved patriotic naïveté with the criminal mess at the Watergate Hotel ("the President lied" is how my father explained it to me). The Hell's Angels beat groovy anarchism to death at Altamont, along with a fan of the Rolling Stones. And in the Hollywood Hills free love was slaughtered and the blood wiped everywhere by Charles Manson's lunatic family—all high on drugs, from what the TV said. Peace, love, racial harmony, and progressive politics were *not* the inevitable offspring of drug use. That was obvious. The "counter" part of counterculture remained, the general "fuck you" attitude, but hippie-happiness had passed into nostalgia for us teens in the late 1970s.[17]

The meaning of drugs was in flux. Marijuana, Kent State, LSD, Vietnam, Black Power, Summer-of-Love, Franz Fanon, *Fear of Flying*, *Fear and Loathing*, *Naked Lunch*, the Weathermen, Ken Kesey . . . it all churned in my anxious boy-mind, pressurized, about to blow. Our nation convulsed, but why? For what? What side was there to join? Drugs as a political project were dead ("turn on, tune in, drop out" was for old people). All that remained was the dope. By the late 1970s disco and punk fought with "classic" rock for our tribal loyalty, but all music was soaked in drugs, even pop (David Cassidy!) and country-western (Jonny Cash!). Altered consciousness was not a path to political revolution, or even social transformation, just a way to hang out. New psychoactive compounds arrived from the margins and seeped into suburban bodies like the martinis and cigarettes of the previous generation. Ronald Reagan would return us to sensible haircuts and avuncular authority in 1981, but this had no effect on the drugs. They were here to stay. "The emergent drug cultures of the 1970s proved far more accommodating [than the 60s' counterculture] to the mainstream of American capitalism."[18] And so they endure.

The origins of what I am calling "suburban dealing" are in the 1970s, as illegal drugs moved from the "counter culture" to the American mainstream, but this was hardly America's first dance with dope. Cannabis had long been popular with certain groups, like agricultural workers or jazz musicians, and the first U.S. cocaine epidemic occurred way back in the 1890s.[19] Beverages infused with coca—the plant from which we get cocaine—were fashionable, and even considered medicinal, from the middle of the nineteenth century through the first part of the twentieth. By the dawn of the twentieth century cocaine was among the top five pharmaceutical products in the United States, and it was hardly only medicinal.[20] Vin Mariani, for instance, the leading brand of coca-infused wine, was lauded by actors, writers, politicians, and even the Pope. By 1900 the catalog from Sears, Roebuck, and Co. featured a "Drug Department." It was one of the first sections—after "Groceries," before "Veterinary Supplies." The offerings go on for pages, and generally promise cures without listing ingredients. The first four advertised compounds take up most of a page, and are "Tobacco to the Dogs" (to stop smoking), "Somon" (for sleeplessness), the "50-Cent Liquor Cure" (to curb excessive drinking), and "Reliable," which promises a "cure for the opium and morphia habit." The "Reliable" label assures us that "no poisonous narcotics" are in the bottle, which would seem important because it was meant to get people to stop abusing poisonous narcotics. Opioids were a significant enough component of the general pharmacopeia that their *absence* was worth mentioning. This whole chemical smorgasbord—and the additional elixirs to get you off of the drugs—was available cash-on-delivery through the U.S. postal service to every house and hamlet in the nation.

So drugs have long been popular in the USA. What changed recently is the ways drugs get to customers, and the meaning they have in the culture—two things that are intimately related. Originally Americans could procure drugs as they would any other commodity, but as the twentieth century staggered forward laws became more restrictive. Even beer was banned during Prohibition between 1920 and 1933. Of course, legal changes do not necessarily have the intended impact and as laws tightened Americans turned to the informal economy for substances they could no longer buy legally or get a doctor to prescribe.[21] In urban areas there were established zones for such contacts, the "bad part of town" or the "wrong side of the tracks," generally poorer communities where policing was lax.[22] But then, only a few decades before the Internet opened a pipeline of pornography into tidy suburban lives, the counterculture brought powerful psychoactive substances into outlying schools, homes, and hangouts. There were new drugs, and new ways of getting them. Middle class white people were set to become the nation's best customers.[23]

Suburban dealing works differently than the urban kind, as we will see, and this transformation of the commodity chain had significant consequences. Not least of these is the way "Americans ingesting lots of drugs" morphed into a more elaborated "drug culture." While our media and politicians remain fixated on cartels and gangs, and on flagrant, street-corner dealing, the boring reality is that most Americans get their dope from people exactly like them: everyday suburbanites. Such deals happen indoors, out of sight. They happen among "small groups of loosely linked entrepreneurs rather than large, highly structured criminal syndicates."[24] And these networks form the economic basis of today's middle-class drug culture. That's the primary thing we explore in this book, through the words of the dealers themselves. The underlying premise is that changing economic behavior is intertwined with changes in culture, but we will also see that the economics of suburban dealing illuminates some stark problems in conventional economic theory more generally.[25]

Consider the mundane logistics of my first deal: I got a quarter ounce of hashish from a friend of a friend for $50. Grams went for $10 so I figured the seven grams represented a potential $20 profit. I got my package at school, a fragrant clod like a small, dried turd. I did not have a scale to weigh it, so I asked a different friend to help (he had stolen a triple beam from the biology lab, which must be where 90 percent of drug scales came from). At this friend's house it turned out that my ostensibly seven-gram quarter-ounce was really about 6.5. I gave the friend with the scale most of the .5 to thank him and I divided the rest with a razor into six one-gram pieces. But I actually made them .9 each so as to get myself 6/10ths of a gram for personal use. I felt bad about this, dishonest, but I knew that nobody would weigh an individual, retail gram and my profit margin was slim. I took my personal stash over to visit the original friend who had set up the deal. We smoked part of it and I gave him the rest in appreciation for setting everything up, though I suspected the missing half gram had gone to him. In any case, I was down to six grams. My girlfriend wanted one for herself and one for her friend Gina, so I gave my girlfriend two. Eventually Gina paid me for hers, but not quickly, and of course no girl ever pays her boyfriend for drugs, so that gram was gone. A guy from my swim team wanted two grams, which I gave him, but we ended up smoking most of it together, so I couldn't really charge him full price. I think I got $15 from him. A kid in math class wanted one, so that was $10.

I could not find a buyer for the last gram and the weekend came around and we were all "partying" in my friend's garage.[26] He had a musty, old couch and some twinkly Christmas lights set up. It was our unofficial clubhouse. Our parents were asleep so we decided to go see the Led Zeppelin movie, *The Song Remains the Same,* at midnight. My friends were older, and one had a car, so I provided the dope and they drove. They also drank beer, which they stole from one kid's dad. I didn't drink, but the driver was exuberantly puffing hash while chasing codeine pills with swigs of Schaefer (or something cheap) from squat, brown bottles. This caught up with him. He could not effectively walk out of the movie when it finally ended and the mall police were called to inspect his mumbling body on the lobby floor. The cops were scary, but nothing came of it. They let us leave after calling the loaded kid's parents from a payphone. They confirmed that the codeine was prescribed to him from an accident he had suffered. While my prone friend had the car, he obviously couldn't drive it. Being relatively sober, or at least not drunk, I was elected to convey us all home. It was 3 a.m. and all I had to do was keep the car between the white lines of our deserted suburban streets. So despite being fifteen years old and lacking a license, I got us safely to where we needed to be. As a parent, I know, this sounds nightmarish. As a young man it was heavenly.

Still, my initial foray into dealing *cost* me $15, a huge chunk of my investment capital. This seems pretty stupid from an economic perspective, especially because my jobs delivering papers, cleaning pools, and making donuts paid minimum wage at most (about three bucks an hour). But I used my 6.5 grams of hash to become better friends with a guy on my swim team, to initiate a relationship with another guy in math, to make my girlfriend happy and improve her standing with her friend (and my own standing with her friend, which was a plus). Even better, I got to see a movie with older kids—at midnight!—and I drove a car for the first time. What is difficult to untangle from my current perspective is the mixture of bliss and banality all this involved in 1979. Drug dealing came with a lifestyle, a community, a way to be social in the world that was at least partly economically self-sustaining. The business, if we want to think of it that way, can only be understood if we attend to the calculating (my grams that were not full-weight, but were designed to appear that way) and the friendship (nearly all of my "profit" was cheerfully given away). Suburban drug dealing combines self-interest and sociality, calculation and altruism, in ways that are not commonly discussed in economics textbooks.[27]

The suburban dealing in this book refers not to the physical location of sales but to the way in which they are done. *Suburban dealing* precludes anonymous transactions and operates entirely through "friendship networks of user-dealers."[28] Some retail dealers in urban areas restrict their business to trusted associates, sell safely indoors, or only deliver to private residences.[29] However, such dealers necessarily compete with other urbanites who benefit from riskier, more profitable, street-level transactions. Street-level transactions draw anonymous people into commercial relations, like most market interactions in capitalist societies. This is the central genius of markets, after all, and the basis of capitalism itself. Imagine trying to sell hamburgers or houses *only* to people you happen to know and trust.[30] This is the challenge that suburban dealers face, and the reason that street level dealing, where possible, is more lucrative but also more dangerous. Drug policy expert Mark Kleiman refers to this distinction as "discreet" versus "flagrant" dealing, but he means more or less the same thing as my suburban / urban distinction.[31] The important element is the presence or absence of anonymity. Lack of anonymity changes everything in economics, and in human behavior more generally.[32]

In these terms, suburban (or "discreet") dealing is beset with "transaction costs."[33] This means you must cultivate the social relations that sustain the sales, build the networks of people to buy from and sell to.[34] This takes time and effort. Much hanging around is called for, "partying," time spent doing things together (often doing drugs together) and developing trust.[35] Legitimate businessmen do this too, of course, from the three-cocktail lunch or the private booth at a sporting event to the round of golf on Saturday with the boss. But it is much less dangerous to invite new people to your golf club than to your dope transaction. Inviting someone out for a drink is less risky than offering him a line of cocaine. But sharing danger builds trust, trust builds friendships, so drug connections build high risk/high reward social networks.[36] So when Levitt and Dubner claim in their book *Freakonomics* that "a crack gang works pretty much like the standard capitalist enterprise," they can only mean the part of the gang that undertakes anonymous, street-level sales.[37] They cannot possibly be talking about the way most drugs are sold in America.[38]

By "suburban," then, what we mean is the distinct situation in which transactions are *only* possible through networks of kin and friends, networks that must be patiently nurtured. Suburban drug dealing is in this sense deeply embedded in its social context.[39] The logic of transactions in such a milieu is very different from the more purely calculative reason necessary for anonymous sales—of illegal drugs or any other commodity. After all, calculating profit and loss in the legal economy is relatively easy. Calculating the price you might demand for an ounce of cocaine that your sister's fiancé's best man wants to pick up at her wedding—or even whether to sell to him, since selling drugs at her wedding might upset your sister—*that* is a great deal more challenging. It is challenging precisely because it represents an element of the human economy,[40] the way actual known and knowable people transact stuff as opposed to exchange conducted by the atomized monads of conventional economic theory.[41]

By the late 1970s, when the stories in this book emerge, LSD remained popular in the suburbs, but no longer promised transcendence (only a day-long high); magic mushrooms were a "natural" alternative. Pills were swallowed insouciantly (amphetamines and Quaaludes most often, not many opioids yet) and pot was everywhere, even in junior high school hallways. Kids smoked joints openly while walking to school (at least at my Southern California school), and geeky punks like me spent years on the fringes of the pungent clouds only hoping to be hip some-day. Heroin, PCP, and methamphetamine were present, though not very widespread. The rural meth crisis and today's spectacular pills-to-heroin (and more recently fentanyl) tragedy were still far over the horizon.[42] I cannot confidently say what percentage of the kids at my high school were buying, selling, or using drugs. I can say that I didn't know anyone who was *not* doing these things.

By the 1980s the real action was cocaine. The champagne of illicit drugs, expensive, erotic, not yet for sale in the dismal markets of the school bathroom: it was "non-addictive," "Vitamin C," the "rich man's aspirin," a sexy "chick magnet" and crystalline symbol of a land beyond suburban boredom. Fashionable people in movies wore coke spoons on gold chains to show how cool they were. "Coke adds life" was un-ironi-cally splashed across billboards. It seemed everywhere and yet hard to get.

As others have pointed out, cocaine was an ideal high for a 1960s generation giving up ritualized rebellion for real jobs.[43] It was, after all, a drug you could ingest at work, and one that required a good job to afford. Coke facilitated what we might borrow two French words to call *faux outré*, a way of being rebellious while drawing a salary. Few people could do that high on heroin or LSD. In other words, cocaine melded rebellion, conformity, and high-class consumerism into bright, white lines on a mirror (or on a desk or on the toilet paper cabinet in the bathroom stall). It did not take long for basketball player Len Bias to die of a coke-induced heart attack (in 1986), and crack use to explode among the urban poor.[44] Thereafter cocaine became something dirty and dan-gerous again, like it had been after our nation's previous cocaine scares.[45] But for a weird cultural moment, cocaine was queen.[46] The core of the drug dealers in this book lived through this time. The rest grew up in its shadow.

WHAT IS A DRUG DEALER?

To understand dealing in a context wider than my own experience I decided to track down former dealers, interview them, and hear how they managed their "careers in dope."[47] I started with social media, and some of the people I knew in high school, but through their suggestions and other contacts I ended up with a much broader array.[48] Nine people agreed to talk on tape and I did at least one long interview each. I sometimes spoke to them multiple times over the course of days, and I spent at least some time informally socializing with all of them (and sometimes quite a lot of time).[49] I was particularly interested in why dealers went into business (it was not simply to make money), how they conducted business (several different ways, I discovered), and why they quit (few of them suffered any legal consequences, so that was not the answer to the last question).[50] At first, however, some denied that they had been dealers at all. Since I only interviewed people who admitted that they had sold illegal drugs, this was confusing. People willingly spoke with me about their drug sales, but did not consider themselves to have been "drug dealers," even a few who sold pretty significant quantities and made quite a lot of money. Why?

It seems an issue of self-image. Whites do not recognize themselves as drug *dealers* even when they are dealing drugs. There are fairly sensible reasons for this, both scholarly and more popular. For one thing, the vast majority of research on drug dealing has focused on poor communities and the people who have been arrested in them. A disproportionate number of such people are black or Hispanic. The folks who get caught and prosecuted are the objects of most drug research, and they look nothing like my friends from high school, or most of the people in this book.[51]

Probably more importantly, white invisibility in drug dealing is sustained by what we see in the media, especially police dramas in films or TV.[52] It is an easy plot device to code bad, violent guys as drug dealers. Greed—and the violence attending it—is portrayed as the essence of dealing, with addiction acting as both the spur to the industry and the downfall of the dealers. Shows like *The Wire* update the stereotype somewhat, and depict dealers relatively humanely, but here still the business is mostly something black people do, and most of them are presented as bad, or as victims, or as people who are bad because the only other option is to be a victim. A series like *Narcos* shines light into the other side of the business, the production and trans-shipment end, but little of this matters to the operations of suburban dealing (and anyway, few suburbanites identify with Pablo Escobar). Invariably, the bad hombres who sell drugs—the ones in prison, in sociological studies, and the ones on TV—have skin many shades darker than the average American drug consumer or dealer. Suburban dealers do not fit our cultural profile. They are not black, or brown, or dangerous; they are not ruthless, addicted, or victims of circumstance. They are, like I was, deliberately entering the "business" on their own terms to fulfill needs only marginally economic. It is hard to frame them—and hard for them to see themselves—as desperate monsters or unwitting dupes.[53]

To be fair, Hollywood has tried to capture suburban dealing, usually quasi-humorously as in *Pineapple Express* or *Weeds*. *Weeds* in particular made a good start, but it does not take many episodes for the main characters to fall in with dangerous (read: brown) dealers, and subsequent scenes swirl with weapons and threats. Or *Breaking Bad*. The series starts convincingly (albeit with a desperate man making poor decisions for financial reasons, which is not how most dealing starts) but the business almost instantly turns ruthless and violent. It seems that we cannot contemplate drug sales without relying on images of violence, addiction, and despair.[54]

By contrast, in my own limited career, I rarely dealt with a black person or Latinos. I never saw a gun (except once), and in general I never knew a dealer who had one (the gun I saw was in the hands of a customer gone nuts over a girlfriend). I bought drugs from my friends and sold to friends—just like everybody else I knew. Almost all of us were white and middle class, though for the book I interviewed a few people who worked the seams between the poor and the middle class or between the middle class and elites. Fundamentally the type of enterprise I am calling "suburban" means everyone either knew who he was dealing with or knew someone who did, but also that sales were as much a social event as a business transaction. Fair play was ensured by simple decency or the threat of a tarnished reputation. When people misbehaved, as they sometimes did, gossip could quickly put them out of business, unable to buy or sell. In the suburbs illegal transactions happen within a dense social context, reputation is everything, and relationships are fundamental to the way substances change hands. Much of this is true in dealing more generally. But in the suburbs every sale is *both* an economic act presumed to be selfish *and* an expression of interest, friendship, or solidarity. This upends the typical economic way of understanding behavior and any brute notion of "self-interest." And it makes such dealing hard to study, hard to bust, and, unfortunately for us parents, almost impossible to eradicate.

In fact, the illegality of the market was precisely what made it possible for someone like me to be involved.[55] I did not have to compete with legitimate, better-capitalized businesses run by adults. I did not have to negotiate with cartels or gangs or stand on street corners and expose myself to the dangers of selling to strangers. Perhaps most importantly, I did not have to try and sell dope for lower prices than the people who did stand on corners. In my suburbs the only choice for young people to be part of the drug culture was to buy from other kids (like me) or drive into the city. Few took the second option, if for no other reason than few of us could drive. Anyway, cities were scary and full of dangerous people. There was, in other words, no easy way for urban dealing networks to directly reach middle class suburbanites. They needed *entrepôts*, which is essentially the job of the people in this book. Such middlemen used their position to have more fun for less money than they otherwise might, and to be the sort of young men that their peers valued—strategically and selfishly, for sure, but also for reasons that extended far beyond material benefit.

Thus, in terms of basic business practice, I was a bad drug dealer.[56] I lost money. But this is to misunderstand the motives and behavior of these sorts of dealers, and the possibilities opened for them by the illegal nature of drug sales.[57] What drugs did for me—freshman year and a while after—was to make me relevant in my social world. Drugs were a reason to call me up, to stay in touch, to bring me along. I had something to contribute, something people wanted. Ergo, *I was wanted*. In a drug culture having drugs is vital to having an identity, to the very possibility of being a comprehensible human amongst others. Having good drugs, and cheap drugs, made you that much more estimable and interesting.

Drug sales and ingestion are key ways to initiate, catalyze, and solidify friendships. This intimate interplay of identity, sociality, and economics gave rise to a specific kind of drug culture in the late 1960s and early 1970s. As near as I can tell the patterns established are still in place today, and are how the latest illicit chemicals are doing their (frightening) work on today's youth.[58] Cultures perdure longer than the people who comprise them, and they are not easy to deliberately change. Even when individuals grow up and get sober, as most people in this book have, even when the drugs have changed and the music has become unlistenable, the established mode of transacting dope in the suburbs continues. *That* song has remained the same. And it cannot be understood using conventional economic theory.[59]

PLAN OF THE BOOK

The first chapter after this is about the materiality of cocaine and cannabis. While chemistry is not destiny, the practices that form around drug use, and the way drugs are bought and sold, have something to do with the chemical composition of the drugs. For instance, cocaine renders people talkative, agitated, and it wears off quickly. This impacts what people do when they ingest it (they do not take naps or practice yoga), and it patterns the way commercial transactions happen (lots of repetitive sales to people trying to stay high). So we begin here, with the substances. While the dealers in this book traded in everything from heroin to psilocybin, ketamine to crystal methamphetamine, by far the most dominant drugs in our account are cannabis and cocaine. This first chapter explains the history of these two drugs and something of the way they impact human brains. It also delves into what I mean by "culture," since I am making the case that drug dealing is a cultural phenomenon.

The next chapter is called *Cities and Suburbs* and focuses on the economic context of the suburbs. It contrasts two dealing models through interviews with José and Doug. José sold marijuana in what I call the suburban way, but he also worked as a crack vendor on street corners in Bridgeport, Connecticut, in the anonymous, urban style. Doug, who is white and from the suburbs, sold mountains of powder cocaine, all behind closed doors. Neither narrative ends very happily, but the contrast between them illustrates the limited social possibilities for men of color[60] selling crack in the urban way versus white men selling powder cocaine. The point of this chapter is to establish what I mean by "suburban" dealing, and to give a sense of how it contrasts with what we tend to imagine as "drug dealing" more generally. Today José is an electrician, happily married and raising two children in a home he owns himself. Doug is a divorced construction worker and recovering alcoholic.

After this we have *Dealing with Privilege*, the story of Brad. Brad went to an elite, East Coast prep school. He sold nearly everything under the sun, and huge amounts of it, and by his telling he ingested formidable quantities, too. It was a wild career, begun when he was about fourteen and done by the middle of college. Today he is a pediatrician, a husband, and a dad. Extending the lessons Doug introduced, Brad shows just how advantageous it can be to have access to good schools, forgiving authority figures, and moneyed customers as friends.

Following this is *Ambivalent Economics*, where we juxtapose Wayne, a businessman from an agricultural state, and Arthur, a banker who lives near the beach in Southern California. Wayne is a strident Republican; Art is a Democrat. Wayne begins by explaining that selling drugs is the same as every other business, but he ends up showing the many ways it is not. Arthur begins by saying that he never was a drug dealer—since he had no intention of making money—but moves on to admit that he in fact made significant amounts. What I take from the contrast between Wayne and Arthur is that trying to transact commodities among friends confounds American models of proper behavior—even opposing models of proper behavior. Neither Wayne's framing of his dealing as a rational business decision, nor Arthur's denial of economic interest in his behavior, manages to capture what happened when they were dealing.[61] This represents a main theme of the book.

Our next chapter is *Ambivalence Revisited: Drugs, Money and Manliness*. We briefly return to Wayne, who talks about how cocaine created possibilities for sex. We then meet Woody, from Colorado, who explains how drug dealing is different when done out of a bar rather than an apartment, and from this he gives another perspective on cocaine's role in romance and dating. Pete, the final person we meet in this chapter, relates even more graphically how masculinity, sexuality, money, and cocaine were interlinked in his era. There is much in Pete's interview about how it is the money—not the drugs—that creates both potential and problems, but cocaine itself does become a problem for Pete. Throughout our discussions he castigates himself as a bad businessman and inadequate man for his failure to capitalize on the opportunities that drug dealing presented.

After moving to another state, Pete turns to growing marijuana, which is the subject of the next chapter, *The Culture of Cultivation.* This features Pete, of course, and his explanation of why growing cannabis is a different sort of business than selling cocaine. While both activities were illegal at the time of our interviews, selling a commodity and producing one for sale turn out to be significantly different in terms of the practices involved and the personality traits that fit with them. I also interview Mary, an indoor grower in Northern California and the only woman in the study. Both Pete and Mary are politically conservative and their ideologies map on to their explanations of their illegal businesses in fascinating ways. Pete and Mary have other jobs, but marijuana growing has become part of their self-cultivation, their identities.

The final two sections deal with quitting drugs, and especially cocaine, first from the vantage of lifecycle changes, and second from a broader, more cultural perspective. *Ambivalence Renounced* returns to Woody, who sold out of the bar, and we meet Simon. Woody explains how marriage and having a child—just "getting old," in his terms—inspired him to stop selling drugs. Simon is much younger, only in his mid-twenties at the time of our interview. He explains why he never sold cocaine in the first place, why he focused on drugs that he found to be morally acceptable, especially cannabis, and why he was done dealing by the time he was twenty-four—when some of the men we have met were just getting serious about the business. Perhaps what is most striking in this section is that drug dealing is one choice among others for middle class whites. When they want to quit, they do . . . *because they can.*[62]

The penultimate chapter is *The Rise and Demise of Cocaine Culture.* Here we return to elements of all the interviews to examine how the culture of cocaine worked, and how it changed. Cocaine moved from being unproblematic and seemingly ubiquitous (in the era of Doug and Wayne and Art) to something avoided even by drug dealers (by the time of the much younger Brad and Simon). Everyone seems to grow out of cocaine, or at least everyone who manages to avoid death, addiction, or jail. But the entire culture shifted, too. This is one lesson we take from looking at "successful" drug dealers,[63] by which we mean the majority who do not become entangled with the criminal justice system: most people tire of drug culture no matter the dictates of the dominant society or its legal system. It seems that some drugs, at least, are a young man's game.

There is an afterword to all this, *In the Shadow of the Sixties*, where I ponder the "why does it work this way?" question. I do not believe there are easy answers, but I look for help to neuroscience, economic anthropology, and especially the classic sociology of Marcel Mauss's seminal essay *The Gift* (1950). Dealing provides a platform for socialization and the establishment of a specifically masculine identity, and this plays an important part in the reproduction of a drug culture. The economics cannot be understood without the culture. And while the illegality of the substances is not in itself the cause of our heartaches, it is clearly part of the way drug culture endures. The ambivalent economics of dealing drugs brings people together. Such socially generative economic transactions, combined with the general American penchant for pharmacological recreation, suggests that conditions are not hopeful for curbing drug culture. Finally, I will argue that the ambivalence inherent to drug dealing reveals important lessons about how humans produce and reproduce their world, lessons obscured by conventional analysis.

I have to say that it is hard to find the right tone for a book like this. Drugs have harmed many people and savaged communities.[64] In speaking with people about this project I am often presented with personal trauma that drugs have caused, stories of pain and loss, the waste of human lives and time, the degradation and death of loved ones. The current opioid crisis is especially productive of human misery, even compared to the methamphetamine and cocaine epidemics that preceded it.[65] Sometimes people assume that misery is what I'm writing about, and they look stricken when I admit that this is not my topic. But it is not.

The destructive capacity of mind-altering drugs is awful, well-documented, and while we might need another book on that (or film or TV series), the present one is not it. Instead I am aiming to reveal something else: the crazy *normalcy* of drug dealing in the American suburbs, the story of the vast majority of drug dealers who are never caught, never imprisoned, never sent to rehabilitation, and who therefore do not commonly find their way into criminological or sociological studies. It is about the ways in which drug dealing is socially productive, the way exchanging substances can be a platform for personal identity formation and group cohesion.[66] I will not defend anyone's bad behavior, or argue for or against legalizing particular drugs. Instead, I want to explain where we are and how we got here. Drug culture has penetrated deeply into American life—white, middle-class life. We need to understand it better. The interviews herein hardly complete such a task, but offer a starting point, a framework for grasping this enduring and peculiar feature of our contemporary world.[67]

NOTES

1. All subjects were protected by a Certificate of Confidentiality issued by the National Institute of Drug Abuse (NIDA). All names and some other identifying characteristics have been changed. See Frank on "why study people's stories" and the relationship of "authenticity," truth, and democratic politics (2002:109).

2. On "retirement" from dealing see Waldorf and Biernacki (1981) in Page and Singer (2010:63).

3. There is no denying that violence sometimes accompanies the drug trade, and scholars seem confident in assuming that this violence emerges from lack of state oversight of the market. Jacques and Allen, for instance, write, "The virtual anarchy that characterizes illicit drug markets increases violence among persons involved therein" (2014:90). Suburban dealing is not violent, but it is anarchic in the sense that the state is absent. The mistake is to assume that the lack of state surveillance leads to violence. See Graeber (2004) for a review of the relationship between anthropology and anarchy.

4. I rely on Becker (2007) for permission to stray from social scientific rhetorical orthodoxy. See also Maher on the virtues of "combining ethnography with autobiography" (2002:311), and Geertz's quote above about ethnography and "confession" (1967:25).

5. This notion of a "drug culture" is longstanding (Langer 1977), and we will have more to say about what exactly this means below.

6. See Bonnie and Whitebread (1970) for a thorough, if now dated, review of American marijuana prohibition.

7. Schaffer Library of Drug Policy, "A Fiscal Analysis of Marijuana Decriminalization," DrugLibrary.org, accessed June 4, 2018, http://druglibrary.org/schaffer/hemp/moscone/chap1.htm.

8. I am not suggesting that girls necessarily perceive risk better, or that they do not take risks. It does seem clear that risk operates differently for girls and boys. See Cepeda and Valdez (2003), Dunlap et al. (1994), Fitzgerald (2009), Friedman et al. (2003), and Sterk (1999).

9. Gupta writes, "The war on drugs has been a war on communities of color. The racial disparities are staggering: despite the fact that whites engage in drug offenses at a higher rate than African-Americans, African-Americans are incarcerated for drug offenses at a rate that is 10 times greater than that of whites" (2011). As Alexander points out, "between 1980 and 2000 the number of people incarcerated in our nation's prisons and jails soared from roughly 300,000 to more than 2 million. By the end of 2007, more than 7 million Americans . . . were behind bars, on probation, or on parole." And clearly, "Convictions for drug offenses are the single most important cause of the explosion in incarceration rates in the United States" (2012:60). Racial disparities extend beyond the criminal justice system, obviously. Conley (1999), following Du Bois (1903), focuses on economic disparities as a significant legacy of slavery and segregation. Dressler et al. note the impact of racial categories on health, because "the chronic, allostatic load generated by this continuing adaptation to enduring structures of inequality, then generates observed health disparities" (2005:45–46).

10. For a broader overview of wealth disparities in the United States, see Lui et al. (2006), and for a history of how we think of equality in economics see Adler (2011). On the economic foundations of racial inequality, Du Bois puts it eloquently: "To be a poor man is hard, but to be a poor race in a land of dollars is the very bottom of hardships" (1903–1906). Obviously, economics is not all there is to discrimination. DuBois also writes "So dawned the time of *Sturm und Drang*: storm and stress to-day rocks our little boat on the mad waters of the world-sea; there is within and without the sound of conflict, the burning of body and rending of soul; inspiration strives with doubt, and faith with vain questionings" (1903:7–8).

11. See Sales and Murphy (2007) on the significance of class analysis in studies of drug dealing. Their "findings suggest attention to social class, that is, the social charac-

teristics of sellers and the availability of types of sales settings (public vs. private) is critical to developing a sociological understanding of drug markets" (2007:919).

12. Drug dealing has most often been studied in the guise of "deviance" by sociologists and criminologists, from classic work by Howard Becker (1963) to a range of textbooks with those terms in their title now. In anthropology, drug use and sales have generally been examined from a medical anthropological standpoint, which is also attentive to culture. See Kleinman et al. (1997), Page and Singer (2010), and Singer (2006).

13. Virtually all scholars acknowledge the linkage between race, class and privilege in drug dealing, as when Fitzgerald writes, "Disadvantage predicts poor drug use outcomes" (2009:267). As a counterpoint to the vast literature on discrimination against people of color, see Conley (2000) for a vivid memoire on whiteness in America, Adler (1985) for an examination of "upper level" white drug dealers, Jacques and Wright (2015) for an ethnography of dealing among middle class young men in the suburbs, and Mohamed and Fritsvold (2010) for work on drug dealing in college dorms.

14. Murphy, Waldorf and Reinarmen write eloquently on how people "drift into dealing" and how these "deviant careers" operate (1990).

15. See Visweswaran for a critical engagement of the failed attempt by anthropology to substitute "culture" for "race" (1998).

16. Becker writes of drug users "learning to perceive the effects" (1963:48).

17. Neo-hippie culture will somewhat surprisingly reassert itself in the suburbs later, as Brad explains, with an ongoing culture of the Grateful Dead and younger bands that pick up that mantle, like Phish.

18. See Gootenberg (2009:310). See also Karch (2005) for a good overview of the history of cocaine with an emphasis on the failure of states to contain it over the *longue durée*. As will become clear, my argument is that drug sales in suburbia do "capitalism" differently than other commodities, and this is key to the durability of drug culture.

19. In Gootenburg's 1999 edited volume, Joseph Spillane writes, "Cocaine quickly passed the test of consumer appeal—the legal supply of the drug increased roughly 700 percent between 1890 and 1902" (1999:21). See also Musto (1989).

20. "By the turn of the century, the dollar values of cocaine sales ranked among the top five products of United States pharmaceutical manufacturers. By the late 1890s, many observers came to believe that the popular consumption of cocaine posed a serious threat to public health and to public safety" (Spillane in Gootenburg 1999:21).

21. The notion of the "informal economy" is generally attributed to Keith Hart.

22. Obviously, while policing in poor communities is lax in terms of making them safer, it is robust in the sense that a much higher percentage of the poor are incarcerated than are the wealthy.

23. See Winant and Omi (1994) for a discussion of "racial formation."

24. See Natarajan (2006:171).

25. I will use "conventional economics" and not dwell on the admittedly important distinctions between "neoliberal" economics and other varieties. I only point to what seem to be the basic, uncontroversial assumptions of most economics (Hill and Myatt 2010, Mitchell 2005).

26. "Party" as a verb was first used by e. e. cummings in 1922, but it took decades to catch on. In my interviews it means roughly "socialize with drugs."

27. See Bauman (2009) and Cohen (2014).

28. Page and Singer (2010:95).

29. Scholars even call this "middle class," as in a case where a female crack dealer used "techniques common among middle-class dealers rather than those more typical of her inner-city location" (Dunlap et al. 1994:1).

30. "Actors in illegal markets need to trust exchange partners in many more dimensions than actors conducting legal economic activities. At the same time, the means available to these actors to enforce trust are much more limited; they more closely

resemble pre-modern trust devices than modern ones" (Beckert and Wehringer 2013:17). See Wherry (2013) on the cultural underpinnings of markets.

31. See Kleiman et al. (2012).

32. See for instance Charness and Gneezy (2008), and Franzen and Pointner (2012). For a broader summary of morality in economics see Adler (2011), Bowles (2016) and Etzioni (1998). For a perspective from economic anthropology see Chibnik (2011), Hann and Hart (2011), and Wilk and Cliggett (2007).

33. See Allen (1999).

34. Beckert and Wehinger write that illegal trade is costly insofar as "personal relations . . . are much more demanding to organize because the risks are much greater than in legal markets" (2013:18).

35. See Carey (2017) for a fascinating contemplation of the ways trust operates in Western social science, and the different ways other cultures see mistrust as more sensible and central.

36. Carolyn Nordstrom has written extensively on trust in the illegal economy (2007). See especially chapter 14 "The Cultures of Criminals."

37. See Levitt and Dubner (2005:103).

38. This is in a section where they assert that "The first trick of asking questions is to determine if your question is a good one" (2005:89). The question they ask is "Why do drug dealers live with their mothers?" To me, this is a terrible question. A better one would be why mothers let drug dealing sons live at home, and to me the answer is precisely that such moms know their kids have few options in the legitimate economy, and that drug sales and use are part of a larger cultural dynamic that they know and understand. In any case, Phillipe Bourgois answers the Levitt and Dubner question in the very title of his book, *In Search of Respect: Selling Crack in El Barrio* (2003). Young men seek things more precious than money.

39. The notion of the "embedded" nature of economic behavior in social contexts comes from Karl Polanyi (1957). Polanyi argues that typical economies are embedded in social relations while in capitalism social relations are embedded in the economy. In this sense suburban drug dealing is more "traditional" than capitalist. This was apparent to me from my early anthropological work in a Moroccan village (Crawford 2008). Here I found much in the mix of calculative reason and social obligation that reminded me of suburban drug dealing.

40. I take this notion of the "human economy" from the book edited by Keith Hart (2011), though many others use the term too.

41. "The 'quantum' of economics is the optimizing individual. All of economics ultimately boils down to the behavior of such individuals" (Bauman 2005:vii). Gary Becker writes that "the economic approach provides a framework applicable to all human behavior—to all types of decisions and to people of all walks of life" (in Friedland and Robertson (1990:18). Desai suggests that in addition to real economic decisions being "embedded" in society (Polanyi 1957, 1977), a second flaw in conventional economics is that "Economics in textbooks dealt with static economies in equilibrium. Capitalism is a dynamic disequilibrium system" (Desai 2002:254). It is not only on this basis that he argues "economists . . . do not respect common sense" (Desai 2002:184).

42. On the methamphetamine crisis see Reding (2010).

43. Waldorf, Reinarmen and Murphy do a fantastic job of detailing drug use in a white-collar workplace (1992).

44. On the vilification of crack see Levine and Reinarman (1997).

45. An interestingly parallel thing seemed to happen when cocaine was first rendered illegal. While coca-infused soft drinks were consumed by white people in soda fountains, the law took no notice. But as the marketing of Coca-Cola expanded to include bottled drinks sold to blacks, lawmakers decided its energizing effects ought to be a crime. Pendergrast writes "The bottling business had one unfortunate, unforeseen consequence, however. No longer simply a soda fountain drink for upper-class urban white professionals, Coca-Cola was increasingly consumed by blacks. Sensa-

tional stories of 'Negro coke fiends' attacking whites caused many to fear the widespread availability of Coca-Cola. As the century turned, so did public opinion, and in 1900 Candler [who had founded the Coca-Cola company] found himself under intensified pressure to reform his 'dope'" (2000:84).

46. Musto (1989) argues that cocaine use rises and falls as each new generation learns anew of its downsides and abandons it. Singer (2006) makes a similar argument.

47. *Careers in Dope* is the title of a 1973 book by Dan Waldorf.

48. See Biernacki and Waldorf (1981) on "snowball sampling," Waldorf et al. on "chain referral" sampling (1992), and Sagalnik and Heckathorn (2004) and Goel and Salganik (2010) on "respondent driven sampling."

49. Page and Singer observe that "Ethnographers studying drug use succeed or fail based on access to networks of informal social relations among drug users and/or dealers/distributors" (2010:15), and I certainly found this to be true. Plenty of dealers refused to speak with me, and I am deeply indebted to those who were willing to talk.

50. See Waldorf et al. on the complexity of quitting drugs (1992).

51. There are a number of exceptions to this general tendency. See Adler (1985), Jacques and Wright (2015), Mohamed and Fritsvold (2010), Murphy, Waldorf, and Reinarman (1990).

52. Ultimately the "careers in dope" (Waldorf 1973) in this book provide evidence that the "whole concern with illegal markets as the source of evil or organized crime in modern America may be misplaced" (Reuter 1983:187).

53. Scholarly work is less likely to portray dealers in moral terms, as evil, than as victims. For instance, see Kleinman et al. on "social suffering" (1997). Middle class whites would not seem subject to this framework, though see Braverman (2015).

54. Beckert and Wehinger write, "In illegal markets, formal institutions involved in securing property rights are beyond reach for the actors. Social ties play a pre-eminent role as a functional substitute, but these are nonetheless inferior to the real thing" (2013:21). It is notable that the "real" way markets are thought to perform depends on structural violence inherent in a state.

55. On "the idiosyncrasies of the drug markets," see Caulkins and Reuter (2006). As we will discuss in the conclusion, what counts as an idiosyncrasy depends on your standpoint. Economists assume a context of state power to ensure contracts and anonymity among social actors. Both of these conditions are historically rare, and so conventional economic theory is poorly situated to evaluate the majority of "economic" transactions. Caulkins and Reuter suggest that economists "should not be content with presuming that elementary market models apply in all cases" (2014:2). Lindgren and Grossman (2005) discuss "social interactions, markets and politics" but give us very little sense of how such "markets" actually work.

56. Originally, I hypothesized that drug dealing helped build entrepreneurial skills that translated to the legal economy. This was not borne out in my interviews, but other scholars have found this effect. Fairlie, for instance, writes, "drug dealers are 11%–21% more likely to choose self-employment than non-drug-dealers, all else equal" (2002:538). See also Frith and McElwee (2007).

57. Bourgois (2003) writes of dealing for "respect." Fitzgerald writes that "Small time dealing certainly means a lot more to Moira [a heroin dealer] than simply economic benefit, or the running of a business or the means to fulfilling a dream of material wealth. The proliferation of relationships that comes with being the centre of social and drug market activity is a core outcome for Moira. . . . She used her sociality to extend her economic capacities, and reinforced her sociality through economic advantage" (2009:267).

58. Friedman et al. suggest a common "non-hostile" view towards drug dealing among youth (2003).

59. Browne and Milgram quote the economist Levitt as claiming "morality is how people would like the world to work; economics is how it does work" (2009), but most of the essays in Browne and Milgram demonstrate the many ways this is not so. There

is no way to disentangle economics from morality because there is no way to remove the social (and therefore cultural, moral) context from individual decision making. See also Desai's discussion of Hegel's notion that freedom is the realization of a moral community (2002:30–31), and his argument, taken from Marx, that freedom can only be a collective state of being—not a state of being free from a collective (2002:5).

60. I find this phrase ungainly and prefer "people of the global majority" to refer to those with more melanin than I have (a group that includes the vast majority of the planet's inhabitants). It is, after all, an obvious fact that white people (so-called, though we're really more peach, pink, or pale) are a minority on the planet.

61. Mohamed and Fritsvold argue that this is common with "dorm room dealers," that "framing their own criminality as a rational business decision was, in part, an attempt to absolve them from self-identifying as criminals" (2010:50).

62. Lui et al. (2006) demonstrate how wealth—in terms of capital and opportunities—accrues to whiteness. What drug dealers show is how this can be utilized to transition out of the illegal economy. Royster writes of "networks of inclusion and exclusion" and shows that "Other things being equal—and in this study they are—the stronger one's network, the better one's chances of making stable labor market transitions" (2003:176). For middle class whites, the networks developed through drug dealing are "stronger" because they have more "well-placed contacts" and "contacts [that] can exercise influence differ significantly for blacks and whites" (2003:145).

63. There are obviously other definitions of "success" (Dunlap et al. 1994).

64. For help with detoxification, see https://www.samhsa.gov/find-help/national-helpline.

65. See Boeri et al. on "myths of methamphetamine" (2009).

66. My original presumption was that heroin users are not very social, but this is contradicted by the evidence. See Bourgois and Schonberg (2009), for instance, on sharing in this drug community—especially in trying to avoid withdrawals, or Hoffer (2006) on the discipline required of heroin users in securing their daily supply, and heroin dealers in providing it. None of the dealers I interviewed spoke much about opioids, but in general it would seem to me that the physical effects of that class of drugs would make them poor candidates for the social drug taking that is the focus of the book. Opioid addicts are generally seeking to avoid withdrawals and keep from being sick. This is different than trying to get high, and especially from trying to get high with other people, though perhaps that does not diminish the socially productive nature of opiate exchanges.

67. This was not an easy project. It was hard to find subjects, and even the people who formally agreed to speak with me were often reluctant. We shuffled around trying to get started, to get them talking. Some did not show up for appointments. Others talked about everything but our main topic. A great deal of shame adheres to illegal drugs, in other words, and for my own part I was reluctant to reveal to my own friends, colleagues, and family what I was working on. It is telling, I think, that this book has occupied me for something like six years and my own (now adolescent) children have no idea it exists. I have not lied, exactly, but I certainly *ambiguated*. And while this has been eased by my children's determined incuriosity towards all things parental, that's not the whole story. The fact is that these are tales few want to tell. As a nation I think we are reluctant to take stock of our recent past, and how it made us what we are. As a father, I know I am.

ONE

Cannabis and Coca, Chemistry and Culture

Most chapters of this book focus on transactions, the movement of things from one person to another, mostly things like cocaine and marijuana. But we will begin with a few words about the substances themselves. It makes intuitive sense to start with what we might call the materiality of drugs, the composition of the "thing in itself."[1] This is at bottom of how we think of drugs, after all. Drugs do things to us, they have "effects" that our culture tends to tell us are independent of our selves. The humans who take the drugs are considered the objects of the action rather than the actors themselves, at least post-ingestion. For Americans, drugs have most of the agency once we've decided to take them. We "take" a drug, but then it "gets" us high, for instance. They act on us. We are the object of the verb.

But it is important to remember that there is far more to drugs than chemistry.[2] The effects of what we ingest do not flow straightforwardly from their molecules. Our own personal biochemistry matters, too, as does the context in which the drugs are taken. People learn to use drugs from other people, and they understand the experience in ways that are derived in part from others. The meanings of drug experiences change over time—both over our individual life trajectories and in broader cultural terms. Whenever psychoactive drugs are operative in a human brain, that brain is both receiving signals and trying to make sense of them. Much of this "making sense" happens through cultural frames of reference, ways we have learned to make sense of the world. In short, to understand cannabis, coca, or any other drug, we have to consider both chemistry and culture.

1

CANNABIS

Despite dramatic changes in American society, and in U.S. drug culture, cannabis has been a staple of our drug diet for forty years. The National Institute of Drug Abuse reported in 2010 that over the "35-year history of . . . research marijuana use . . . has displayed patterns of gradual increase and decrease, with no long-term trends consistently upward or downward."[3] Robust, continuing surveys by the Substance Abuse and Mental Health Services Administration (SAMHSA) confirm the same thing. In other words, since the 1970s marijuana has been the foundation of American illegal drug use, not least in the suburbs, and this foundation seems stable. Decriminalization in some states, and legalization in others, is probably changing this, but it is hard to imagine that these changes will lead to Americans ingesting any *less* pot than they commonly and consistently have done.

This should be unsurprising. *Cannabis sativa L.*—including what we call marijuana—is one of the oldest plants used by humans, with evidence of its manufacture into fiber as many as twelve thousand years ago in Taiwan, and hints of its psychotropic use five thousand years ago in Europe.[4] Intoxicating preparations of *Cannabis* are associated with a long history of medicine and philosophy in the Indian subcontinent, and have been noted by writers across the Old World, from Pen Ts'ao Ching to Herodotus and Rabelais. "Definitive records of the medicinal and physiological effects of cannabis are found in the earliest pharmacopoeia in existence," according to one scholar.[5] People have used cannabis for a long time. There is no real doubt about this.

Cannabis sativa L. was first formally classified in the West by Linnaeus, the Swedish botanist who developed our modern taxonomic system (thus the "L," for Linnaeus, at the end of cannabis's Latin name), but it is not actually a very simple plant to classify. For one thing, it is morphologically quite variable. Male plants grow somewhat differently than females (males produce better fiber but no edible seeds or intoxicating flowers), and some varieties grow in a sprawling fashion to twenty feet while others remain small and compact, only a few feet tall. Some argue that there are four Cannabis sub-species (*sativa, indica, afghani,* and *rudentalis*), while most consumers are familiar with only two (*sativa* and *indica*).

The *sativa* and *indica* strains are recognizable for somewhat different growth habits and different cognitive and emotional effects. *Sativa* behaves more like a hallucinogen (which can mean anything from making you contemplative to silly or paranoid) while *indica* is generally more corporal (rendering you relaxed, sleepy, or mellow). Some growers assert that you can influence the effects of the plants by how you harvest them, with an early harvest (especially of *sativa*) leading to an energetic, social type of high and late harvests resulting in more of a can't-get-off-the-couch variety, especially in *indica*. Most widely marketed contemporary varieties are hybrids of the two strains. Still, the majority opinion among botanists is that *Cannabis sativa L.* is a single species. Despite the fact that thousands of cultivated varieties (or "cultivars") are bred for specific qualities, any *Cannabis* male can reproduce with any female.

Importantly, some cultivars have no psychotropic effects whatsoever. What we call "hemp," for instance, is properly *Cannabis sativa L.* and has been grown for thousands of years for food (it has edible seeds), for fiber, and for use as paper. Hemp is the majority fiber in the pants I am wearing as I write this; it provided the paper for the Magna Carta and Gutenberg's first Bible.[6] Before synthetic substitutes, hemp was essential for ropes and sails, and seaworthy vessels needed *Cannabis* as much as lumber. The explosion of European trade in the seventeenth century generated a voracious market for hemp and so *Cannabis sativa L.* was one of the first great global commodities—a prerequisite for sailing, and thus a key ingredient in the spread of cotton, sugar, coffee, tobacco, and more. Because hemp made sailing, and thus trade possible, desire to farm more of it spurred colonization and helped give birth to our current world system.[7] Capitalism was born of cannabis, you might say, or at least alongside it. However, one could smoke a bale of hemp and experience little more than a headache.

Other strains of *Cannabis* are powerfully intoxicating, pleasantly so for many people. The main reason for this is that some varieties have a chemical called *delta nine tetrahydrocannabinol*, or THC. This is mostly found in oils secreted by small trichomes, or hairs, on the female flowers, though THC is found in lower quantities in other parts of the plant. THC influences what is called the endocannabinoid system of the human brain, a system that, among other things, impacts mood, appetite, memory, and the experience of pain. While THC is the most significant psychoactive substance in marijuana, it is not the only one. In the words of one expert, "more than 400 distinct chemicals have been extracted from the cannabis plant, 66 of which are unique. . . . These 66 chemicals are collectively known as cannabinoids. Many cannabinoids are isomers of each other, that is, they have the same chemical formula (such as that of THC: $C_{21}H_{30}O_2$) but different arrangements of atoms."[8] Furthermore, some non-isomers seem to influence the effects of marijuana and according to the European Monitoring Centre for Drugs and Drug Addiction, these "closely related substances that occur in cannabis include cannabidiol (CBD) and, in aged samples, cannabinol (CBN), both of which have quite different pharmacological effects to THC."[9] These different substances combine in the brain to create a variety of sensations and effects. Growers use careful breeding, harvesting, and curing to maximize the specific effects desired, and they stabilize their product through cloning (which ensures all the plants are identical) and proper storage.

Cannabis has an astonishing range of uses—25,000 in one florid estimation[10]—and consequently its cultivation by humans affords it one of the most extensive ranges of all plants, thriving around the world from temperate to tropical zones. *Cannabis* has been part of the agricultural heritage of North America at least since the 1600s, when the Virginia Company required each Jamestown resident to grow one hundred plants, and the governor to grow five thousand.[11] *Cannabis* continued to be grown widely, especially for fiber, until the late 1930s, when it was declared illegal in the United States because its intoxicating variant, by then called marijuana, was newly prohibited. It is generally accepted that the reason for making it illegal was primarily its popularity among non-white and immigrant groups, particularly Mexicans.

There is no obvious visual distinction between an intoxicating version of *Cannabis sativa L.* and a non-intoxicant, so marijuana prohibition effectively killed the lucrative hemp industry. After prohibition acreage devoted to growing *Cannabis* plummeted, but then surged during World War II as the government suspended its ban to offset hemp shortages created by the war. The pre-war United States maximum of 16,000 cultivated acres (around 1888) increased to 146,000 acres in 1943, but fell precipitously after 1945, when the United States went back to importing its hemp from the more than thirty countries that still allow its production, principally China.[12]

Today, despite millions of dollars spent to eradicate it, marijuana is grown in all fifty of the United States and the District of Columbia. In 2010 over 10 million plants were destroyed and, obviously, many more survived and found their way into the legal and illegal drug markets.[13] In sum, *Cannabis* is cultivated worldwide as hemp; it grows wild as a weed across much of the United States; and it is laboriously nurtured as an intoxicant both indoors under lights and outside in hidden farms. *Cannabis* has been used by humans for longer than we have pursued agriculture, and it appears to be one of our first domesticated plants.[14] From this perspective, the use and persistence of cannabis in the United States is less curious than our sense that its presence is novel or noteworthy.

But things are obviously changing. Legalization in some places and decriminalization in others have led to a surge of interest in both medical and recreational varieties, as well as a resurgence in the commercial potential of hemp (thus my hemp pants). Very high-potency strains have been developed along with a bedazzling selection of cannabinoid combinations aiming at everything from the alleviation of pain, nausea, and seizures to treatment for glaucoma, social anxiety, and depression. New forms and preparations of marijuana facilitate the ingestion of these varieties—from candy and pills to topical oils and waxes—and new e-cigarette style devices allow consumers to vaporize (rather than smoke) the plant or its derivative waxes and oils. (A vaporizer works by heating the substance to a temperature high enough to vaporize the cannabinoids but not to ignite the carbon structures of the plant. It is thus technically "smokeless.") All of this is transforming the relationship between mainstream American culture and its favorite intoxicating plant.

COCA AND COCAINE

Cocaine is a simpler drug than cannabis, at least at the molecular level. $C_{17}H_{21}NO_4$ is the chemical formula for cocaine hydrochloride, HCL, the key psychoactive substance in what is bought and sold as cocaine. There is nothing else in the plant that seems to do much to humans. However, the actual powder sold as cocaine includes a variety of adulterants added by producers and dealers. Sometimes these are just filler, as in vitamin B or lactose, and other times they are meant to enhance the perceived value of the drug, as when dealers add Novocain (to increase the numbing effect) or different kinds of stimulants (to increase the perceived potency of the drug, the sense of being accelerated). Whatever it is packaged with, cocaine can be swallowed, injected or smoked. Standard formulations absorb easily through mucous membranes, like the nasal passages, and so in the suburbs it is generally inhaled or "snorted."

Cocaine must be differently formulated for different modes of ingestion. To smoke it, for example, the sniff-able version readily available in the suburbs has to be rendered amendable to vaporization. Users turn powder cocaine into a substance that can be smoked by mixing it with baking soda or ether—"cooking it"—and the result is called "freebase" because you have liberated the base cocaine from its bonding agents. This allows it to be easily heated and smoked. However, this also makes it kind of gooey and hard to manage. Freebase is not a very marketable product and so people who want to ingest cocaine by smoking it have to cook powder cocaine one batch or hit at a time. This facilitates a ritual sort of solemnity, at least sometimes, as the high is brief and the cooking has to happen repeatedly. Smoking freebase allows people to consume lots of cocaine in very short periods of time, so it is extremely expensive and dangerously addictive. However, in the 1980s enterprising cocaine dealers discovered how to prepare smokable cocaine for the mass market, how to make hard, thus transportable and saleable "rocks" of cocaine you could easily sell and immediately smoke. This was known as "crack" for the crackling sound it makes when heated. It was a huge marketing success.

However ingested, cocaine crosses the blood/brain barrier with little trouble. Smoking and injecting get more of the drug into the body quicker than other methods (in a few seconds as opposed to minutes), and this produces more of a "rush" or a surge of intoxication. Inhalation—snorting cocaine—has less of an initial "rush" experience but the slower intake makes the drug's effects last longer. Whatever method is used to deliver the chemical, the impact of cocaine fades quickly. Whereas a single dose of heroin can last five hours, and LSD up to half a day, cocaine's impact starts to diminish in as few as fifteen minutes. The relatively short duration of the cocaine high impacts how it is used socially. To stay high on cocaine is really to get high over and over again, though habituation means that many people take more and more to get the same high. The repeated need for drugs increases the amount of social activity between users and dealers; people tend to use up their supply and want more, which, along with being wide awake at uncommon hours, stimulates repeated social interactions and sales. Coming down from a cocaine high can mean fatigue, depression, or anxiety. The solution to this, often, is more cocaine.

In the brain cocaine reduces dopamine re-uptake (the extra dopamine signals pleasure through the *mesolimbic dopamine system*, the brain's reward pathway) and it alters norepinephrine and serotonin receptors (raising your heart rate and making you feel energetic, talkative, or ebullient). Cocaine is also a vasoconstrictor (it slows bleeding) and an anesthetic (it dulls topical pain). These last two qualities are what makes cocaine useful for surgery, especially of the eyes, nose and throat. But it is the former set of characteristics that facilitated cocaine's rise as a global commodity.

In 1860, German chemists extracted HCL from *Erythroxylum coca*, a nondescript shrub (with several varieties) that grows primarily in the Andean nations of Bolivia and Peru. Liberated from its uncomely shrub and purified into crystals, cocaine quickly became a key ingredient in a wide variety of medicines and tonics. Coca infusions and cocaine-laced pills and powders were said to be good for everything from hay fever to neurasthenia, sluggishness to menstrual cramps. "Inca cocaine" was touted as a solution for teething babies, though personally I would question the wisdom of giving a stimulant to a fussy infant no matter how effective the analgesic qualities. Hucksters sometimes promised improbable cures for conditions ranging from nervousness and sleeplessness to alcoholism and "the opium habit." Some products advertised to cure alcoholism were largely made from alcohol—port, wine, or malt beer infused with coca. It is hard to see how someone wanting to quit booze would be helped by coca/alcohol cocktails, or how someone quitting "the opium habit" or suffering from sleeplessness would benefit from a stimulant. There seems to have been a strange obliviousness to the effects of the drug as we now understand them in a large number of the proposed claims for coca's medical efficacy. This underscores the point that the impact of any chemical is about more than its molecules.

By 1863 Angelo Mariani had perfected a "wine tonic" and it rapidly became the most popular coca-infused beverage in the world. The historian Paul Gootenburg, in his masterful study of Andean cocaine, notes that Mariani solved several problems associated with merchandizing the coca plant. First, he dignified its use by combining it with wine from

Bordeaux. This meant users did not have to pack their cheeks with wads of coca leaf, as Andean Indians did. The wine had the added benefit of enhancing the effect of the drug, since Europeans relied on relatively low grade dried leaf, and alcohol magnifies the impact of the alkaloids in coca. Mariani also adopted strikingly modern marketing strategies, using celebrities like Jules Verne and Sarah Bernhardt to bolster claims for his product, and he cleverly deployed images in his advertising to associate coca with the "noble savages" of the pre-Colombian past instead of the degraded peasants of his era. Queen Victoria, Thomas Edison, and Ulysses Grant were all enthusiastic proponents of Vin Mariani coca-infused wine. After 1878 Pope Leo XIII awarded it a medal. Incidentally, surely, he turned out to be the longest living pope so far.

Competition was fierce and Mariani was hardly alone. Dozens of producers vied to provide coca-alcohol combinations. When some U.S. counties flirted with alcohol prohibition, producers switched to a sugary base to replace the booze. Thus commercial "soft" drinks entered the American lexicon as delivery systems for coca. Such products were all the rage during the second half of the nineteenth century, but were gradually eliminated in the twentieth. The Harrison Act made cocaine (and coca infused products) illegal in 1914 and the drug came to be associated with deviant subcultures instead of movie actresses, celebrated generals, and religious leaders.

In sum, America's first great embrace of coca started after the Civil War. Its popularity surged but then petered out around World War I. While still to be found in large cities and among some subcultures, cocaine mostly disappeared from public view in America until the late 1960s. Then, of course, altered consciousness came back into fashion, often as a political or social statement rather than in the guise of a medical intervention. At that point cocaine reemerged, first in subcultures where it had never entirely died, as among jazz musicians, and later as the plaything of bohemian elites.

In general, plants like *Erythroxylum*, from which we get cocaine, produce alkaloids to protect themselves. Alkaloids taste bitter and can be toxic in large doses, though humans have a particular affinity for a few of them. Caffeine, morphine, and nicotine are among our favorites; other well-known alkaloids include quinine and strychnine. It is notable that the alkaloids that seem to cause the most trouble (arguably cocaine and morphine) are also the ones that tend to be ingested in highly concentrated forms. Pure caffeine is toxic, for instance, but it does not matter because it is not generally used in a pure form.[15] Instead we drink it in small doses in coffee or tea. Nicotine is even more toxic—purified it serves as an insecticide—but few people would think to administer these distilled alkaloids to their bodies, and they would likely die if they did. Instead, traditionally, we smoked small doses of whole tobacco leaves instead of concentrates. This limited the damage. So, while smoking cigarettes kills far more people than cocaine or morphine, this happens not because it is concentrated into something dangerous. The real issue is that nicotine is highly addictive, the plant containing it causes cancer, and you can buy it at any corner store and administer it as many times a day as you want over a lifetime.[16]

As a culture, however, we ingest cocaine in highly concentrated forms and this is a different sort of problem. We do not stuff leaves in our cheeks, or drink tea from coca, but instead inhale concentrated cocaine through our noses (or we smoke it with pipes). Even though retail level cocaine rarely ends up being very pure, great effort has gone into extracting cocaine from coca and consolidating it in a form that has a rapid and profound impact on the brain. So, the danger of coca comes less from the plant than the way we culturally choose to ingest it. The point is that while *Erythroxylum* is hardly unique in producing pleasurable alkaloids, concentrated HCL is a product of our specific culture, and its problems lie as much in that as its chemistry. We can blame the drug for doing bad things, but this begins with us doing bad things to the plant.

After all, Andean people revered *Erythroxylum* and enjoyed it for upwards of eight thousand years. They grew, harvested, and cured the leaves, and either made tea or packed the coca in their cheeks, adding lime to facilitate the release of the alkaloids. Regular farmers seem to have used coca, but it was in some circumstances the special privilege of royalty. We find evidence of its ceremonial uses in their tombs. Reportedly the plant helps with fatigue, encourages alertness, and is extremely useful for altitude sickness. And yet indigenous Andeans never suffered any obvious social disorder or personal decomposition from coca; we have no record of epidemics of drug use, of Inca-period drug prisons, Aymara crack addicts, or indeed of any Andean society making an effort to protect people from the shrub. Today many South Americans resent the equivalence of the (relatively harmless) coca plant, native to their region, with its obviously problematic derivative, cocaine. No less than the President of Bolivia has said that *la coca no es la cocaina*. What he means is that foreigners, and most especially North Americans, have the real interest in concentrated cocaine hydrochloride, and it is the North Americans who ingest it in doses that would stagger an Andean farmer. Cocaine is what Euro-American culture decided to do with coca. Others just thought to make tea. This should make it clear that chemistry is not destiny. Cultural norms matter.

CULTURE AND CULTURAL CHANGE

While the main thrust of the book is about economics, and while chemistry matters to the transaction of drugs, a few words are necessary about *culture*. Clearly cultural understandings play a role in how we use drugs and sell them. We do not concentrate caffeine and snort it, but we do concentrate cocaine. We do not smoke purified nicotine, or at least we had not until recently, but instead use the whole leaves. And while we do concentrate alcohol, we have strict laws about how concentrated it can be. Similarly, it did not occur to me alone to concentrate or sell cannabis. It was a thing people did long before I got involved, and I learned about it from others, and copied them.

Later in the book I will make the case that economics are embedded in culture.[17] We buy alcohol from anonymous people who work in liquor stores, or from bartenders who pretend to be our friends, but we get cocaine and cannabis from our real kin and friends. Some of this has to do with laws, obviously, but laws emerge from norms, convention and habit. Laws are the formalized variant of cultural norms, we might say, or the way dominant groups inflict their norms on everybody else. So we need to think about culture, power, and economics at the same time as we try to understand how and why these chemicals move through our communities.[18]

Clearly the laws around drugs do not accord with the cultural norms of everyone.[19] The people who want to take drugs are a minority, which is one reason that anti-drug laws are on the books. But another reason is that people who break the law do not necessarily want to change it. We all accept the legitimacy of norms we do not follow, at least sometimes. Everyone knows the speed limit, but nobody drives that slowly on the freeway. We do not change the law. Instead we have cultural norms for breaking it. (We may drive seventy miles per hour, but we do not go 120.) Put another way, there are cultural rules for breaking cultural rules. Only one of the dealers in this book actually argues for cocaine legalization. The rest are content to keep the laws as they are—except with cannabis, in those places where it remains illegal. So if people are breaking the law, but accept that the law makes sense, what is going on? Our typical understanding of culture as a way of doing things is too simple to explain this. Culture is a shared way to doing things, surely, but this does not explain diversity within a culture, or the subtle rules for flouting culture. Most seriously, the concept of culture itself does not explain cultural change. So, while culture is important, we need other explanatory concepts too. Sometimes I will borrow these from anthropology and sometimes from fields like philosophy, neuroscience, or behavioral economics.

One way to think about drug culture in particular is through the idea of "subcultures." When groups of people within a society decide together to follow distinct norms that is usually understood to be a "sub" culture. When a subculture is in conflict with its parent culture, then the behavior is usually termed "deviant," though obviously it is not deviant in the subculture. Sociologists and criminologists in particular are very interested in deviant behavior. Deviant behavior still conforms to norms, just its own norms rather than the dominant ones. Moreover, as noted above, people can participate in deviant behavior without giving up the norms of the dominant culture. Sometimes, especially for young people, contretemps with dominant norms is part of the thrill of deviance. Young people in many cultures experiment with alternative norms, and particularly strive to craft norms that separate them from—and annoy—adults. With most of the dealers here, the deviance turned out to be a phase more than a real departure from the mainstream American culture. The drug dealers who spoke with me are shockingly *normal* Americans in a cultural sense. Their deviance involves the application of American norms to new domains rather than a real departure from those norms. I explain this more at the end of the book.

This still leaves us with the difficult question of cultural change. If culture drives our behavior, and if our culturally patterned behavior changes over time, what makes it change? How can we say "culture" is changing (so that marijuana is more accepted while cocaine has become less so) if we're saying that culture determines the acceptability in the first place? It cannot be the case that our culture is just getting more rational, that we are figuring out that cocaine causes far more problems than marijuana. That seems to make sense, and we might wish it to be true, but cocaine and marijuana have both come into and out of favor before, and both have been legal and illegal in the past. It would be a mistake to see cultural change as a rational progression. History shows how wrong this is. Culture is not moving any particular direction or following any singular trend.

I will not belabor the point in the book, but implicitly I rely on an assumption that culture is *dialectical*. While philosophers have many (confusing) things to say about the word dialectical, for my purposes it is straightforward. Essentially, every culture is made up of people. A culture with no people would be . . . an empty room, or something. It would not be a culture. That seems obvious. At the same time, every individual is formed by culture. You cannot have a culture without actual people, but you cannot have actual people without culture.

The first part of this—the "culture is made up of individuals" part—is so obvious that Americans will not need it to be further explained. The second part should be equally obvious, but to most Americans it will not be.[20] This is because we are proudly individualistic, by which I mean that one thing we have in common is that we deny our commonality. We think of ourselves as discrete, separable beings and we value explanations that reduce phenomena to individual behavior. So, we tend to think of societies or cultures as collections of autonomous individuals, as separate persons clumped together differently in different contexts. In these clumps we do not lose our individuality; we might cluster or assemble, but do not amalgamate. I think this cultural understanding of culture is wrong. There is no such thing as an individual without a culture, or a culture that is not comprised of individuals. Still, the behavior of groups of people exhibit characteristics that cannot be explained as a sum of the parts.[21]

Some readers may have to ponder this. What would "you" be without your specific culture? Without your family, history, experiences, without your language and everything taught to you in that language, what's left? Would "you" think the same if you were raised in a different place, with different parents and friends, with a whole different set of life experiences? Considered this way, each person is fully 100 percent constituted by culture. If you doubt this, imagine having no culture at all. How would you speak, bathe, eat, use the toilet, dress, or groom yourself? What would you value? What would you dream?

Human beings lack instincts for our most fundamental activities. Instead we internalize the behavior of other people, we learn to be people from those around us, and this behavior becomes so natural, so normal, that it never occurs to us to question it. Culture substitutes for instinct. Our minds attune to the minds nearby, even the synapses of our brain mimic those with whom we communicate in a process that scientists call neuronal mirroring.[22] Every action of every person simultaneously reflects the culture that gave rise to that person and becomes a part of the culture, a model for others. Some idiosyncratic behavior gets copied. Most does not. But each of us is simultaneously a product of our culture *and* a producer of it in an open-ended, dialectical process of creation.

This is not to say that culture is *sui generis*, subject only to its own dynamics. My argument will be that economic and social practices involved in selling, buying, sharing, and taking drugs all contribute to an ever-changing drug culture.[23] They build and shape, but also canalize and sustain it.[24] These socio-economic practices work with other biological and political processes. Considered this way, a book like this is not simply describing cultural practices, it is also potentially changing what it describes. All narratives about people work this way. Becoming consciously aware of the cultural nature of our behavior can alter its reproduction. So, if we understand how the culture of drug dealing works, we stand a better chance of changing it in ways we might desire. As a parent, that seems worth doing.

NOTES

1. This notion is from Immanuel Kant (2010).
2. This is evident to virtually all researchers in this area. For an overview see Page and Singer (2010).
3. Quoted in Newton (2013:84).
4. See Merlin (2003).
5. See Li in Rubin (2011 [1975]:56).
6. See Newton (2013:26).
7. By "world system" we generally mean the capitalist world market as conceived by Immanual Wallerstein and Andre Gunder Frank.

8. See Newton (2013:14).

9. European Monitoring Centre for Drugs and Drug Addiction, "Cannabis drug profile," EMCDDA.europa.eu, accessed on June 19, 2018, http:// www.emcdda.europa.eu/publications/drug-profiles/cannabis.

10. See Clark (2011).

11. See Clarke and Merlin (2013) for an exhaustive study of the history and ethnobotany of cannabis.

12. See Newton (2013:40).

13. Allen St. Pierre, "Whack and Stack: 2010 Marijuana Cultivation Eradication in America," Norml, published June 27, 2011, accessed on July 6, 2018, http:// blog.norml.org/2011/06/27/whack-and-stack-2010-marijuana-cultivation-eradication-in-america/.

14. See Merlin (2003), Clarke and Merlin (2013), and Rubin (2011).

15. James Foster, "Documented Deaths by Caffeine," CaffeineInformer.com, accessed on July 6, 2018, https://www.caffeineinformer.com/a-real-life-death-by-caffeine.

16. The legalization of addictive substances would not seem helpful from a public health perspective. Whether it makes sense on political, ethical, or other grounds is a question beyond the scope of this book.

17. This notion of "embeddedness" is typically credited to Karl Polanyi (1957, 1977). The discipline of economics takes economic behavior to be a discrete domain. Polanyi, and many economic anthropologists, dispute this assumption. See also Block and Somers (2014).

18. The general idea that laws are formalized versions of culture can be traced to Emile Durkheim; Max Weber is the classic source for ruminations on the "how" of state power, though more recently Foucault is generally cited. The idea that power is necessarily implicated in culture (as "ideology") is usually attributed to the Marxian tradition.

19. See Waldorf, Reinarman, and Murphy (1992).

20. See Rosenfeld (2014) for a review of the American faith in choice.

21. Obviously, this is a hallowed observation, one that many would credit to Durkheim's concept of the "collective conscience" or to Marx's "sociological apperception." The realization that our selves are social is akin to what C. Wright Mills called having a "sociological imagination" (1959). See Kropotkin (1902) for a classic view of the matter.

22. See Bloch (2015) for a bio-culturally based assessment of Durkheim's fundamental sociological insights.

23. Sharing is vital even for homeless heroin addicts. Bourgois and Schonberg write: "Initially we thought that the homeless constantly pooled money and shared ancillary paraphernalia out of economic necessity when injecting heroin. They were generally unable to raise enough money to pay for a bag of heroin alone before beginning to feel withdrawal symptoms. When the price of bags dropped threefold, however, from twenty dollars to seven dollars during the second year of our fieldwork, sharing did not decrease. We realized that cooperating to purchase bags is not simply a pragmatic, economic, or logistical necessity; it is the basis for sociality and establishes the boundaries of networks that provide companionship and also facilitate material survival" (2009:83).

24. Fitzgerald, too, finds this type of relationship between economics and sociality, as when he notes that a dealer "used her sociality to extend her economic capacities, and reinforced her sociality through economic advantage" (2009:267).

TWO

Cities and Suburbs

Urban dealing is relatively well understood. Criminologist Mangai Natarajan writes "the vast bulk of research on drug dealing is concerned with retail or 'street level' dealing. Ethnographers have assembled a considerable body of knowledge about how drug dealing at this level is organized and carried out, the kinds of individuals involved, the roles they play, how they avoid detection and prosecution, the extent to which they use drugs themselves, how they package and adulterate drugs, the street price of drugs and how much profit they make. In contrast, ethnographers have rarely been able to gain access to the earlier stages of the drug distribution process, known as middle or upper level dealing."[1] So we know about street-level, flagrant dealing; we do not well understand the higher levels or other types of drug organizations.

In contrast to scholarly work, more popular media has been fascinated with "upper level dealing," drug kingpins, or, as Levitt and Dubner put it in *Freakonomics*, "the top of the pyramid."[2] The television series *Narcos,* for instance, is about Pablo Escobar, not the people who sell his drugs on Miami streets or in distant suburbs. From *Scarface* to *Blow*, Hollywood loves the drug trade. In reality, of course, "beneath every big-time dealer who may approximate the stereotype there are hundreds of smaller sellers who do not."[3] We will examine two of them, "José" and "Doug." José exemplifies "the vast bulk of research" in that he was a street-level dealer at least part of the time. But Doug's suburban dealing is what this book is primarily about. The point of the chapter is to show that Doug's operation—the kind less frequently studied—is economically distinct. Despite being mostly retail, it is not "street level dealing" in the sense Natarajan is discussing, nor is it "upper level."

JOSÉ

José was born on a military base in 1980. His father had joined the army and his mother was a homemaker. The family moved frequently — the vicissitudes of army life — and upon release from military service they returned to their native Puerto Rico. José went to school there for a few years before settling in Bridgeport, Connecticut when he was nine. That's where he considers himself to have grown up. He now works as an electrician during the day, but takes other part-time jobs to support his wife and kids. José has a mortgage and hopes to own his house outright someday, and he's proud of this. He is the only one of his neighborhood friends who has managed to stake this claim on middle class life. Most have remained renters, and few have jobs as good as José's.

Bridgeport is a poor city and the schools are among the worst in the state. One website ranked the district 175th out of 176 in Connecticut, though the methodology of the ranking was unclear. Another ranked the district 183rd out of 184. The poverty is obvious. There are thirty-six schools in the city and in twenty-five of them at least 90 percent of the students qualify for free and reduced federal lunch program money; 14 of the 36 schools have at least 97 percent of the student body receiving federal lunch aid. By contrast 2 percent of the students qualify for federal lunch program in Fairfield, the adjacent town where I live and work.

José's mother had relatives in Bridgeport (his father's family lived sixty miles away in the Bronx, New York), and while some might portray his neighborhood as dangerous, José recalls it as a warm environment alive with family and friends. He never talked about his city or his community as a bad place to grow up, even if some bad things happened there. It was home. Like other boys across the country, José played sports — he especially loved basketball despite a lamentable lack of height — but he was not very interested in the academic parts of school.

José started smoking marijuana in 1992 when he was about twelve. Uncles and older cousins introduced him to it, and the way he told the story there was nothing unusual about this. At first José got his drug money from his family. For instance, José would go by his father's work, ask for a few bucks, and pool this with his friends to buy small, five-dollar bags of marijuana and food to enjoy with it. He was very descriptive about the food — the ethnic diversity of the city made for a wonderful variety of options: from Cuban sandwiches and empanadas to Vietnamese pho, Chinese fried rice, Jamaican salt fish, and all sorts of locally made cakes and sweets.

This arrangement didn't last long, however. By the time he was ready for high school an uncle from California moved to Bridgeport and sold cannabis in larger quantities. José began skipping school to smoke with his friends (in abandoned buildings — there were many to choose from) and he needed more money to do it. He and his friends started shoplifting to make the necessary cash. They would take the bus to the north end of town (it was a straight shot from his house, he said) and pinch expensive cologne from department stores at the mall. They'd take the bus back to their neighborhood and sell the $60 cologne for $10 to "Middle Eastern" guys who ran the corner stores. With this they'd buy their five and ten-dollar bags of marijuana and, again, food to share. It is notable, I think, that for José food and pot go together. Both are enjoyed socially, amid the company of others, with the give and take of conversation and bonhomie.

By age sixteen José himself started selling pot to avoid stealing. "I was trying to get my own supply so I could distribute it to my friends," he said. There was no monetary profit in this. It was simply to have pot, "to party." The point of life for these young men was to hang out and enjoy time with friends, and marijuana was portrayed as an essential ingredient in this homosocial bonding activity.

In 1996 José was seventeen and he decided to "move up" from selling pot to crack cocaine. The rationale was simple: It was "a lot quicker money . . . way more addicting . . . a short high . . . and it sold better." Importantly, José never smoked crack himself (or almost never: a cousin once slipped it into a joint). With marijuana sales José's profits literally went up in smoke (or he ate them once he was stoned and hungry). With crack it was pure money. Moreover, the crack went "to a different crowd." His own friends were sixteen or seventeen; they didn't tend to have jobs; they could not afford cocaine in any form, even the relatively cheap crack variety. Essentially, José started his crack business to subsidize his (and his friends') cannabis habit. And while his friends would hang around with him as he sold the drugs, the actual customers were an older demographic because, as he said, "to get to that drug [cocaine] you had to pass through marijuana." The people who had "passed through" were in their twenties and thirties, generally white, and had jobs and cash. There was no fencing stolen property or credit or other sorts of informal economic arrangements. It was all anonymous, straight cash for dope.

José found his crack supplier through his mother's boyfriend (his parents had split up by then). This boyfriend had an old pal in a gang. The pal, or the "gentleman," as José called his supplier, would drive up in his car and usher José into the back seat. While José obviously knew the identity of the dealer, he had to pretend that he did not. The gentleman would hand "a bundle" over the seat to José, a Ziploc bag with twelve vacuum-sealed, ten-dollar rocks of crack. It was José's job to sell these and return $100 to "the gentleman." For every twelve bags sold, José made $20. Often customers would buy the whole bundle for $120, so he could make twenty bucks on one sale and be done for the day. The twenty bucks, of course, would immediately be spent on marijuana and food for the crowd that was hanging out with him.

I asked José how he found customers for crack since his friends could not afford it. His answer was intriguingly entrepreneurial. "That starts by . . . marketing yourself. You stand out on the corner . . . [the customers] know where to come in the neighborhoods when they see the crowds together, the guys standing around smoking pot, hanging out, they ask do you know anybody? Who's got some around here? And from there, you're like, I do." In this scenario José's friends perform a service. They seem to be just "standing around smoking pot," or "hanging out," as they call it, but the crowd they form signals potential customers that drugs might be available. Friends serve as advertising, and, as we will see, they also facilitate sales. Anonymity does not characterize the whole street-sales enterprise, only the final transfer to the consumer, the explicitly "business" part of the deal.

But José was not in a gang, so another aspect of his business was to choose a corner that was not already claimed by gang-affiliated crack salesmen. The search for such a place led José to the wealthier part of town. This had the advantage of avoiding the "real criminals" (from José's perspective) and of being more accessible to relatively solvent white customers. As José said, "The reason I got going on that block was because there was no one else around. . . . [The block] was in the north end. Really quiet. Crime in general was low." In other words, José sought to sell crack in a low crime area because it was safer, and because there was an under-served market for it there. This seems perfectly economically rational. He noted that his locale was "right off the main road . . . customers didn't have to go deep" into neighborhoods they saw as "bad." He understood that buying crack from a racially diverse group of boys could feel dangerous to his white customers because, as he put it, "the crew is Spanish and black." With his establishment in a relatively good part of town, and his friends along with him, business went well for José. He was "simultaneously hanging out and making money." The appeal of the dope career was that it combined work and leisure. The "work" was selling crack; the leisure was spending the profits on cannabis to share. These two were brought together, but they remained fundamentally different transactions: selling happened with strangers while sharing happened with friends. The business empowered José to live the life he wanted with his friends.

Until it didn't. One day José was in a nearby apartment playing video games and smoking pot with his buddies. Someone came and told him that a customer was down in the street looking to buy. José went out and found a white woman in her mid-twenties. She had a black eye, which was "typical among crack heads" since fighting was common among them, so to José the woman appeared to be an authentic customer. She bought the whole bundle, all twelve individually wrapped rocks, and as she did cops descended from every direction. José put up no resistance. The woman was an undercover police officer; the cops had staked out the corner from every side, and they had video surveillance of everything José had been up to. Evidently the area was "low crime" for a reason—the police kept it that way. José was seventeen years old and headed to jail.

After José's arrest the police did not take him to the station directly. Instead they transported him across town to a "special narcotics place," an "unmarked building." There they tested the drugs and started interrogating the boy (without a lawyer, notably). They knew he was a bit player and they wanted the name of his supplier. "Obviously, I didn't give the guy up, that's why I did my time and why I did my programs. There was no way I could give them information. Forget it. You come out, you're dead." José knew to keep quiet.

The police did not believe that José didn't know the name of his connection and they finally took him to the city jail. His father refused to bail him out. The assigned public defender was overworked and unsuccessful at getting him out on bail. And worst of all, the other inmates were all gang affiliated and abused him physically and psychologically. They took his food. They took some of his clothes. They threatened him. He was terrified. José found that he knew people in jail, and some were even old friends, but they were junior members of the gang and "there are rules." They were not allowed to stick up for him, "they couldn't get their hands dirty unless you were part of it," i.e. unless you were in the gang and at a level where you were allowed to make decisions. So his gang-affiliated friends watched sheepishly as José was mercilessly traumatized.

After a week someone from "upstairs" (the older people who had been arrested were upstairs, those under eighteen downstairs) came and told the boys to stop harassing José. Though he is not sure how it happened, José thinks that his mother's boyfriend heard about the violence, and since José had not revealed the name of the gang-affiliated supplier, the boyfriend was able to speak to the gang leadership and get José some relief—not protection exactly, but at least relief from the worst of the maltreatment.

After a week and a half inside he was allowed a plea deal and was made to attend "programs." These involved an electronic surveillance device, restrictions on his movement, anti-drug classes, and so forth. After about a year he was able to get a part-time job (in fast food) and there were fewer restrictions on his time and movements. The trauma of the arrest prevented José from moving back into crack dealing. But it did not keep him from selling marijuana. Working with his younger brother, he gradually got back into business, buying modest amounts of pot that he sold to friends. There "was a little bit of a sliding scale . . . you're just kind of selling for the smoking of it." He was not looking to make money, just to subsidize his social life. The business was mellow, not dangerous.

Until it wasn't . . . again. One day someone came to the door and said that there was a guy outside who wanted pot. José's brother had some for sale, but José "had a weird hunch about the guy." He knew the buyer by reputation, and while the potential customer lived in a nearby neighborhood, no one knew exactly where. José did not want his volatile younger brother involved with someone he suspected of being "a really bad human," so José went to make the sale himself. He followed the guy for a few blocks, and when the man said that he needed to go back to his apartment for money, José followed him further. Suddenly, in an alley behind a video rental store, the guy put a gun in José's mouth and took his money, his pot, and his gold chain. "I was crying, I was scared. Terrified." It was "way more extreme than being in jail."

As José concluded, "That was like the last straw. I knew that if I stayed doing this there was one of two things . . . I was going to end up dead or in jail for a long time. Both of which I wasn't cut out to do. Even though for a while, I thought I was cut out to do it." José's career in dope ended when he was eighteen, and today he does not smoke marijuana, though "I still dream about it," he says. José believes that his ability to stay calm was what saved his life, and that his brother, who was much more aggressive, would have resisted and would have ended up dead. Of course there was no way to tell the police about the "really bad human" because of the illegal drugs, and because José was on parole. The "really bad human" went on robbing, and worse, for years.

From a scholarly perspective, the drug dealing economy is far more complex than the "urban versus suburban" model we are using, so it is worth pausing to examine how José's story fits in the larger picture. First, all business involves personal transactions, or in Keith Hart's terms, a "tension between the impersonal conditions of social life and the persons who inevitably carry it out."[4] Drug dealing is no exception to this. José's crack business involved deals with strangers, and this had consequences, but the final anonymous sale to the consumer was only a small part of a much larger network of more intimate associations.

What this points to is the complexity of drug dealing networks. Researchers Curtis and Wendel, for instance, studied nearly four hundred people involved in the drug trade, including 147 heroin dealers in New York alone, and tried to sort out what they found. In the simplest terms, the research suggested that "Two primary axes of differentiation were indicated by the data: the technical organization and the social organization of distribution. The technical organization of distribution refers to issues such as the physical location, policies, procedures, technology and equipment employed by distributors. The social organization of distribution refers to issues of cooperation, differential responsibility, and power and authority among distributors."[5] From this they argue that "(1) street-level sales; (2) indoor sales; and (3) delivery services" are the three main ways drugs are transacted, and "(1) freelance distributors; (2) socially bonded businesses; and (3) corporate-style distributors" are the main ways drug networks are organized.[6]

In these terms we can see that José's marijuana business was generally "freelance" (he was working on his own) though occasionally he might be classified as "socially bonded" (when he worked with his brother). His sales of marijuana were of the "indoor" variety most of the time, and only very occasionally of the "delivery" type, as when he went to a friend's house to hang out and he would bring the marijuana with him. Both of these would be classified as "discreet" by experts like Kleiman.[7] Only once does José report selling marijuana to a stranger, and this ends badly. In fact it ends his career as a dealer. By contrast, José's cocaine sales were always and entirely "street level" and "freelance" (as well as "flagrant" in Kleiman's terms).

If such typologies are useful for sorting out a bewildering complexity, it seems to me that there is a preeminent distinction between flagrant, street-level sales and everything else. The central issue with José's crack business was the anonymity at point of sale. This makes such deals efficient in a classic economic sense. Buyers and sellers can find one another in an open market. But it also renders the sales dangerous because there is no relationship beyond roles of buyer and seller, no trust and no loyalty. The "legitimate violence" of the State stands behind standard business relations.[8] If you try to walk out of the grocery store without paying, the police will come get you. Similarly, gang violence sanctions much street-level dealing. If you rip off the gang-affiliated guy on the corner, another guy—likely more than one—will come find you. José had neither type of support, and along with his inexperience, this made for a short career.

There was no way that José could sell crack like he sold marijuana. He didn't have the customers, and even if he found a few, he could never access as many as fast as he did standing on the corner. José never made friends with his crack customers. He nurtured no relationships, developed no social networks through his sales. Such urban sales are socially vacuous, just like the rest of the mainstream economy (at the retail end, anyway), and this is why scholars like Levitt and Dubner can argue that decision making structures relevant to anonymous transactions are universal (2005). However, not all drug sales are anonymous.

One place they surely are not is in the suburbs. There are only "discreet" (in Kleiman's terms) "indoor sales." Such deals operate with a different economic logic, and have different social outcomes. José's marijuana sales were suburban, in my terms, because they were focused on the friendships developed through the transaction and the social ingestion of the drugs. Indeed, the point of the drug sales *was* sociality. As this shows, suburban style deals do happen in the city (they may even be dominant there too), but there are not, and cannot be, flagrant and anonymous sales in the American suburbs. This is made evident when José's business intrudes on the "good part of town" where things are "quiet" and he is summarily shut down by the police.

Moreover, in an economic sense, José is clearly "freelance" in his crack business but he does not, in fact, have much control over it. The product arrives measured and packaged for sale, making him more like a paid vendor or a franchise operator than an entrepreneur. He has no ability to impact the quality, weight, or prices. It is all standardized, and not by him. Partly this is due to the fact that crack cannot be easily adulterated (while powder cocaine can be), but the central point is that suburban dealing involves many more independent decisions, more socially integrated communities, and much more entrepreneurial latitude than José's freelance crack dealing. Doug's story will illustrate this, as will most that follow.

DOUG

Doug was born in 1964 in Gloucester, Massachusetts but moved at a young age to live in the suburbs of Portland, Oregon. His father stayed on the East Coast and was mostly absent from Doug's life. According to Doug his father was a serious alcoholic and when the old man did visit it was, embarrassingly, to ask for money. Doug's mother had a white-collar job as an accountant, and managed to invest in her own house in a suburb where Doug went to middle and high school. The neighborhood was solidly middle class—with three-bedroom, two-bathroom houses, tidy yards, trees to climb, and schools that were generally safe. A quick Google search shows Doug's school now is in the top 10 percent in the state. While it is 87 percent "minority" now, when Doug went there it was dominated by whites like him. The only significant ethnic minorities were Latino, though there was a growing Asian presence. Something like a third of the students today take advanced placement classes and go to college. In Doug's time the school mostly served the children of working-class whites, along with professionals ranging from social workers and teachers to doctors.

Today Doug has the gnarled physique of a lifetime's physical labor. He is over six feet tall, with leathery hands and an ambling, bow-legged gait. He speaks with a hint of a stutter sometimes, one that remains from childhood. Doug is melancholy for most of the taped discussions we have. The questions I ask bring forth troubling memories. But Doug also has a wry, self-deprecating sense of humor and he is thoughtful and articulate about the world he is describing.

As he tells it Doug first smoked marijuana when he was twelve. He did it with some people he "met at a community center" and he was caught by the police that very first time. "It's been a pattern my whole life," he joked. "I don't think that was even the first time I was in the back of a cop car, but I was definitely in the back that night." Doug describes his childhood as "fairly abusive" and he attributes his early pot smoking to that. By fifth grade he was a regular consumer. About 1978, in junior high school, Doug met Connor, whose older brother sold cannabis and "we decided to do the same thing." As he explained, "it started out to get a good deal for myself, a good deal for friends, and it worked into selling pot at school." Then at age fifteen Doug's mom evicted him for misbehavior and he moved two doors down to Connor's family's house. Doug and Connor were buying four to eight ounces at a time (a quarter to a half pound) and selling $10 bags. Initially they measured it by fingers (a one-, a two-, or a three-finger bag referred to how full it was), but then they got a scale. At that time quarter ounces went for $10. "It was horrible pot," he said. Doug also worked at a restaurant busing tables, which is how he got his money to invest.

One day Connor had gone to school and Doug remained at his house because "I had just scored a half pound of weed. I had just gotten it, I hadn't taken anything out of it yet" and the cops "kicked in the door." Doug made no attempt to escape—it wouldn't have mattered, there seemed to be dozens of officers swarming the house all with weapons ready—but it got worse from there. "When I got busted at Connor's house the phone kept ringing . . . and everybody from school . . . who wanted to buy weed from me, man they kept calling and the cops kept picking up the phone. The cops would say 'Doug's busy, come on by.' Before you knew it we had like thirty different kids around the house in handcuffs. If they didn't go to jail their parents had to come get them. I got about 30 people thrown in jail." In the interview I protested that it was hardly Doug who got the other kids in trouble (in fact, while they were threatened, they didn't actually go to jail), to which he responded, "Yeah, but I'm the one who paid for it come Monday morning. Come Monday back at school, they didn't remember it was the cops." This was his junior year of high school.

Significantly, Doug *was* back in school on Monday. The police arrested Connor, too (in class at school) but they were both released on bail after less than two hours. And they were never prosecuted despite the fact that in addition to the marijuana the police also seized a notable cache of amphetamines. Still, the experience "put the kibosh on me selling, for a little while at least," said Doug, and he moved back in with his mom.

It turned out that a "little while" was about a year. "I got booted out of the house again right before I graduated high school . . . and I started selling weed again." Doug got an apartment with a roommate and worked to pay his own way. "Then I broke my leg real bad and the only way I could pay the rent was to sling dope. So I started selling coke. I was 18 years old." Normally Doug balanced his drug selling with his work in a restaurant, where he had moved up from being a busboy to a cook. But "I was in a cast for a year and couldn't work." With the marijuana he was "not really making any real money. Just getting my pot for cheap or free was all that was really designed into the pricing plan." The transition to cocaine was both obvious, and, because of his disability, economically necessary. "There was a great need for it in the early 1980s. It was everywhere. Everybody was selling coke. Everybody was doing coke. So I jumped in and started making money."

Leaving aside the question of why he was able to make money if in fact "everybody was selling," I was curious how the business worked, how he found a supply of the drug and customers to buy it. Doug explained "coming out of high school I had a lot of friends. All of my friends smoked pot, and a lot of them were graduating to coke. The customer base was no big deal. It was finding [the cocaine] that we had issues with." Here fate intervened. Doug's new roommate had a very high-level source for cocaine. Classically handsome, non-smoking, uninterested in taking drugs, the roommate defied most stereotypes of a dealer, but somehow he had developed foreign connections, people with boats and direct access to imported cocaine. Doug said, "For the longest time the best deals I got were straight through my roommate. . . . Everybody was paying $2,000 an ounce for coke and I was paying $500 an ounce. It was a GREAT deal. All of my friends were getting awesome deals. And the people who were not my close friends were still getting an awesome deal in comparison to what everyone else was selling it for. That's how I cleaned up. I made a lot of money. Everybody was getting $100 a gram and I'm giving . . . a sixteenth [of an ounce] . . . a gram and three quarters for 80 bucks." Doug sold drugs for less than half what his competitors charged. Later we will discuss why more profit was not "built into the pricing plan," as Doug had put it for marijuana.

For Doug, "there was never any guns, never anything like that."[9] The business was basically non-violent. But that didn't mean that there were not a few scares. One time, for instance, a supplier panicked and flushed two kilos of cocaine down the toilet (that is two thousand grams, more than four pounds). The supplier blamed it on Doug. "They came to me and they were going to kill me. They weren't very happy we'll say." But it did not take more than an explanation to set things straight. "I told them what the real deal was. They went back and before you knew it" the problem was solved. The supplier had "a nice tee shirt business, a Corvette. I saw him about two weeks later driving around in a fucking Pinto. And he didn't have a business no more. So I have a feeling those guys got paid."

Later in the interview Doug responded to more questions about problems with the law and their relation to quitting the business. He said, "I never really went to jail. I hung out in jail for a couple hours. That's about it." He emphasized that the constant challenge was to secure a cheap supply, that "connections dried up." I asked him why they "dry up" and he explained by telling me how he eventually quit dealing with his roommate. Essentially, Doug said, "I got scared. I had a feeling we were being watched and getting ready to go to jail. We were getting ready to get arrested at least. So I told my roommate and I split. I found another place to live and I moved within about a week. My roommate said I was crazy, didn't know what I was talking about. But about a week later he too moved. He felt the same thing." It turned out to have been prescient. Still, "[the roommate] couldn't leave the money alone . . . so he supported the guy down the hall. Gave him all the drugs. Gave him all our customers." And [this person] was arrested after about a week . . . and went to jail for three years."

After this Doug and his partner "both got out for a while," but when Doug ran into the former roommate a year later he was getting large amounts of high-quality marijuana from Northern California, and beginning to ship cocaine to Hawaii and bring cannabis back from there too. "He was pretty heavily into it. And he was doing quite well money wise . . . but we had gone our separate ways. I didn't want nothing to do with him and he didn't want nothing to do with me." It seemed like the two dealers were safer operating separately, and in their own ways—the partner was getting too big and Doug was using too much—and so that connection "dried up" in Doug's terms. The partner moved up the chain and sold larger and larger amounts of drugs across a wider geographic territory. Doug became steadily more mired in his own consumption and poor economic choices. So the demise, for Doug, came not swiftly via the criminal justice system or violence. It was a slow erosion. Addiction, as he called it, and other costs of the drug lifestyle, weighed on his health, his sanity, and his economic stability.

The economics are key. On one hand, Doug's increasing consumption was obviously making it difficult to turn a profit. He said, "I was out of control . . . and had to walk away. There's an old adage 'don't get high on your own supply' and we all laughed at it. But if it ain't the truth. . . . "[10] Still, "I was never solely a drug dealer. When I first got out of high school and broke my leg and I couldn't work for a year . . . yes, at that point I couldn't work and drugs were my sole income" but otherwise Doug had steady jobs, first in restaurants, then as a mechanic, and finally in construction. "I basically just realized I couldn't make any money selling drugs. I was just doing too much coke and had to stop. That was the eventual thing: I just didn't have any more money"—either to spend or to invest. There was more than a touch of sadness in this part of the interview. "The hardest part about walking away, though, is having that pocket money." I asked if he thought he was addicted to the money or the drugs and he replied, "I was equally addicted to both. It was killing my life, it was killing everything, you know?" Doug was completely done selling by age twenty-four. He had to get away from it. "If I've got that big pile of coke in front of me, I'm going to do it. Like alcohol now."

Doug considers himself an alcoholic and does not drink. He has been alcohol and cocaine-free for many years.

While Doug blames drug consumption for his downfall, this was not the only issue. He also talked extensively about the amount of cocaine he gave away, and this is confirmed by others I interviewed. Some of this went to his girlfriend. "She was just taking as much as she wants basically," and this seemed to Doug perfectly reasonable. However, "It turns out I was supplying some of her girlfriends, too, and that I didn't know about." According to Doug this was "against the rules." "She wasn't taking the risk. It wasn't her money going in. She was taking advantage of the situation. She took full advantage of the situation. . . ." Still, Doug stayed in the same committed relationship the entire time he was dealing, which would seem rare at that age, especially for a coke dealer. "In high school it was just pot, and the chicks didn't really put out for pot." He laughs. "I hear cocaine was a real good way to get laid, but I never used it to get laid. My bad. I missed that opportunity."

So, Doug was using too much and his girlfriend was taking too much. And he was selling for half what others charged. This put strains on his business. But in addition to all this, he also admitted: "If anybody came to the house, lines were on me. I'd give anybody lines." It is worth pausing here because all of Doug's business passed through his house, which suggests that all of his customers were given free cocaine in addition to the great deal. This seemed surprising in a business sense, so I asked, "wasn't your house always full of people?" "It was!" he laughed, "and so why did you do it that way?" I queried. "I just liked having friends," Doug replied. But then he considered this more carefully. After a pause he said, "I actually have no idea why I did it that way. It just seemed . . . I don't know, it all just flowed. Most people weren't going to come by and glom [i.e. illegitimately take] lines from me. Most people come by, you give them a line or two, they buy some coke and go on their merry way. That's how most people were doing it. There were only a few people around who would take advantage of my hospitality, my generosity."[11] Doug expanded on this to some degree and estimated that each customer spent about a half an hour "partying," that is, hanging around Doug's house accepting his gifts of cocaine and occasionally offering some of their own. (Some of their own that they had just bought from him.)

In terms of economics, this generosity at the point of sale is a *lagniappe*, a gift essential to the conclusion of a sale.[12] You find it in some market situations, and I found this with every suburban dealer I interviewed. Most dealers stressed that gifting was an essential part of the business, though whether it was "real" business or "truly" a gift was a matter of confusion and debate. As we'll see, some claimed that the lagniappe was merely strategic, a way to lure in customers. Others claimed that it was "real" generosity and that they "partied" with people because they wanted to, because it was fun, or because sharing was the culturally appropriate way to ingest drugs. Some said contradictory things in the space of a single interview—they were self-interested *and* altruistic—or they alternated between explanations within one interview or across several. However, all suburban dealers gave away free drugs to their customers in the context of the sale. It seems to me that what defines a lagniappe in this context is that it is *both* strategic and a gift at the same time. The apparent distinction between the two is illusory, as we will discuss in the conclusion. Separating self-interest from sociality is part of our cultural heritage, a way Americans make sense of our behavior, but analytically this is confused.

With all of his free-yet-obligatorily given cocaine,[13] and repeated deals with the same people, Doug engaged his customers deeply. They shared time and pleasure, conversation and friendship. He sold them cocaine for a profit, but moderated, sometimes subordinated, his business interests. Doug gifted, sometimes dramatically, and others reciprocated with friendship, further sales, and return gifts from the drugs they had purchased from Doug only minutes before. The social bonds this generates in the suburban economy compounds its safety. After all, only an explanation from Doug was required to ensure that the loss of four pounds of cocaine—many thousands of dollars' worth—was falsely blamed on him. Ultimately the person who panicked and forfeited the drugs paid for them without dramatic violence—only the loss of capital, a business, and a car. While downgrading from a Corvette to a Pinto was a shocking loss of status, it paled in comparison to the terror José experienced—in jail and out—for pathetically small amounts of drugs.

José lacked even minimal control over the pricing of his cocaine, he spent no time with his customers, and so had little possibility of building the social capital, trust, and contacts that Doug managed. José did not have to navigate the ambivalent economics of gifts and counter-gifts—at least in his anonymous sales—but he did not reap the deep, human rewards of such grappling. Market efficiency has its price, too. While neither José nor Doug had particularly happy experiences with drug dealing, Doug's was made significantly more profitable, and less dangerous, by the social context in which he operated. This is at least partially explained by the intimacy of the suburban drug economy and the moral ambivalence upon which it turns.

NOTES

1. See Natarajan (2006:171–72). For other typologies of dealing "levels" see Waldorf et al. (1992:78). Murphy et al. suggest five discrete modes of becoming a cocaine seller (1990), and see also Dorn et al. (1992).

2. Relying on the excellent ethnographic work of Venkatesh (2000), Levitt and Dubner write that "a crack gang works pretty much like the standard capitalist enterprise: you have to be near the top of the pyramid to make a big wage" (2005:203).

While this may be narrowly true, the much larger, spurious conclusion they draw from this is that all economic organization is like "a standard capitalist enterprise." I aim to show how wrong this is.

3. See Murphy et al. (1990:322).

4. See Hart (2005:1).

5. See Curtis and Wendel (2000:128).

6. See Curtis and Wendel (2000:132).

7. Kleiman (1991)

8. Max Weber (1946) is the typical source for the idea that "legitimate violence" is fundamental to state power. In other words, citizens have to internalize the laws for complex societies to function.

9. This stands in sharp contrast to urban dealing, where "regular displays of violence are essential" (Bourgois 2003:24).

10. See Waldorf et al. on "controlled use" of cocaine (1992:140).

11. This resonates with a dealer who explained why he spent all his money and drugs, "I just wanted friends" (Bourgois 2003:91).

12. See Crawford (2016) for an initial discussion of this term. I learned the word from a Society for Economic Anthropology listserve, though I cannot remember who brought it to my attention.

13. This paradox comes from Mauss, who urges us "to emerge from self, to give freely and obligatorily" (1990:71). We discuss this more in the final chapters.

THREE

Dealing with Privilege

One clear theme that emerged from the previous chapter is that privilege has much to do with how dealers work, and the consequences they suffer (or don't) for dealing. We saw José and his friends struggle to pool enough money to get pot to smoke, and occasionally even shoplift. We saw José risk selling crack openly to strangers to make pitiful profits (up to twelve sales to make $20). And we saw him try to sell marijuana to friends (in the suburban style) but fail to compete with the more economically efficient street dealers.[1] José took a chance selling cannabis to a stranger and nearly paid with his life.

By contrast Doug moved vastly more cocaine than José, thousands of dollars' worth at a time. He had little trouble finding friends who could be customers, who had the cash to buy his drugs. Doug had numerous encounters with the police, but never did any time in jail nor did he experience any violence beyond threats. While neither José nor Doug had much support from government or family, Doug had other resources—middle-class friends with money to spend—and his business model was thus resistant to police interference.

This chapter extends this theme of privilege with the story of Brad. Brad grew up in suburban New Jersey, the youngest son of teachers. He was not rich, but his parents were well-educated and Brad had the opportunity to attend the elite, private schools at which his folks sometimes worked. His mother in particular was very supportive. She did not throw him out of the house for misbehavior (as Doug's had) or refuse him bail (as José's had). Brad was an accomplished athlete, and despite his middle-class roots, he played basketball in some of the grittiest cities in New Jersey. He therefore acted as a kind of *entrepôt*, a middleman who could move between urban (often black) culture and elite (generally white) private school life. This turned out to be a lucrative intersection.

BRAD

Brad is lanky, tall, whip-smart, and funny. His blue eyes fix on you in conversation and his head tilts attentively to catch your words. After college he worked for several years assisting the disabled. I have a disabled daughter, and that is how we originally met. He is now a doctor, married, with rambunctious children and a very successful wife.

It was somewhat of a surprise to me when I mentioned this book project and he volunteered to tell me about his dope career. Our first taped interview lasted nearly three hours. As an author himself, a researcher, and former drug dealer, Brad had a multifaceted view of my project, and he had much to say about it. His initial interview is much longer than the others, longer in total than when I interviewed other people multiple times over different occasions. Since Brad is younger than most of the men profiled in this book, his story illustrates how widespread drug dealing has been in suburban America, and how persistent it has remained over time. Brad shows what a normal part of middle class culture the ingestion of powerful psychoactive drugs had become — from my era through his. It also demonstrates some striking consistencies from my far earlier experience on the West Coast to his later in the East.[2]

However, Brad was not a particularly precocious explorer of alternative consciousness. The youngest of three children in a two-parent suburban household, he was a dedicated jock and his focus was on that. His older siblings were into drugs, he said, and he was aware of it, but his early misbehavior was limited to "raiding someone's parents' liquor cabinets on a weekend" and other acts he—and many other suburbanites— considered benign. As he put it, "I had close friends who were smoking pot and doing stuff like that but I was pretty clear that I didn't want to get into it because I wanted to be an athlete. I wanted . . . a college scholarship. . . . I would try to get good sleep on the weekends so I could play whatever tournament I had and that sort of thing." The fact that Brad was thinking of college when he was barely done with middle school is itself indicative of a certain social class.

In 1997 Brad was fifteen and his father died of a heart attack during a morning jog. This did not immediately plunge Brad into the world of drugs. Initially, instead, something like the opposite happened. "After [my father died] . . . my mother was a total mess and I became very much her primary care giver. My brother was living at home but . . . he was pretty much an alcoholic. He was . . . holed up in his room most of the time. . . . And my mom was sort of distant . . . not able to function . . . she went to her job but when she came home she wasn't able to take care of everyday tasks."

The loss was catastrophic for the whole family, but especially for Brad, the youngest. He had idolized his father and with his passing Brad sought to care for his traumatized mother. "I didn't want her to stay home alone, so I never slept out anywhere. If I went to a party I would go for a couple of hours and come home. I was bound to my home and I . . . maybe . . . drank a few times in that period but still had never tried any drugs or anything like that." While there seemed to be some sort of dysfunction going on (an alcoholic brother and a sister who disappears from the narrative), Brad's immediate response to the death of his father was an *increased* sense of responsibility. This turns out to be a central element of Brad's character, but one that only fully asserts itself after some rather dramatic misbehavior.

Freshman year of high school was hard. Then the "summer [after freshman year] one of my closest friends invited me to go for a week to the beach with him and his family, their . . . family vacation. That was the first time I stepped out of that post-traumatic family experience into another space. We rented a house at the Jersey Shore, Long Beach Island, and that friend was among my friends, who were all jocks, but were starting to smoke pot and that sort of thing." An uncle of the friend was a "prolific pot smoker" and was well-supplied with a cannabis variety they had even named after him. So "we smoked pot in this sort of wooden outdoor shower of Long Beach Island in a beach house. And yes, you know . . . when I look back at . . . how all that stuff happened I think in some ways it was sort of a release . . . after this pressurized experience of . . . you know, after my father died."

He also switched back to public school. Both Brad's parents were teachers and while his elementary education had mostly been in the public system, he had later switched to an expensive private school where one of them worked. This had advantages in terms of sports (they had a terrific basketball program), but it also meant that Brad was away from the friends he had grown up with. After Brad lost his father, he decided to return to public school and the comfort of boys he had known from childhood.

"I entered the world of pot smoking at that time. I wasn't doing any other drugs, but I started smoking pot . . . hanging out with those guys . . . we were friends but we had separate worlds. Sometimes we would be at parties, they would go off and smoke pot but I wasn't part of their regular pot smoking ritual. But that year I became part of it. So we would finish school, and some people would go to soccer practice and those of us who didn't have soccer practice would go in to the woods and smoke pot for hours and then go and get pizza and then go home." The social aspect was paramount, the sharing of pot and pizza, the camaraderie. Brad worked doing childcare in the afternoons in the summers, and that helped pay for his dope smoking. But his father's passing put pressure on the family's finances.

"When my father died he didn't have life insurance or anything like that and my mom was a schoolteacher. She had three kids; my sister was in college, at an expensive private institution. And we had a little bit of money that was a social services thing that came because I was still a minor, and my mom sort of used that to pay the bills and stuff. But money had become an issue in our house. It was always an issue in the sense that we went to a private school and other people would go on these lavish vacations and we would go visit my grandparents. But if money was a huge drama, it had been kept between my parents. Now that my father was gone the money problems had spilled out into the family. So when I started, I was basically buying pot with the lunch money my mom would give me and I just started feeling this huge shame about it." It was the shame of financial dependence—and a desire to be independent—that would lead him to begin selling cannabis.

"I started to see . . . these other people were smoking lots of pot and providing other people with pot. They would open up a massive bag and roll a huge joint and we would all get really stoned and the thought hadn't hit me until around this time that some of these people just sell pot in order to smoke it with no limits. So that was the sort of thought that hit me, that allowed me to enter that realm. I wasn't thinking of it as this really lucrative domain, but it was something that allowed you to smoke pot without having to tap other financial sources." In other words, selling pot would allow Brad to "smoke without limits"—to share ostentatiously—without straining his mother's limited resources.

"So there was this guy who was a senior that year and he sold pot and I had become friends with him and I would smoke with him and that sort of thing. And you know, it must have been maybe a month, not long after I had started going to school [in the new place] that I thought that I should save up some money and buy some quantity of pot and try to basically . . . the thought that I had in my head was that I would buy these half ounces and sell dimes [ten dollars' worth] and nickels [five dollars' worth] to friends and have some quantity left over that I would smoke myself. . . . I hadn't really registered the idea that if you buy a half ounce you get it for less. I thought a nickel was a nickel and a dime was a double nickel. I hadn't really processed this idea that the more you buy the cheaper it is." He goes on, "I played basketball, I didn't play soccer, so I would hang out with these [non-soccer-playing] dudes. It was pretty much the black kids at our school and the poor white kids. And we would all go to the woods by the library and smoke a bunch of pot. And I would sell them all the nickels and dimes, but I also had this schwag shake [bad pot, leaves and bits that would break off and settle in the bottom of the bag] that I would accumulate and I would roll these big blunts and so [these customers, friends] were benefiting from my surplus, but then I was also selling to them at just the standard rate at that point."

In the interview I was interested in the sources of the money, the way the kids who were not selling managed to get money for drugs. Brad explained, "there were for sure a lot of people that had . . . unproblematic sources of cash in their household, from their families. Almost none of us were working because we all played sports, after school and on the week-end, all of us, my closest friends, we were just playing sports constantly. One of my friends . . . was really poor and worked at the ice cream shop that was owned by the football coach, who got him a job there so he could make a little money. But my friends . . . nobody was rich but everybody was sort of confidently middle class. No real fear of economic backsliding . . . I have no idea what the ins and outs of it were, but these were people who could produce money for pizza, or for whatever, with-out having to generate the income themselves. But when I went into it I don't remember thinking . . . 'it will be from these guys' parents that the money will come,' you know what I mean? It was just like there was this thing that happens, there are a lot of kids around here who were buying pot, someone's going to sell it to them, no one in our grade really sells . . . so if I got it I would be able to provide it to my friends." Brad's original motivation to sell drugs comes down to an interesting combination: 1. A desire to be independent of his mother's money and save her limited resources, 2. Wanting to provide pot to himself and his close friends and, 3. A willingness to provide pot more generally to everyone in his grade who desired it. Brad's original drug business combines business acumen, public service, rugged American individualism, and devotion to family. It was not a simple decision to profit, but an array of desires that together pointed him toward a dope dealing resolution.

I asked Brad to explain some of the mechanics of the business, how he decided on pricing and quantities and so forth. He responded, "I don't really remember the pricing at that point. I think there were these little bags that were nickel bags or dime bags and you would basically stuff them. And then once it was stuffed as full as it could be, that's a nickel. And once that other one is stuffed as full as it could be, that was a dime." This sort of sale by volume of the container is common for low-level dealers before they acquire a scale, before they operate in bigger quan-tities and work more professionally via selling by weight.

I then asked whether everyone got a standard price and Brad replied, "Pretty much. I can vaguely remember times where there was this guy, he was one of the poorest guys around. . . . His mom was a crack addict, his dad was also a crack addict,[3] he had three siblings that were all from different fathers and they all lived with their grandma; I think she cleaned houses or something like that. He was one of the poorest kids around, and he was also pretty much my best friend. He was one of the best athletes too. I can vaguely remember him scrounging . . . seven dollars for a dime. I remember I would give him special deals and things like that. And there were times where he only had nine dollars and I would just give him a dime . . . or smoke him out [i.e. share pot] or whatever." This combination of generosity and commerce, the way gifts of drugs and friendship intertwine with a profit motive, is fundamental to the suburban drug economy.

The next turn in the narrative involves getting busted for the first time (but not the last) *and* getting fingered as a police informant. "Sometime in November I go to gym class . . . early and the senior guy who sells me pot isn't there yet so I propped the door open to the gym locker room, there is an indoor entry door and exit door. And his locker is straight in there and I prop it open so he can still get in because when the bell sounds, they shut the door and it gets locked. I wanted him to be able to get in so I could get pot from him and then run out to gym. So he comes in and he's getting the pot out and I think he gives me eight quarters [quarter ounces, seven grams each] or something like that. I had maybe worked my way to two ounces at a time by then, all in separate plastic bags and I'm handing him the money and this guy, Mr. . . . he has an Irish name, it doesn't matter but this big, fat . . . bullish, balding, red-faced, white-haired guy who was my first period English teacher walks in and I sort of, you know, go like that [Brad motions like he's hiding something], and I have this money in my hand and go like this [trying to look casual] and he stops and walks away and I ask my dealer, I'm like, 'I think he saw' and the dealer is like, 'Ah nah, no, he didn't see.' And I give him the money.

"I'm sort of stressed out, I'm like 'maybe we should put the pot some-where else, he saw' and the dealer's like no, no don't worry about it. So I take it, and I think he wrapped it up in a shirt for me and gave it to me to stuff in my locker, my gym locker. So I stuff it in my gym locker and I go out . . . on the soccer field. I see the Irish teacher come out and he's sort of the supervisor of that period. And he talks to my gym guy and [they go back in] and there's stuff happening and I'm just sort of like 'fuck, you know, shit.' And we are coming back in from playing and the dealer's shirt was all ripped from the game and we come back into the locker room and I just see the Irishman standing there with the vice principal and some other guy and they say, 'Mr. [Brad's-last-name'] and that kind of thing, and I'm just like, 'fuck,' and I think the dealer bolts down the locker room a little bit and there's someone else over there to take him and he's just sort of freaking out and everyone is standing there and they wait until everyone changes their clothes and everyone gets out of the locker room and they go through the dealer's locker and they make him open it. And he opens it and they pull out this, you know, a massive brown paper bag with shitloads of pot all separately bagged in there. Big wad of cash, and you know, that definitely equals two [i.e. 1 + 1 = 2, it's obvious], there's no way that doesn't equal a conviction for dealing. So the dealer is like, 'fuck,' I remember him punching the locker and sort of freaking out and then we go to my locker. He had this long locker be-cause he was a senior and I had this little stubby locker because I was a sophomore."

"I had this bag of shake [the 'schwag' mentioned above, the leaves and bits that fall off] . . . and I would keep it in my boot, I would sort of shove it in my boot so if I got searched by someone they wouldn't find it. . . . My boots are on top of my stuff. So I was sitting there and they open [my locker] and there it is [the bag] with a little bit of schwag shake. And they're like 'Ah ha!' And I'm like, 'oh fuck' because there are these other eight bags, these other eight quarters wrapped in this shirt. And I'm like, 'AHH FUCK' you know, and I punched the locker too, and they say, 'JUST RELAX.'"

At this point "they ceremoniously take everything out of the locker and then he shakes the shirt that has all the stuff wrapped in it and nothing comes out and they put it in this pile and I'm thinking, 'thank fucking God' and then there is this sprawling pile. But then one of the men begins really checking this pile carefully and putting the things he has checked in another pile. And the shirt with the pot is sort of . . . spewing towards this other pile and I'm being theatrical and at some point I make this big hullabaloo up top and slide the shirt over to the other pile down low and they're like, 'Just relax!' Ultimately what happens is they end up shaking my other stuff and they don't find it. And they're thinking 'the dealer sold you pot that you were going to smoke yourself,' so I'm not considered a dealer at this point. So we go and they put us in separate rooms so they can really get the story."

"Just like on TV," I say.

"Yeah and there is this whole drama, and the police aren't there yet, it's just the vice principal and the principal and everything. I'm a new student there and everybody also knows that my father just died and there is this easy narrative for me. I'm an athlete, I was going to be the star of the basketball team, I was an athlete and I stumbled onto this pot thing. So they talked to [the dealer] in this one room and they talked to me in this other room and I'm sort of, you know, just dreaming up what's going to happen if I just sprint to my locker and just grab the bag and run into the woods and throw it somewhere, you know, I'm just trying to figure out what the hell to do. And I don't know exactly how it all worked out. I never mentioned anything about selling, I just said 'I don't know anything, I don't know what's going on. This is the first time. I don't know.' I think I just denied everything and then they said we could call someone to let them know what's going on and I called my brother and just said 'come pick me up.'"

The upshot of this is that the other dealer, who was "from a poor family [and was] selling to make money," gets kicked out of school permanently. Brad, because of his reputation as a good student, his family situation, his value to the school as an athlete, and the fact that only one bag of pot was discovered, is suspended for two weeks. It probably also helped that he is white. Brad did still have to go to the police station and be fingerprinted, and he undertook the other rituals of the criminal justice system, but nothing permanent was added to his record and he spends no time in jail or on parole. Brad was not able to explain to his senior friend what happened, however, and since Brad seemed to suffer no legal consequences, and because he was new to the school, the class-mates and customers of the dealer assumed that Brad was a police infor-mant, a "narc." The failure of the police to find Brad's drugs led many to think he worked for the police.

By now Brad's mother was at a loss for what to do. "My mom was a mess emotionally and she had sort of no disciplinary control over me. . . ." Brad ponders for a second. "She had some control over me through massive bursts of emotion and guilt loading or things like that but you know, there were no limits, she couldn't actually set a limit. She couldn't be, like, you can't go to this house and stay there because you got in trouble at school and you are also in trouble at home. She wasn't able to do that. They used to be able to do that kind of do that stuff with my brother and sister before my dad died, but you know. . . ."

So Brad spent the two weeks that he was suspended from school at a beach house near where he had initially smoked pot. "His [the friend with the beach house] parents were away, his grandmother . . . could barely remember her own name and was supposedly watching [the friend], and they have three floors and he has this loft up top that is this pot / sex lair that we hang out in all the time. . . . So I end up at my friend's house and we are just smoking massive quantities of pot and, you know, I'm trying to think about the rest of that year."

Luckily for Brad's business his own classmates (i.e. the sophomores) knew him from elementary school, they knew his family, and trusted him. Brad still had customers. What he lacked was a supplier and at about this time he happened upon a good one. It came through another of his friends: "So 'Elliot' was a basketball buddy, he's one of my best friends growing up, and he went to the private school with me for a while. He came from a similar economic background as me, you know, lower middle class basically, he was on the lower side of it I guess, and he had gone on a scholarship to the private school, and then he had left to go to a different private school and got kicked out of there, two different private schools he got kicked out of, and ultimately went to a community college and got his GED. But . . . he hung out with this guy who was sort of a Phish tour pot guy that he had met at the last private school. . . . This guy, 'Collin,' he was maybe a couple years older than us and he had . . . one of those fucked up vans that you see on the Phish or Grateful Dead tour with the curtains in the back and there's a makeshift bed in the back and you're driving around the country on Phish tour always high on something, usually acid or coke. He was a sort of nut."

"So Collin had massive quantities of pot all the time and Elliot had seen that you could make good money and do lots of drugs by selling pot, so he also was starting to sell . . . around the time when I [first] got busted. And so I started getting pot from Collin. Collin . . . had friends in Vermont and he would drive up to Vermont and get this amazing, super high-quality pot, grown by hippies in Vermont, or grown by someone who knew what they were doing. . . . It was really something that had been grown with care and transported with care and you could look at and inspect and have some sense of quality and smell the chemicals and all that kind of stuff. It actually had a smell, you know, the smell would seep through your pocket and fill the room and this kind of thing, so you had to start double bagging it and put fabric softener sheets around it to absorb the smell and that sort of stuff. You could actually hold the stem and see the crystals on it." So Brad partners with Elliot, who shares with him this source for very high quality cannabis. This provides a practical introduction into the larger world of drug dealing, and eventually a social identity where this dealing makes sense. Brad is still only half done with high school.

At this point Brad has not taken any other drugs, but the amount of pot he is selling has increased dramatically. He gets a pager and develops a code for talking on the telephone (something "lame," as he puts it, like "do you want to meet on *eighth* street or *fourth* street?") that his "mom figures out immediately." He is not making a lot of money, however. "It wasn't a huge profit. . . . Let's say we would get an ounce for $300, we would sell the eighths for $50, so that's $400, and then we would probably end up smoking an eighth, or a bit more, but you would make $50 bucks off it or $30 bucks or something like that. I remember there were times people were selling ounces for $400 and we would have to sell the eighths for $60, and so we're not making huge amounts of money but were making enough to smoke, and we're slowly building a little bit of money." The parallel with the West Coast dealers' experience is striking.

The big issue for Brad, however, is financial autonomy. At this point "I am no longer taking money from my mom for lunch and shit like that . . . like I told you before my mom never cooked. My dad was the one who cooked. So drug money would go to pizza . . . and doing . . . stuff. It . . . gave me this sense of independence that I could provide for myself and I think I had this idea that in some way I was taking a burden off my mom financially."[4]

However sensible this seemed to Brad at the time, he was clearly creating all sorts of trouble for himself, and anxiety for his mother. "I was constantly in trouble at the public school, never again for drugs but constantly for other things I was in the principal's office. They are basically ready to kick me out. I'm being suspended all the time for disciplinary stuff and yelling at teachers. I'm kind of mess so we decided . . . to go back to private school." He manages to convince the private school to take him, but only if he repeats sophomore year. "I still had these dreams of getting a college scholarship. I was playing on travel teams and that kind of thing. And I starting playing that season for the private school and I was scoring lots of points and I was in the newspaper and that sort of stuff and those dreams were sort of happening. . . . It seems like this school will allow me to sort of redeem myself for the basketball thing, give me a chance to try to stir up some interest in me as a college player."

Meanwhile Elliot has quit school, or been kicked out, and is attending community college (at age sixteen), but he and Brad continue selling pot. They are not partners, strictly speaking, but much of their business is conducted together. As Brad describes it, they had a "monopoly within at least a large circle of people on the good pot. [Collin was Elliot's connection, but for the kids still in school] I was the only person who could get really good pot." The relationship between Elliot and Brad survives one bad deal: Elliot didn't have all the money for an ounce of pot, but he passed what he bought along to Brad without telling him it was underweight. Brad sold it as an ounce, and when the customer came back and demonstrated that it was short, Brad, trusting Elliot, got into an argument with the customer. Elliot admitted this much later. The point is that while things were not always rosy, even when deals went bad there was no danger of violent retribution. The argument never amounted to more than aspersions cast and reputations dented.

Then Collin sells psychedelic mushrooms to the boys and this opens a new world for Brad. "That fall of junior year Elliot gets some ounces of mushrooms so I get maybe an ounce of mushrooms and do it with a bunch of friends and it's just this mind blowing, amazing experience. We're all in the woods and it's just unbelievable. . . . I had . . . maybe four or five friends and we all ate a certain amount and then I sold some eighths to some people and you know, a certain buzz happened in our grade, some people start asking for them." Brad had purchased the mushrooms to sell even though he had never tried them. As he experiments with harder drugs, Brad is at the same time coming to think of them as commodities. The "system" for selling mushrooms was the same as it was for pot, he says. Same source, same customers, better profit margin. This was also the case later when Brad moved into selling ecstasy. "We started doing ecstasy, and like everything else, there was a pattern in place. Collin could get ecstasy, we wanted to try to get ecstasy, so I would get . . . twenty pills. . . . Ecstasy costs $20 . . . but with Collin we could get it for . . . $13 or $14 and we followed this same sort of pattern."

At first the hallucinogens did not fit well with Brad's identity. "Growing up I was very much basketball, I had Air Jordans and I played basketball in places like Trenton, which is the inner city near us, and I sort of dressed that kind of way. I had baggy jeans and that was my style. At home I hung out with a lot of hippies. My parents were hippies, my brother was a hippie, you know, in our room we liked to listen to Phish and Grateful Dead and Jimi Hendrix and Led Zeppelin for hours and hours when I was a kid and I knew all that music, but I sort of identified as this sort of rap basketball guy so . . . this whole mushroom/hallucinogens experience wasn't my thing as much. . . . I had a gold chain and played on this travel team, we all had our gold chains. We couldn't wear them during the game so we would all put them on our coach and he would have like thirteen gold chains on as we would play, you know, everybody would have the puffy jackets." In the interview I asked about the significance of the puffy jackets and chains and Brad laughs. "The chains were huge you know and they had these massive medallions. None of them were actually gold, they were sprayed gold, you know. I remember buying this chain that was partly gold color and partly silver. And I was like, 'you don't have it in gold?' and they were like, 'yeah, we can have it in gold, just come back in a half hour' and you could literally just see the guy spraying it in the back. . . . At first I smoked pot with the black kids and then, you know, I started smoking pot more with my hippie buddies who were more suburban."

The suburban faction of Brad's friends was changing. "My core group of friends that I had grown up with were . . . guys I had played sports with . . . they were also growing their hair out now and sort of experimenting with being hippies. It was very much the in-your-face Birkenstocks, corduroy pants, tie dye shirt, growing your hair out kind of thing. And they all did it at the same time, end of sophomore year. All of a sudden everybody that used to have a short suburban cut no longer did. All of a sudden the soccer team had pony tails and, you know, we were just screaming pot as we walked down the street of this suburban town. And they were all playing music and would go to these shows . . . you know, Phish or whatever it was. But I hadn't been really into that scene yet. I was sort of drifting into it at this point, so was Elliot, who had a sort of similar trajectory. He grew up even closer to Trenton and was similar. Most of our friends were black when we played basketball and that was sort of our reference point, and then we were both sort of drifting into this more hippie thing." Brad had experimented with cannabis with his "rap basketball friends," but his transition to harder drugs accompanied a movement to white, suburban, neo-hippie culture.

Brad attended two Phish shows in the summer before his junior year, which he found "really awesome, an incredible experience, this whole other space . . . it just felt like a parallel universe." By the following summer he saw more than a dozen shows. Before, during, and afterwards he was ingesting and selling LSD, MDMA (the active ingredient in Ecstasy), and, in particular, large amounts of marijuana. He tried cocaine in conjunction with these other drugs, and he was drinking alcohol as well. "I remember as school started I was trying to go back and think about how many times I ate mushrooms or acid that summer and was like 'whoa, thirty times in a summer' or whatever it was. And I remember when school started there were people at the private school I didn't see much and they were saying 'what happened to you?'" I asked Brad what that meant. "I was losing weight. And whatever . . . it did to my face or my persona, my personality, it was visible to outsiders." He had also returned to selling drugs at the private school, which was more lucrative because the kids had better incomes. "I'm making money off these kids and, for me, it's not morally problematic. And for them it's not problematic because they have money and really I'm their only hope for getting pot, you know? They really can't get pot from anyone else. And I'm selling mushrooms to some of them. And so I do have this division between my public school friends and my private school friends."

About this time Brad began reading the Beat writers that his dad had once been interested in, and Brad would read them provocatively, at school, instead of his assigned material. This made for an odd fit with private school culture. Brad was arrested for possession of alcohol (twice, because he would supply kids with booze that he got from his older brother), he received numerous traffic violations (he went to traffic school high on cocaine), and then he wrecked his sister's car (nobody was hurt). Finally, Brad was called into the headmaster's office and accused of selling marijuana (he had pot stuffed in his underwear at the time). Brad never suffers any serious legal consequences from any of this despite the fact that "it was probably clear to a lot of the teachers that I did drugs . . . because I would come to school really stoned. I smoked a bong before school a lot of the time and . . . we would eat mushrooms on Sunday and I would come to school on Monday still tweaky." And it was not just teachers. In his bucolic town "it was pretty clear that the cops knew that I was at least major fuckup, if not a drug dealer."

The arrival of cocaine accelerated the "train wreck" that Brad describes bearing down. "And it was again with cocaine this same kind of pattern, we would get an eight ball [3.5 grams] or we would get seven grams, and we would sell the grams and then we would have a certain number of grams left over. Or we would look at it and be, like, okay, we got this for 'x' number of dollars, if we sell all the grams at a normal price that means that these other grams are ours to do." When they could, Brad and Elliot combined other drugs with Ketamine, "a whole shitload of 'K' . . . we just did outrageous amounts of 'K.' I had no idea what it would do to you but I just loved it," and then "to balance out" the edginess of cocaine "we used to crush pills up and snort them too, we would . . . crush up Xanax and Valium, Klonopin and stuff like that." As Brad explained, at first it seemed that any drug could be plugged into their system. "We . . . had the hang of this deal. You would get a bunch of something, sell part of it, use the rest of it, you make a little bit of money and then on it turns. . . . "

But cocaine turned out to be different. "One thing that I can distinctly remember that changed was that the kind of panic that people would have, and the kind of obsessive calling you that people would do; people would just harass you in a whole different way for coke than they would for pot or for mushrooms. . . . " Brad continued, "People would lose their shit and start calling you over and over and over again. It freaked me out, I hated it. And sometimes they were even close friends. And it felt like a different thing, I felt more guilty giving people their first bit of coke than giving people . . . their first mushroom trip, which almost felt like an honor or something. It was like you were opening up a space for someone with mushrooms whereas with coke, it just had a dirtier feel. . . . People really did seem to lose their willpower once they got a hold of coke. You know, they just really seemed to get obsessed with it." Ominously, Brad adds "I always really liked it, but almost from the beginning I wanted to stop doing it."

Stopping did not turn out to be easy. Brad and Elliot "never . . . ever just did small quantities of stuff," and so trying to hide cocaine from girlfriends and loved ones was impossible. "We would end up doing huge amounts of coke and Elliot would just sit there looking like a lizard, and so he would always get us busted." (Here he means "busted" in the sense of being conspicuous, not arrested by the police.) As their cocaine consumption rises, Brad and Elliot are coming to buy pounds of pot—$4,000 or more at a time—as well as Ecstasy and other drugs, and the stakes are getting significantly higher. They are buying from a new class of professionals, people who supported themselves by selling drugs, and who more or less lived nomadic lives on the psychedelic rock concert circuit. But Brad also worked with "other people that had more suburban lives . . . maybe even had a job but augmented their income by selling pounds of pot or something like that. You know, they had maybe done it when they were younger and they had kids now and they didn't make enough money with their job . . . these people were more . . . in the woodwork of the normal community around me." In the same way that Brad and Elliot had earlier linked the "inner city" culture of basketball to suburban public schools and to their elite, private school, they were now the link between nomadic professional dealers and their settled suburban customers. Quantities were going up, prices down, and Brad was sometimes clearing $1,000 a week despite his Brobdingnagian levels of personal use.

Monetary success accompanied personal disintegration. "I was continuing the nosedive. And I was really constantly trying to stop myself, you know? And especially with coke." For instance, he and Elliot went with Brad's family on vacation to the Outer Banks of North Carolina and they decided to get clean on the trip, to have a "natural vacation." But "two days later we're calling Elliot's girlfriend to have her next-day-air a package with Ketamine and Ecstasy and other pills to my grandfather's P.O. box. I told him it's this special CD that we needed and I don't know . . . it's someone's birthday, I have no fucking idea. We get that package and we do all those drugs, we get another package sent, you know we are both desperately trying to stop ourselves but every two days. . . ." The minute they get home they buy cocaine, which had become, by now, a thing that Brad says was "ever-present."

So again in the summer Brad followed the band Phish on tour. He attended as many as sixteen shows that summer, he was doing a lot of coke, and visibly disintegrating. "I'm looking super skinny and . . . a mess all the time and then . . . we were going to a Phish show in Jersey. I hadn't been home for a while and my mom is just thinking that I'm a mess . . . I need clothes, I mean I've been on a string of shows for a couple weeks and we are going on another string. I need clothes and I sent my girlfriend by the house to get some and she comes with this bag and she says, 'there are clothes in there and your mom put something in there, I don't think you want to see it. It's your choice but you can just tell me to give you the clothes and I'll give you the clothes and you don't have to see what she put in their right now.' And I'm already way high and of course I want to see it. And my mom had put in there this picture of me and my dad roasting marshmallows on a family vacation in Shenandoah or something like that, maybe the year before he had died. And I think she had written on the back something like, 'what if your father could see you now,' or something devastating like that. And I went to the show and I sought out heroin almost immediately and got outrageously high on heroin."

By now Brad is being fronted—supplied on credit—ten pounds of pot at a time. He generally has $5,000 in working capital, and he is getting maybe four times that on consignment. He uses part of his money to help bail out one of his drug suppliers, who had been arrested. This puts him in the good graces of the arrested man's business partner, which further drops the price of the cannabis and increases Brad's profits. But even the professional dealers are worried about Brad. They intervene to steer him away from heroin, despite their own lavish drug habits. Brad says, "They're pretty much out of my league they're so fucked up," but they clearly have an avuncular relationship with Brad. He moves to their "inner circle," he says. "We really had built trust over time."

Just after this arrest Brad and his new inner circle move on to the next show, one in upstate New York. "And then we meet up in Albany and we just get outrageously high on acid and we're doing pills. I black out. I don't remember after a certain hour. But we don't sleep all night. . . . Phish usually has these parking lots which are basically wombs. You know that cops roam, but it's pretty easy to not get busted there. You sort of have to be ridiculous and blatant to get busted. The show at Albany is in the middle of the city so there is nothing that belongs just to the venue, everything belongs to the city. So the city cops are there, and I remember . . . we were drinking these massive Long Island Iced Teas and I'm still half blacked out and I'm like, 'I need to get some coke.' And [my friend and supplier] does too, he needs to get coke. So we go down and I buy two eight balls [eighth ounces] from this guy I know from tour, just this quick hand off because we know the cops are around and I just stuff it in my pocket."

"So I sit down on this bench and I go . . . to take a look at what I got and the girl next to me said, 'Don't do that here.' And the guy next to me is wearing this flannel shirt just sitting there just hanging out just reading the newspaper." He is, of course, a cop. Brad is immediately arrested. "And then I go in and have to sleep in jail, in prison, and I still remember this tiny cell and I still remember this guy had sort of etched in . . . he was counting down the days, and people had etched in all sorts of madness on the walls about how they're losing their minds. I remember doing push-ups and thinking, 'I think you just got to do push-ups when you're in jail, that's just what you got to do, get some of your energy out.' They brought us some shitty gruel . . . it wasn't gruel, it was this plastic little container that was, you know, like brown canned corn and various types of shit. You had to take a shit on this metal thing that had no cover or anything that was just in your cell. And people were just . . . going nuts, yelling shit. It was sort of like a holding block, people weren't there too long term. But some people had been there for longer periods of time and I went walking and there was an older guy who had a box of books under his bed and he called me over and was like, 'Young man, you look like you might want a book.' You know, he gave me a book."

"I went and made my one call, called my mom, she was going to try and bail me out. . . . She taught at . . . private school and so there was a rich person who had money that she had access to. So she had [the rich person] wire money to bail me out." Brad had been behind bars for less than twenty-four hours, and his official record listed only a misdemeanor. Upon release he and his friend immediately ventured into the seediest part of Albany in search of cocaine. All they could find was crack, the variety of cocaine formulated for smoking, which was unfamiliar to them. "I think we tried to snort it and it was terrible and I didn't know what to do with it. I don't think we smoked it." Even by the year 2000 crack and powder cocaine remained culturally distinct, their use both socioeconomically and racially segregated. Experienced white dope dealers were still ignorant of crack and how to use it. Brad sums up, "So that was how I started my first semester of my freshman year at college. I tried to explain to my expository writing teacher that I was in jail when the paper was due and he said 'that's your fault.'"

The move to college had been bittersweet. The basketball offers from the Division I schools had fizzled out or been rescinded ("my grades were too low"), but Brad managed to get accepted at a big state school. Instead of living in the dorms, he got a basement apartment from which he could deal. At this point Brad had not exactly hit "rock bottom," but he had begun to change paths. He was going to his classes. He had reduced his LSD and other hallucinogen intake to something more periodic than continual. He was avoiding cocaine, and certainly not selling it regularly, though when he and his friends were home from college they would sometimes splurge. He was still selling very large quantities of marijuana, but at college this was not seen as legally or ethically problematic. And he had begun seeing a therapist.

Elliot had gone first for therapy as a condition of legal trouble and Brad followed. "I got to this point where I was like, 'I'm out of it, I don't have control over what is going on any more, maybe I'll give this a try.' And this therapist actually turned out to be really cool. . . . He was having me read … Carlos Castaneda and . . . those books. It was, on the one hand, adding to this romantic image of tripping and hallucinogens and peyote . . . and all that kind of stuff. But on the other hand he was really teaching me how to examine myself in this more controlled kind of way . . . to experience life with more depth, but in a more controlled way."

There is no decisive break, but Brad decides that the local state college keeps him too immersed in the drug scene. He applies to a prestigious, out-of-state university and he gets in based on his college grades. There he reinvents himself as a serious student. The rest is mostly positive history. Away from drugs, Brad works hard, graduates with honors, gets a job working with disabled children, and becomes professionally and personally involved with several prominent academics. From there he applies to a top graduate program, where he earns a PhD and then he moves on to medical school. It is, to me, an astonishing tale. Had Brad not been intellectually and athletically exceptional, it might have been a very sad story. If he had been poor, Latino, or black, where would he be now? If his mother had no access to the money to get him out of jail and clear his record, would Brad have been able to find the success that he did? If he had never found his academic niche, or been introduced to a competent therapist, where would he be now? How many people are in prison because they lack the social and economic resources that Brad was lucky to have? Privilege is at the core of suburban drug dealing.

NOTES

1. See Adler (2011) for a discussion of "efficiency," and particularly the transition from a utilitarian notion of equality as efficiency to the now accepted notion of a transaction being "Pareto efficient" and divorced from any notion of equity.

2. Obviously this does not cover all of our vast nation. It is unclear to me if drug dealing works like the people in this book describe in a suburb in Alabama, or small-town Iowa. I am aware that nine interviews do not approach the standards of a proper sample required to make solid sociological case for all of the United States. I am intrigued that all of the interviews are aligned on the most fundamental issues.

3. "Crack addict" became a term of moral opprobrium rather than a description of a condition; you would not hear Brad, or other dealers, similarly say "cocaine addict" despite the fact that crack *is* cocaine. As we will see, while he was dealing powder cocaine, Brad did not even know what crack was or how to ingest it. See Levine and Reinarmen (1997) on vilification of crack cocaine.

4. Mohamed and Fritzvold find this "desire for independence" among the dorm room dealers they study (2010:58).

FOUR
Ambivalent Economics

By now I hope to have established the main themes of the book. First, we contrasted Doug and José to make the case that suburban dealing is a distinct phenomenon. Its lack of anonymity ensures that the economic dynamics are different from street-level ("urban") sales. Urban dealing—like the mainstream economy—is efficient because it allows for quick transactions among strangers, at least at the retail level. The suburban underground economy is restricted to people we know. It is "structurally inefficient."[1]

We also saw that suburban sales depend on certain advantageous conditions. If you live where there are no street level sales, and especially if you are white and middle class, it is safer to become a dealer. You stand to benefit more and suffer less than the poor. You do not have to compete with street level transactions and your behavior is excused by society much more readily than the same behavior committed by (brown) people of the global majority, even if, like Brad, your behavior is wildly transgressive.

The previous chapters also raised the issue of the ambivalence of suburban drug dealing—the main topic we take up in this chapter. Dealing is a business, but among friends, a circumstance that complicates the calculative logic. Profit is necessary, but profiting from friends is awkward (at best) and subject to elaborate social rules. Dealers are, in some sense, capitalists who can't properly capitalize (or ought not to capitalize) and they struggle to make sense of this. Doug admitted that he "didn't know why" he gave away so much cocaine, or why he sold it for prices far below what he could have. Brad talked about the camaraderie of his drug dealing connections, his partnership with Eliot, and also the importance of friendship among the professional dealers with whom he became part of an "inner circle." Maximizing profits—or being seen to—would jeop-

ardize such friendships. Of all the things about which we might econo-
mize, our intimate relationships are perhaps the most fraught.

In this chapter we explore this ambivalence further. We will meet
Arthur, who operated a kind of cocaine collective while in college. He
claims to have had no interest in making money. In fact, the interview
began with him emphatically stating that he himself was never a drug
dealer because, as he said, "it was never about the money." If you are not
intending to make money, you are evidently not a "dealer," at least in
Art's mind. So he is perplexed when, in querying him about how prices
are set by drug dealers, Art came to admit that he adjusted how much he
charged based on the relative friendship of the customer.[2] This certainly
seems to involve an interest in making money. In fact, it's putting a price
on friendship.

We also hear from Wayne, who, by contrast, initially claimed that
cocaine sales were "all about the money," and that drug sales followed
standard business practice. But later he too shifts positions. He tells me
that "of course" he gave away nearly as much cocaine as he sold, as if
such a thing would be obvious in business, and that many people to
whom he sold coke would turn around and consume it with him—in
essence giving back the drugs they had just paid for. He struggles to
frame this in terms of conventional business practice.

Art and Wayne raise the difficult issue of combining altruism with
interest, the calculation required to profit with the concern for others that
is necessary for human relationships.[3] They understand a drug dealer
needs to profit, and they understand profit in particularly American cultural terms. Profit is good and necessary, in its context, even for Art (who
considers his dealing venture to be the wrong context for profit). However, both men in this chapter sold exclusively to friends, some closer
friends and some more distant. Art first claims no interest in profit because of this. He downplays the for-profit side of his transactions. Wayne
ignores the friendship side of the equation, the special deals and gifting,
the lagniappes, in order to emphasize the centrality of profits. Both positions are blind to the uncomfortable possibility that suburban drug dealing involves assessing one's friends economically.

Many economists would say that is, in fact, exactly what is happening,
but I think this is too simple. In our culture genuine friendship should be
disinterested—a good in itself, a situation in which you care for a person
and do not treat him or her as a means to an end, especially an economic
end. Yet friendship is also about being *interested* in the friend, in their
welfare and camaraderie, in spending time with her or him. A friend is
someone you enjoy, someone whose company in itself gives you pleasure. Otherwise, what is a friend? So friendship has to be interested *and*
disinterested at the same time. To have an authentic friend you must care
deeply in certain ways, but guard against caring in other, more selfish
ways.

Drug dealing exacerbates this conundrum. It adds economic definitions of interest—as a premium paid on an investment, and as our singular motivation in terms of "self-interest"—to the already vexed interest/
disinterest tension inherent in relationships. Drug dealing calls people to
perform friendship in situations where trust is vital, money is at stake
(sometimes quite a lot of it), and the stakeholders are often intoxicated. So
in this chapter we explore the knot of dis/interests at the nexus of the
friendship-business enterprise.

ARTHUR

Art's parents are civil servants. They are far from rich, but they received a
small inheritance, invested wisely, lived frugally, and raised their only
child in a safe, affluent town on the Southern California coast. As a child
Art lived inland from the gate-guarded mansions directly on the beach—
he still does—but his schoolmates had homes in these exclusive coastal
communities. Like the rest of the men in this book, Art started experimenting with drugs in high school, but unlike the others Art never sold
until he went away to college. There he met two other young men freshman year. Almost immediately Art and his two colleagues formed a kind
of drug buying collective, and this grew into a much larger operation.

The boys shared capital and drug sources, discussed prices and contacts, and split both the drugs and financial rewards of their operation
casually. Art claims that they never had an argument, and that making
money was wholly beside the point. The legitimate use for money was
for *the collective* to have fun. They spent their earnings on dinners together, drugs to consume, concert tickets, and other collaborative pleasures.
They were, he says, generous to those outside of the collective, too. For
Art, cocaine in particular facilitated a powerful communal identity via
shared business operation. All of the boys graduated on time. His two
friends have gone into desirable jobs in the financial services industry.
Art is vice president at a bank.

Art's grandparents were immigrants from Asia, and he still carries
with him a pride in their history and appreciation for their suffering
when they came to America. Of course, he would never call himself
"Asian," but would instead talk of his particular heritage. He is physically strong, a distance runner, diver, hiker, and camping enthusiast. He is
rabidly outdoorsy, from my perspective, loves sports, and is a huge fan of
almost any intoxicant. For Art, control is the key. He does not drink on
weekdays, but indulges to excess on weekends. When I visited Art he
had several different types of marijuana vaporizers and a medicine kit
full of different cannabis strains, but these are generally reserved for days
off work. He will take almost any pill, and seemed to especially favor

combining opioids and alcohol. If he could still find cocaine in his present milieu, he would probably take that too, at least on occasion, under control. In the good old days, when he could get cocaine, he did a lot of it. The drug figures prominently in his personal narrative. But these days during the week Art wakes by 04:00, runs several miles, reads at least one newspaper, has a healthy breakfast, and arrives at work punctually, wakeful, and, if not enthusiastic, at least responsible. He seems a remarkably regimented man.

Art was born in 1967 and describes himself as a typical high school student in the 1980s. He began his narrative by saying "the gateway drug, of course, is alcohol," which he started consuming in sixth or seventh grade. He managed to access marijuana by seventh grade through a friend's older sister and when I asked if this was normal he asserted that "not a lot of people did, but I don't think it was rare." What I found most striking in his story was the collective sense of adventure. Everything was "we." Unlike Brad, who was clearly singular, even extreme, Art presents himself as a young man of his times, just going with the flow, as when he says "everyone in the neighborhood was on the same wavelength," and "even if they didn't do drugs they didn't care if you did." The picture you get is of a happy, privileged group of friends and acquaintances eager for adventure. Intoxicants were part of the adventure.

By his junior year of high school Art experimented with LSD. He and some friends took it at a huge, oceanfront mansion, watching *Hendrix Plays Berkeley* and *A Clockwork Orange* on a videotape machine that must have been novel at the time. In the interview I suggested that the latter film was probably a bad idea for a first acid trip and after thinking about it he replied laconically, "yeah, I think we turned that off." Later in the year friends ventured up to someone's vacation house in Lake Tahoe and "we had some coke up there, too." While he was not sure, Art thought that might have been the first time he did it. He did not see it as very significant.

Not all of the kids were wealthy. It was a mix. Some worked for a gardening business owned by one of the high school teachers. Others took shifts at the local gas station when not in school. In those days it was not strange for the children of wealthy families to still have jobs in order to "be responsible." Art himself "worked a little bit after school, but," he reminded me, "I also had rich friends. You know, they just had money."

Art went to college at the University of California, Santa Barbara. In his freshman dorm he met two guys from the Bay Area, Shawn and Tylor, "and they used to get these half kegs . . . pony kegs, that's what they called them . . . I'm not sure how they got it but they said that it was pretty common for them and their friends to get a pony keg and then drink it before they went out to do whatever. But those guys, I met them, and in the first week they had blow and they were like 'hey, do you want to do a line?' and I'm like 'yeah, fuck, that's cool.'"

Art expands on this in a different interview, and on the importance of friendship to the purchase and consumption of cocaine, its "natural progression," as he calls it at one point. "I think it was kind of a normal evolution. Obviously when we were in high school and someone was like 'hey I've got some coke' we were like 'absolutely.' We all wanted to try it. It was just one of those things where it wasn't that readily available. And then I get to college and I meet these guys and they say you want to do a line? I'm like 'yeah, sure.' And fuck, this is cool man, and . . . they're turning me on and I'm saying I'll get some coke, I'll buy some, and . . . turn you guys on. And they say we get it from our buddy, and he's coming down, and I'm going, 'let's get some more!' It was one of those things where right away . . . I think if you're in that . . . I don't know if the right term is 'mindset,' but it's like this guy's offering me, or these guys I just met . . . obviously we're friends enough that they're offering me a line and I'd like to reciprocate but I don't have access to it. If you can get more, I'll buy some and turn you guys on. So right immediately they're like 'oh that's cool.'" The reciprocity was the point. Cocaine was expensive. One didn't enjoy it with just anybody. Shawn and Tylor made Art feel special and he was determined to show that he appreciated it. The way to do that, of course, was with more cocaine.

He is very explicit about this. There is honor involved, status. With drugs "if someone offers you something you want to reciprocate. You don't want to come off as being chintzy. Especially when you're doing coke. That's how I looked at it. If someone offers me a line, I want to offer them one, not like they're like going [Art sniffs lightly] I didn't even get a hit. I mean, to me, if I make someone a drink, I want them to go 'whoa, this is a little strong.' I don't want them to think I'm chintzy on my alcohol. And if I'm giving someone a line, I don't want them to think 'I didn't even feel that.' It's not even worth doing. It's probably stretching the question [of how he got started dealing] but it's just wanting to reciprocate. I just wanted them to know 'wow, I really appreciate it' because obviously you can't go down to the corner and get some coke. . . . It's not like offering someone a Gatorade. [sarcastically] 'Hey, you want a Gatorade?' With cocaine it's like wow, man, I really fucking appreciate that."[4]

Through cocaine Art bonds with Shawn and Tylor and the three become friends. Other students quickly come to see that the three have access to drugs. Says Art, "[Shawn and Tylor] knew someone from home and they would get like a quarter ounce and bring it to school in the dorms. I'd just hang out with them and they'd sell a little bit. This expands over the course of the year. And then by our sophomore year they ended up meeting someone locally, in Santa Barbara. And it would be the kind of thing like 'hey, you guys can get coke, can you get me some? If they wanted a gram and they'd give us a hundred bucks but we can get an eight ball [3.5 grams] for a hundred and twenty bucks, and so it's like yeah, give us your hundred bucks. Yeah, I'll throw in the twenty bucks and we'll do the other two and a half grams. And then somebody would say hey, I heard you got them a gram. Here's fifty bucks. And then you'd sell to them off that [i.e. off of the two and a half you have left]. And so we're like fuck, we can get a quarter ounce for cheap . . . and so you get a little bit more, but people are basically just fronting you the whole quarter ounce for whatever they want." In other words, the buyers are supplying the capital up front for the entire purchase, leaving the collective to do what they like with the 50 percent (or more) of the cocaine left over.

Like most of the dealers we met so far, the crucial element is finding a connection at wholesale prices. That is what these three young men accomplished, mostly, it seems, through luck. Thus far in our conversation it seems like Art has two categories of people in his cocaine life: the members of his collective (Shawn and Tylor, with whom he shares everything, and from whom he would never consider profiting) and everyone else. Everyone else seems to pay standard rates, $100 per gram in most cases, while the collective is acquiring 3.5 grams for $120, then later 7 grams for $200. Obviously, the profit margin is astonishing and soon the guys are moving to more wholesale transactions, selling 3.5 gram "eight-balls" rather than buying them. As Art says "it would just be where . . . people would offer 'here's three hundred bucks for an eight ball.' And we were like fuck, man, we can get an eight ball for a hundred and twenty bucks. And so then it's like, yeah, OK! I mean, you know, depending on who it was. If we didn't really know them that well we'd say yeah, give me your three hundred bucks."

This intrigued me, the "depending on who it was" and "if we didn't really know them that well." Obviously they were not selling to strangers, only other kids in the dorms, friends, at least nominally. So it seems like Art is suggesting that there are more than two categories of customer (the collective and all others), that there is a separate group of people "we know well." I wanted to know more about this. Specifically, I asked, "How did the collective decide prices for others and rewards for different members?" His response is fascinating.

"Prices were just the retail price for people who we didn't know. We'd kind of talk about it." He thought a bit and continued, "It was more of a friend thing." How does someone get to be a friend? I wondered out loud to him. Mostly, he responded, if the three members of the collective had consumed cocaine with someone, that could qualify them as a friend. "We would get an eight-ball and maybe charge them eighty bucks [for a gram of it]. We weren't like a 7–11. If it was someone we really knew, we'd give it to them at cost."

In the interview, I was still trying to figure out the logic of who counted as a friend and Art was becoming flustered with me. "For us there wasn't really a set logic," he said. "It was kind of like on a whim because the point was never really to make money, but to get free drugs." Still, I press, there must have been a rationale. Art is emphatic: "That's the whole point of our collective. There were really no set norms. If it was someone we all know, maybe we'll give to them at cost, or maybe make ten bucks. If it was someone like I know this guy, I don't really know him that well, he just wanted to get some coke, and he gets charged full price. And then it's like if I say 'hey I know this guy' then everyone's fine, they get a break on the price. It is *never* about maximizing the profit for us," Art says. "There was really no hard, set rule." But to me "never about maximizing" seems to contain an implicit, if ambivalent, rule.

At this point Art and I discuss a bit of economics, things like self-interest, opportunity cost, efficiency, marginal utility, and other basics taught in any introductory economics course. Art then claims, "I'm not fitting any theory. When you put it in these terms, it does sound weird." So, I say, it sounds to me like you're discussing the proximity of a friend-ship, how good a friend a customer might be, and then putting a price on that. Exasperated, Art counters, "That's totally fucked up though. It doesn't make any sense."

He thinks for a long time and finally relents. "That's exactly what happened. . . . There would be times when I would be, like, look, I know somebody who wants this and I don't know him real well, not like we know so and so but more like so and so, and then it'd be like whatever. The deal was that we're not in it to lose money. So, whatever. You decide. You can't lose us money. You decide." The collective guaranteed autonomy, but expected responsibility. The price would reflect the perceived degree of friendship. This was subjective, and each member had to independently assess the status of the customer and thus the price of the drugs.

In fact, this collective was a unique feature of Art's experience. Nobody else I interviewed had this sort of communal business. Art explains, "I think I still have the bag, we had this little bike bag, but it was just this kind of collective. You'd put in like a hundred bucks . . . people would come and say 'hey can you get me a quarter?' And we'd just throw it in this bag. And then we'd say hey, let's go out to dinner and we'd just grab money out of the bag. But it would just swell with cash." I am surprised and say, "You did it as a collective?" He replies, "That's what I'm saying. We weren't really trying to make money. We'd be like let's go see the Grateful Dead and we'd just buy tickets out of this money.[5] It's really funny that you call it a collective because I didn't really look at it that way, but it was never really something where someone is going 'I need the money, I need to take a thousand bucks' and even if they did we'd be like alright, whatever. But it never came down to that. It was never a problem. Money was never an issue as far as like an argument."

At this point in the interview I compare Art and his friends to some of the other people I've talked with, and suggest that the big difference is that beyond all the profits from dealing, it is the parents of the three who are paying the bills. Art considers this and comments, "I think that I'm the only one of us that worked while in college. But all of us, all of our parents, paid for our college. None of us were on student loans or anything. You're right. That's privilege, obviously. It's funny, as we're talking I realize more and more how . . . I don't want to say absurd, but in terms of the money making thing . . . you're kind of bringing this out as we talk. You're right, it was complete privilege. Nobody was really in it to make money." They weren't in it for the money because they didn't need it. What they needed were friends, bonding, adventure, a sense of belonging and importance. That was the "profit" of drug dealing. They money was a mechanism for sociality—concerts, dinners out, drugs at the end of the day, and other communal pleasures.

To me Art's story suggests that while dealing is often presented as the last refuge of the desperate, it is also the prerogative of the privileged. Art and his friends had the capital, the contacts, and a safe environment in which to sell. They were in school, and so had the time. They kept one another from going too far, from becoming addicted. They got good grades, had a great time, and graduated into productive, upper-middle class life. As abruptly as the collective got started, it came to an end. School over, the boys sat through graduation and ventured their separate ways. They still visit one another periodically, but their dealing days are done, and were done exactly when college was done. They moved on to lucrative, white-collar jobs in the upper echelons of the American mainstream.

WAYNE

Wayne is reluctant to discuss his career in dope. While Brad reveled in the weirdness of his path to success, and José, Doug, and Art were open about their dealing years, Wayne seems embarrassed. He expressed weariness with my discussion, and while there is much laughter generally in our conversations, the formal interviews are punctuated with sighs. He gives me curt answers and does not usually elaborate. Much of what I write about Wayne I gleaned from less formal conversations, sitting in his truck, lounging by his pool, or drinking with him at bars, where his skills as a raconteur are on booming, public display. In the end, Wayne was willing to let me write about him in this book, but on condition that I heavily redact his story. He wants "total anonymity," as he told me, more than mere confidentiality. I try to honor his wishes, but also to fill in the things he didn't or wouldn't tell me on tape with information I learned other ways. I have tried to shape the elements I substituted for the identifying facts so that the drift of the story is consistent with the gist of Wayne's real life.

Wayne was born in a medium-sized city in the American West. Culturally the place feels like a cross between Levittown and Oklahoma, with a preference for American trucks on the road and the radio divided between country music and classic rock. He still lives here, and while he has traveled extensively, he has never lived anywhere else. Probably this has something to do with Wayne's reluctance to explore his past. A sizable chunk of the population here knows Wayne's history and now, as a grandfather and pillar of his community, he would just as soon people forget his wayward youth. Wayne prefers to be known for what he is now, for what he has accomplished as a businessman, father, and grandfather, rather than for the lunacy of his younger days.

Wayne has grown thick in the middle but he retains his steely gaze and powerful hands. His grip can crush my hand and I would not want to fight him. He normally wears boots while at work, flip flops at home, and his large belt buckle rests under a tucked-in shirt straining at its obligations. When he was younger, Wayne was physically daunting, or seemed so to me. At one point he worked laying pipe for oil fields, and at another he was a bouncer in a bar, and both jobs suited him well. One story had him ejecting a violent drunk from a club one night. The man went and got a car and tried to run Wayne down in the parking lot. Wayne jumped up on the hood of the car, and, hanging on to a windshield wiper with his left hand, he beat the man through the driver's window with the right until the car came to a stop. I doubt this is strictly true, and Wayne himself denies it, but that's the way I heard it. If you met him, you would think it possible.

Wayne is different from Art in many ways. Art had the advantage of generous parents and educational opportunities, while Wayne's parents did service work and he himself barely began high school. Art is a liberal Democrat, Wayne a staunch Republican. Wayne will tell you that he doesn't read much, doesn't see why he should, and does not necessarily have a high opinion of people who do (like me, for instance). Wayne struggled to grasp why I would put so much effort into things that pay so little (like this book). He treats me with brotherly concern, as if my schooling has blanched me of understanding the simple fundamentals of human action. Wayne sees people in straightforward, interest-based terms. I think this is common in many parts of America.

If he is typical of the white American working class in some ways, Wayne is exceptional in others. For one thing, despite his early exit from formal education, he is very successful. He owns land, a farm, houses, and the take-home profit from his primary business is approximately four times my salary (and I was interviewing him in a bad year). Beyond this, my own observations, and conversations with people who know him, show that Wayne has a big heart, a powerful sense of justice, and he is generous to a wide range of people. He is open, even brutally honest, but deeply kind. Wayne is also far more astute than you might at first appreciate. I think he uses this to his advantage. Part of his "good ole boy" demeanor is, in fact, an act. But only part. Wayne denies it, but he seems a pretty good guy.

Wayne's mother and step-father worked in several bars around town and Wayne grew up in the social environment of the bar, or what might be better described as a saloon or a pub. He himself worked at one of the same places later in life, and it served as a kind of second home and a base of operations for his social life, and eventually his cocaine business. Wayne ran wild as a young man, getting into trouble with friends and experimenting with marijuana. He first sold pot in sixth grade, in the early 1970s, and he had experimented with other drugs in that era, but not yet cocaine.

Wayne was twenty-one years old in 1981 and cocaine was in the news. It had not arrived in the less hip areas of the country yet, and anyway, says Wayne, "I was oblivious to it because I was a pot smoker. I had never done coke. But I remember the day very clearly. I was doing the Friday night calls. 'Hey, what's going on, party here, party there, what's going on, who's got a joint.' And a friend of mine came in the house as I was on the phone with somebody . . . looking for coke . . . and my friend heard me say to the person on the other end of the phone 'ah coke, I don't really know anything . . . or anybody' and he started waving his arms saying 'no no no, tell him you'll call him back.' So I hung up and my friend said 'hey' and threw me an eight ball of cocaine. First time I had ever seen it. I had heard about it. I had friends that had done it. Until that point I had never tried it myself and I was twenty-one. And I had done a LOT of things by the time I was twenty-one. . . ."

While in larger and more fashionable places cocaine use had already begun its ascendance, it was relatively new in Wayne's milieu. Wayne walked into it in an unusual way: his first taste was also his first sale. He ended up selling part of that initial eight ball, and much, much more after that, becoming a major cocaine conduit in his community. As he puts it, "I didn't come up through the usual social ranks. I kind of got tossed right into the top of it.[6] I was getting coke cheap and plentiful from people who were bringing it across the border themselves. You know, they were giving it to me. Pay me Monday, pay me later. Immediately I had a credit line. The first couple of times the person who introduced it to me made the purchases. He would buy it. Or they would give it to him and he would give it to me. After the first couple of weeks I was partying with them and they were giving it to me direct." It was the "partying with them" that made the supplier/supplied relationship solid. Using drugs together helped build the trust necessary for business.

Like many in the working class, Wayne had moved out from his parents' place quite young and he had his own apartments with roommates. In our interviews there is no talk of his childhood or mention of his family. He functioned as a full-fledged adult from middle school, making his own choices and taking (or avoiding) responsibility for them. This did not mean he was any more responsible than Brad had been, but the two have a very different way of presenting their early manhood. Like Doug (and unlike Brad or Art) Wayne had no real family support, so he was generally dealing drugs in addition to his regular jobs, and he had to be careful as he had no one to bail him out.

I asked him about the risks involved in dealing and he said "If you're a small guy and you're dealing with a lot of people, the risk is there of getting busted. But a first time bust is usually little and the cops would rather have you turn on somebody else than go to jail. Which most of them do [i.e. most people turn in someone larger to get themselves out of legal trouble.] So there's not a huge amount of risk on little bitty shit. You've got maybe a few eight balls that you bought and you've busted it down to sell to people on Friday and Saturday night. There's not a ton of risk involved. We've had cops take it away from us and put us in jail and not press charges. Just to get us off the street. You know, when we were out partying. . . . And when you do get busted, 99 percent of the time it's going to be doing some sort of drug diversion class. And you're probably going to drug diversion class high." It is worth noting that the amounts that were considered trivial by Wayne (and the police who simply took it away from him) were far larger than those that sent José to jail.

It seemed to me that someone in Wayne's financial circumstances would mostly be interested in making money from the drug sales, but he explained that I was at least half wrong. "I dabbled in what I preferred, not what made me money. Most of the people who deal don't make much money. They do it to get high themselves, pay for their own stash, pay for their own party . . . or to make a meager income. It's not to get rich, unless you're ambitious, and that involves a lot of risk. Most people are not into all that much risk. With bigger amounts the police department's interest in you goes up, and the people you deal with get shadier. Risk goes up in different ways. At retail are just average people. At that point they are just financing their own party. It's a much more casual deal. Until you get into people who are severely addicted, and then they get pretty weird and can't be trusted. . . . Some people get addicted to the point that they'll turn to stealing from you . . . just blatantly robbing you."

Despite this explanation of risk, and the comparatively low risk of keeping his business small, Wayne got pretty big—selling ounces at a time rather than "little bitty shit." Wayne moved from just "busting down a few eight balls" to cruising from bar to bar with a supply that would outlast the weekend, and then selling retail full-time out of an apartment. Still, as he explains at this point in the conversation, he was not maximizing profit so much as having fun. He was going to the bars he wanted to go to, and when he got there a whole bunch of people were *very* glad to see him. He was the center of attention. As a source for the hip new drug, Wayne was popular with women and befriended by men.

The sexual opportunities facilitated by cocaine were a big part of Wayne's motivation to sell it, as we'll consider in the next chapter. This nomadic, opportunistic delivery style of dealing evolved into the sale of larger, wholesale amounts out of a series of apartments. There we see much the same situation described by Doug: complicated social dynamics guiding when people could come over, what they would buy, what they would do while there (i.e. how they would share drugs), and how long they could stay.

What interested me about Wayne's interview was the way he described the logic of his business. On one hand, much of his discussion involved the same economic terminology he would use to explain his current legitimate businesses. For instance, the way he described his careful assessment of risk, as we saw above, and the way he talked about his "credit line" would fit in any business class. He was even more explicit about pricing, and he sounded like the beginning of Art's interview when Wayne asserted that "everybody got the same deal" and later that "it's like the cost of baloney at Brookshire Grocery versus Kroger's [i.e. big, retail grocery stores]. Pretty much the same. And the price goes up and down because of supply and demand, and quality." Wayne asserted that cocaine dealing was just like any other business, a view often presented in the scholarly literature, and in wider circulation publications like *Freakonomics*.[7] But I continued to press for details and he admitted "there were never half price sales. But on occasion . . . not as a rule, not on a regular basis but I kind of remember doing bros [i.e. brothers, friends] favors, but for the most part it was what it was."

"What it was" was a commodity. Cocaine sales followed the same economic principles as any other commodity. I did not wholly accept this explanation, however, and so I mentioned that his out-sized generosity was pretty famous, the amount of cocaine that he gave away rather than sold. To this he responded incredulously that, sure, he gave away "TONS" (his emphasis) but he quickly insisted this was an index of good business practices rather than a good heart. As he put it, "consider it advertising. It's healthy for a business to have a healthy amount of new customers. And if you brought in enough new customers, then it was less pain out of your pocket to party." He might have taken his answer, in slightly different terms, from an introductory textbook in a business school. He is arguing, I think, that what others called generosity was really self-seeking economic strategy. He seems determined to deny genuine generosity.

However, at other points in our discussion this profit-oriented framework dissolves and a different logic animates him. Wayne says unequivocally, for instance, that generosity with drugs is reasonable "because no one wants to party alone. So if your friends couldn't afford it, they got it anyway." There is still a hint of strategy in here, as he continues "it was advantageous to be my bro and hang out because they were going to get the residual of what I was doing without buying anything." But Wayne did not see this advantage compromising friendship, or his friends taking advantage of him. "My core group of friends . . . were there before, during, and after the business of cocaine." For Wayne, then, friends are clearly not an instrumental means to an end. They are separate from customers, even if they sometimes are customers, but these friends can still legitimately seek some "advantages" without jeopardizing the friendship.

So, as Wayne expresses it, cocaine functions generally as a commodity, and sometimes one invests part of the commodity to generate new customers. Still, there are instances when cocaine is a genuine gift, as when it is given to friends who "couldn't afford it." As we mentioned above, gifts are not "disinterested" (one has to assess what would be an appropriate gift, whether it is a bouquet of flowers or a pile of cocaine, and this assessment presumes some kind of interest in the relationship). But any gift can only be a gift if it lacks an explicit quid pro quo. In Wayne's terms, it is very different to spend $200 on an evening with a woman, and maybe go home with her, than it is to pay a woman $200 to go home with you. Indeterminacy separates gifts and sales. Gifts must be voluntary, thoughtful (done with some interest in the person), and they cannot be blatantly reciprocal. We discuss this further in the conclusion.

At this point I ask whether I understand Wayne to say that there is a clear difference between cocaine as a gift and as something you sell. "Exactly," he says, but then he sows confusion between the two: "people do that all the time. They come over and buy an eight ball from you, and sit down and do it with you. They pay good hard money for it and sit down and give half of it back to you. That's the purchaser's prerogative to do." To Wayne it seems like choice, the voluntariness, is what turns a commodity (when it was purchased) into a gift (when it is given back to the seller). But I had understood that the seller was obligated by custom or culture to provide at least "a few lines," a lagniappe or a gift to the buyer to seal the deal.

To me Wayne has first said that there is no ambiguity, and then he has given the most ambiguous example I can imagine. He extends my confusion when he admits that "I can say I'm guilty of it too," with the "guilty" here being the violation of solid economic principles. He is guilty of giving. Since he now seems to be saying that cocaine *should* work as a commodity rather than it does work that way, I returned to his baloney example in the grocery store and suggested that commodities are not normally like this, where after a sale you consume the commodity with the seller. Wayne agrees, as he says "You don't go fill up your tank at a gas station and then go inside and give the guy a can of gas and hang out with him. But with drugs it's a camaraderie deal. You want to hang out with these guys. People would want to hang out with me because I was the supplier. So they would buy it and hang out and do drugs with me."

This suggests yet another strategic calculation, that buyers seek to share with dealers to ingratiate themselves, but Wayne continues to be instructively contradictory. On the other hand, he says, "nobody wants to be a freeloader, or at least not many people want to be a freeloader. So they'd buy it from you, and you'll do some of yours, and they'll do some of theirs." We discuss a bit of what constitutes being a freeloader, what's involved, and how you can tell. "You usually get a feeling right off the bat. They come over, usually with someone else. And they [the freeloader] are mooching off of them to begin with. I mean . . . a lot of musicians were freeloader son-of-a-bitches. They thought that because they were a rock star you should want to hang out with them and give them your dope. I thought that was peculiar because you could make them fuckers dance. At one time I had quite a collection of guitars. Bass guitars, electric, acoustic . . . I'd go repo people's musical equipment because they wouldn't pay for what they thought they didn't have to pay for. I'd go 'you got no money? OK, I'll take that, and I'll take that.'"

I tried to return to my main interest and pressed him on this distinction between customers and friends and he said to me "If you come over to visit, you're *invited* to come over and visit. You're not there on the premise that you're there to buy something and then just stay and never leave. You were invited. . . . When you would come to town, I wanted you there. I liked to show off, I liked to have a good time, and that was a great way to do it. Some people are a lot of fun to party with. That's a whole different deal than someone who calls you on the phone and they come over and you want them to hang out for a half an hour and then leave. Totally different deal." So, in the end it seems gifts (to friends) and commodities (for customers) are *totally different*.

So what's the point of dealing? To Wayne, "It was about fucking fun! Financing the fun!" You just had to "be smart about who you were dealing with. After a while I was buying more and having larger quantities around. I had to be cautious and only sell to people that I knew. If anybody new wanted it, there were avenues they had to take to get close enough to buy it themselves. Otherwise they had to continue to get it through a second party. But it also kind of goes up in smoke, so to say, when you're high. Better judgment is never around when you're high. You do stupid shit. I'm kind of amazed that it took me as many years as it did before I finally got busted."

I ask if that's why he quit, because he got busted, and he answered "Not really because I didn't stop after getting busted, I didn't stop for a long time. When I got a young lady pregnant and had a child: that was the major motivator. I'd come to the healthy conclusion that there had to be a better way. There was a desire to get on with my life. To put that part of my life behind me." I asked if there was a transition period. "Yeah, as I was working my way into the mainstream world of jobs I still dabbled in drug dealing. I dabbled for a long time. I dabbled longer than I should have. You know, then it would go long periods between . . . point A and point B . . . even just doing it. Then it just ceased. Coke got harder and harder to get, and the quality got worse and worse. That had a lot to do with it. The networks change, move, go away, die, go to jail and/or the shit just gets so bad it's not worth doing." Even the "bust" Wayne suffered only caused him to serve some weekend time in a local jail. He never spent serious time in prison.

In the interview I was interested in whether this is a general trend in the way people get out of the business, and what factors drive people into the legitimate economy. "It's kind of all of the above. Some do end up in jail. Some get out in rehab, some get out that way. Some people just get tired of it. You know, people grow up. People find love, get married, quit drugs. Some people die. Some people end up on skid row. Some people are still in it. I've got plenty of them who didn't do well. Multitudes of them. A lot fewer who came out of it unscathed. Lost a lot of good people to the dark side. Their lives were just ruined by drugs." But not you? I ask. "I guess it's just my personality. I knew other people who were dealers who were dickheads. Very by the book. And some who were just dumb as rocks—they didn't last long. I was just having more fun than the ones who were dickheads and lasted longer than the ones who were dumber than rocks."

Finally, I ask Wayne about what he learned from the experience, what about dope dealing has been useful in his present, very lucrative, career. At first he's dismissive, he laughs, "For one thing I don't give anything away anymore!" This is, again, good economic logic but I suggest that it is not really true since in our time together he always seemed to pick up the tab for lunch or drinks, and he tipped exorbitantly. "Oh, well, yeah. I've made a lot of my customers today into friends as I did in my cocaine business then. I find everybody's much more comfortable dealing with people they consider a friend. Their wallet is much freer to buy things from people they consider friends. That's why you listen to me talk to some of my customers [in his truck on speakerphone], I talk to them like friends. I don't talk to them like customers. They feel more comfortable around me, more trusting what I'm selling."

So, I think, talking *like* friends is not the same as talking to real friends? By the end of the interview I am still asking if friends and customers are "a totally different deal," if a friend might *really* be a customer, or if any customer might *really* be a friend. It seems tantalizingly ambivalent.

NOTES

1. "The personalized structures typical of illegal markets are a far cry from economists' definition of perfect markets but also far from the much less personalized existing legal markets. If one assumes, in line with economic theory, that the efficiency of

markets is enhanced through competition, then illegal markets are structurally inefficient because of limitations in their potential to develop competitive structures" (Beckert and Wehringer 2013:17). While economists recognize a number of different types of
inefficiency, here I am referring to the simple fact of commerce restricted to personal
contacts.

2. Despite Art being outraged by this form of behavior, it is in fact commonplace
(see Maher [1996] cited in Page and Singer [2010:98]).

3. An instructive example of this difficulty involves economists grappling with
remittances, instances where individuals in one country send their hard-earned cash
to another. Carling writes "In the most cited article ever published on remittances,
Lucas and Stark (1985) laid these motives out as a continuum from altruism to self-
interest. In the middle of the spectrum are mutually beneficial, implicit contractual
arrangements between the migrant and the remittance-receiving household"
(2014:224). So at least some scholars can conceive of motives other than "self-interest."
However, he goes on to suggest that "There is no corresponding theoretical framework within the ethnographic literature on remittances" (2014:225), which could possibly be true specifically about remittances, but which seems absurd in terms of "theory" given the voluminous work emerging from Mauss.

4. Arthur seems to be asserting something more than the cost of cocaine, something about its materiality. On the materiality of the gift—as opposed to gifts being an
empty signifier of social relations—Pyyhtinen writes, "I claim that the importance of
Mauss's essay lies significantly here, in the fact that he takes seriously the gift-object.
However, paradoxically, it is precisely this dimension of Mauss's theorizing that has
been left in the dark over the years. Several anthropologists and sociologists after
Mauss have stressed how the gift plays an important part in the organization of social
life. More often than not, this emphasis on the constitutive role of the gift to relations
is, however, accompanied by an ignorance of the gift-object. It is typical of the studies
of the gift to reduce the gift to a relation. . . . To me, these authors and several others
are too hasty in substituting the logic of relation for that of the object or the thing. They
take as a given what I think is precisely the problem, namely: is the gift a thing or a
relation?" (2014:6).

5. Mohamed and Fritsvold find much the same thing with their "dorm room dealers." Essentially, these sorts of dealers seek to "underwrite the costs of personal use"
(2010:42) and "underwrite other incidental and entertainment expenses," among other
motivations (2010:45). The choice of verbs is telling; most of their subjects are business
majors.

6. Here Wayne insightfully references the different "levels" that dealers enter the
business (Henslin 2008:43).

7. Levitt and Dubner write "In other words, a crack gang works pretty much like
the standard capitalist enterprise . . . " (2005:103). Sociologists and anthropologists talk
less about the money than status and culture, however.

FIVE

Gendered Ambivalence

Cocaine, Money, and Manliness

The previous chapter explored the cultural confusion inherent to conducting business with friends. In suburban drug dealing profit is derived from people you know, sometimes people you know well, and calculation of interests is entangled with camaraderie. Given that friendship involves an implicit interest in the person—and not what you can get out of them—extracting material benefits from friendship is a vexing endeavor. In a typical drug deal the roles and motives of buyer and seller, user and provider, gift-giver and recipient mix and contradict in the space of a single transaction. This gets no easier in the context of romance and sex.

Most of us would agree that sexuality is complicated, and by many accounts, cocaine is associated with sex. Cannabis and LSD might have been culturally linked to "free love" and the hippie movement, but the rise of cocaine brought with it a different sexual ethic. Some make the argument that the chemical substance of cocaine lends itself to this. Some report that arousal is a feature of the drug, arguing that it lowers inhibitions for women and increases stamina for men. Note, however, that this assessment of how the drug impacts sex depends on a specific understanding of how sex works in humans, with women requiring inducement and men needing, or at least appreciating, help with what is called, without irony, "performance."

This is a very culturally specific way of understanding sexuality. This model has little to do with the iconic orgies of Imperial Rome or 1960s Connecticut key-swapping parties, never mind other understandings of pleasure, for instance societies that treat male/male sex as a desirable norm (like parts of ancient Greece or Papua New Guinea), or those that consider the female libido to be stronger than the male.[1] The "coke is good for sex" assertion envisions sexuality in conventional American terms, in other words. It seems a retreat from the more androgynous sexual identity of the 1960s, where men and women wore similar clothes and had similar hairstyles. This suggests that in the 1980s the role of cocaine in courtship and mating represents a return to a more traditional American understanding of sexuality, with an emphasis on sexual dimorphism rather than an extension of the sexual revolution begun in the 1960s.

The cocaine-sex nexus operates two main ways. First, the use of a drug to facilitate sexual connection fits squarely with our mechanical understanding of ourselves. Americans tend to view their bodies as sophisticated machines that can be directed to behave one way or another with calculated instructions in the form of chemicals. We are perhaps only an extreme example of Western, mechanistic understanding of the mind/body relationship, but from this vantage it makes perfect sense that a thing external to us (in this example, cocaine) can change fundamental things about us. It "makes us" do things or want things, or makes us capable of things that we would not otherwise desire or achieve.

However, a second way that cocaine relates to sex is through money and power. Male sexuality in our culture is augmented by power, and power is connected to money. We expect rich men to have beautiful wives, which demonstrates that female sexuality emerges from what we consider physical attractiveness while male sexuality relies on at least an element of status. This is not true everywhere for everyone, but in the American context wealth is often believed to serve as an aphrodisiac for women. If it does not conjure genuine desire, it at least inspires women to accommodate powerful men. In the 1980s context, where women were considered to have naturally less powerful sex drives, men used money and its crystalline avatar, cocaine, to attract mates.

This is all relative, of course. In the context of middle class lives, where most young men make minimum wage or something close to it, having any cocaine at all was a form of conspicuous consumption. Whoever had it was claiming disposable wealth, and was thus commanding attention, including sexual attention. If someone was giving coke away for free, that was notable.

Yet not everyone connected sex to cocaine in this way. Doug had a long-term girlfriend, we recall, though even he noted that he "missed his chance" to use cocaine for sexual advantage. He understood that cocaine was connected to sex, but he personally did not use it that way. Art, by contrast, never mentioned the opposite sex or sexuality at all. For him the bonds formed by cocaine were entirely homosocial—powerful, but platonic. By the time Brad was a dealer cocaine had come down in price and had lost its exotic allure, including its sexual allure. As he made clear, people even denied taking it. Cocaine had become less expensive and unglamorous, even shameful. But in its heyday men like Wayne saw cocaine as a prime way to build masculine attractiveness. We will begin with what Wayne had to say about this, then we meet Woody and Pete. Wayne represents a pretty typical story, I think, a common way men attempted to provide cocaine to women as part of the process of wooing them. Woody explains this further. Pete connects cocaine to sex (and money) in a different way than the other two, but he is insightful about the connection between sex, drugs, money, and masculinity.

WAYNE'S COCAINE SELF

Recall that Wayne's initial response to my question of why he sold drugs was that "It was about fucking fun! Financing the fun!" And his answer to why he gave away coke was that "no one wants to party alone. So if your friends couldn't afford it, they got it anyway." Here he means "friends" as men, which for him are not sex partners. Wayne's main motivation is to hang out with his buddies. But in the interview, he also insisted that cocaine dealing was "lots and lots about sex." I think it is fair to say that in his twenties Wayne was enthusiastic about meeting women, the more, and the hornier, the better. Cocaine was "lots about sex" because, at that moment in Wayne's life, everything was.

In Wayne's world, cocaine needed to be provided to "the girl you wanted to be with, and/or the girl she had brought with her," as he told me. This was *not* trading cocaine for sex, however. The girl's friend (who was not an immediate target of sexual conquest) was as deserving of free drugs as the desired girl herself, for example. The coke was not quid pro quo any more than a dinner date might be, or even a barbeque, where you invited multiple people. The idea for Wayne was to establish himself as a particular type of person, a generous guy, a fun guy, and in this sense the barbeque is perhaps the best analogy. This ultimately would be the kind of man an attractive woman would of her own free will *choose* to sleep with. It was a broader identity Wayne sought, the construction of a self that was sexually desirable. The gifting and consumption of cocaine, like food, was part of building a social world in which this identity made sense.

Cocaine, like alcohol and marijuana, was fundamentally a way to pass the time in company, to "spend time" with people, including women. Note that for Americans "time" is a thing (like money) we "spend." So "spending time" is another variety of expenditure, though it is unclear what type exactly. Is this spent-time a gift (as when we congratulate fathers who "spend time" with their kids) or is it a calculated return (as when you "spend time with a client" playing golf or sitting in special box seats at a game)? Time is not universally understood to be like a "thing" one would "spend," but for Americans it is. Spending time is our way of grasping one of our most basic existential coordinates. We are allotted a certain amount of time; we spend it doing some combination of what we have to do and what we want.

Wayne wanted to spend his time doing cocaine with women. This could amount to a kind of foreplay, at least in that cocaine facilitated lots of talking and getting to know people. There is no denying that people on coke cannot shut up, and while this could be annoying, it also accelerated the rate at which you might come to know a person (for better and for worse). Having a pile of cocaine in front of him meant that at least some women were willing to share—conversation and cocaine, of course, but perhaps more. Wayne recognized that at least some women explicitly liked to combine sex and cocaine, which was one source of its power. But more generally women liked to be around men who had the drug, especially those who gave it away. Such men were "fun," the kind of guys who not only provided drugs, but went out to bars and concerts, picked up the tab for dinners, men who performed a broad array of behaviors commonly associated with the masculine side of heteronormative American mating rituals. The cocaine was added to an existing cultural mix, in other words, the money and social visibility already associated with desirable manliness.

Few women paid for cocaine, according to Wayne. In his view women who bought it "were not that bright. Or else they weren't interested in sex. Because I'd give it to them just out of the prospect." He discussed going through his phone book methodically from one end to the other inviting women over to do coke (people had actual phone books in those days, made of paper). If one woman declined, he went on to the next. Wayne didn't see this as manipulative or sleazy. He did not see it as disrespectful or as an attempt to buy sex. Wayne liked cocaine. He liked sex. And he was searching for women who had the same interests. This seemed to him obvious and commonplace. It also meant that cocaine was a masculine thing, a substance men used to perform masculinity, because, at least in part, women wanted it. If you sought to be a desirable male, and particularly if you wanted to be an alpha male, having cocaine was important. It follows, then, that if you were not rich, selling cocaine was essential to full manhood. So cocaine sales—not just cocaine use—were deeply bound up with masculinity and sex in the suburbs.[2] At least for a while.

WOODY

It is February 2014 in small-town Colorado, cold and brilliant, and Woody finally agrees to be interviewed. He is not excited about this, and he has made that clear. I have followed him around for days, chatting with him and his friends, and he has been willing to say lots of things informally in bars and restaurants, or on ski lifts, but he does not want to face the recorder. He never says this. He just finds a way to do something else whenever I think we might have time to do a "real" interview.

Woody is tall, tan, scruffy, and fit—as stylishly casual as the premier ski resorts he has lived in for decades. On my last day in the state, in his truck on the way to the airport, he agrees to be taped. I turn on the machine and ask him simply to tell me about his career in dope.

"Well," he begins carefully, "I guess, it would start . . . I grew and sold pot. I was sixteen years old, or something like that. It was pretty small time. I had a few plants in my parents' backyard. Never really made too much money off of it. . . . " There is a pause here before Woody moves on to the real story. "But I moved out here to Colorado. I guess the only time I really made money was selling cocaine while I was bartending. My roommate would go buy kilos of blow. Then he bartended and another roommate bartended and I bartended all at different times of the day. So you could pretty much buy cocaine at any time of the day, from 2 p.m to 2 a.m."

I had spent hours already talking with Woody, but none of this had come up. I had not known about the roommates, I had not known about the cocaine. I had just interviewed Art in California and Woody's situation made me think of Art's "cocaine collective" in college, so I asked whether Woody and the roommates worked as a unit.

"No," was the answer. "I would buy a small amount, like an ounce. Or maybe that's not a small amount. In any case I would get twenty-eight grams, sell them for one hundred bucks a piece, and probably triple my money, or something like that." Few people gave me specific information about prices, but this suggests that Woody was getting ounces of high quality cocaine for about $900, twice what Doug had paid (who gave so much away), but still remarkably cheap.

Woody continued, "I sold almost exclusively, pretty much, while I was working . . . I would bring like three grams of cocaine to work with me." He explained that his entire customer base was about twenty people, all friends, people from town. "It would always be friends." They would come into the bar and "usually order a drink and then pay me $103 for their drink." Woody called it getting a B&B, a "Budweiser and a bindle," the "bindle" meaning a small paper envelope of cocaine. Like this, he said, he would "make $300 bartending and $300 selling in a night . . . tax free."

That seemed like a lot of money for a young person, but it also seemed to lack the "hanging out" and "partying" that were so common in the other interviews, so I asked about this, whether there were other ways he sold cocaine.

"Well, you'd throw a couple in your pocket whenever you'd go out, you know, two or three grams. Generally I would work nights, Thursday, Friday, Saturday nights when people were out. But no, I didn't have people coming to my house." I thought that this was interestingly different from most of the earlier interviews, so I asked Woody specifically about the pricing, about discounts for friends, and he replied emphatically that it was "pretty standard a hundred [dollars per gram]." There was no "bro price," as he put it, as there had been for others, and no ritual gifting. Woody explained, "The *only* people I was dealing with were bros. There was no one else. It was just a set deal." I remembered Doug giving "everyone" the bro price, and Art using a sliding scale, where the price would reflect your level of friendship with him or members of the collective. Woody is decidedly more businesslike, in attitude more like Wayne, yet he seemed defensive when explaining his decision, as when he continued, "I wasn't getting a great price, I wasn't buying tons of it. I was doubling my money, but it wasn't like I was getting it for nothing. I got it for forty or fifty bucks a gram, sold it for one hundred. Each transaction I made like $50, or something like that." Initially Woody estimated that he tripled his money, but in response to my questions about friendship and drug transactions he recalls "only" doubling it. There seemed to be some tension around the practice of profiting from friends.

Partly this is because Woody has already explained to me that he didn't really consider himself a dealer. His roommate was a "real" dealer, the one who came face to face with what he called the "cartels." Woody himself was, in his mind, helping people out. "My roommate, he was a little more big time. He was the one who would go and meet the cartel fellas and brought it home. He would not deal with people at night. He only worked in the daytime. It was all prearranged, he wouldn't take any calls. You had to tell him a week ahead of time if you wanted something. That was the wholesale. The other roommate and I were just kind of retail. More, like . . . friends. Friends would get it for a friend. So that was my career arc. I did that for about ten years or so." Listening to Woody, I thought back on my interview with José, who sold something like a tenth of a gram at a time (the twelve packages that sent him to jail equaled about one of Woody's minimum units), and was in business less than a year. Clearly Woody had a much better business model, one predicated on having a great supplier, wealthy friends to sell to, and a context—the bar—where he could sell without having to use his own drugs to "party" with customers.

Like many of the suburban dealers we met so far Woody stumbles on to a high level connection early in his career. Wayne's initial cocaine connections were bringing it across the border themselves, Art met two guys in his freshman dorm who could get lots of coke cheaply, while Doug and Woody both were living with roommates who, it turned out, had access to kilos of very pure cocaine. All of them were within a person or two of connections who were bringing drugs into the country. Woody even showed me the parking lot about an hour from where he lives where his roommate used to meet the "cartel fellas" (suggesting that he, too, had more to do with that end of the business than he's telling me).

Whether or not the "fellas" were really in a "cartel," they were Spanish-speakers ready to unload as much cocaine as they could, and the roommate who dealt with them used extreme caution. It seems that blind luck—meeting someone with a wholesale supply of cocaine—was a large part of what drew suburban dealers into the business, at least the ones I happened to find. The dealers in this book did not usually start small and "move up" the chain. They began their cocaine careers high up the ladder, with familiar contacts who gave them great, wholesale prices, more or less from the day they started selling. It was, it seems, a deal that was too good to pass up.

What is different with Woody is how the transactions are organized. He does not sell out of his house (none of his roommates did either) and so we do not see the style of socializing, ritualized drug sharing, and gifting that we saw in the home sales context. Woody is very clear that everyone he sells to is a "friend," and on this basis he considers himself "small time," yet none of the "friends" get special deals, gifts, or even lagniappes. The friends pay $100 for the cocaine and $3 for the beer. There is no ambiguity about it. We do not see the blended partying-with/supplying-the-party dynamic that we had when the deals happened in a living room, or even when Wayne or Doug sold as customers in bars. The difference seems to be the side of the bar they were on. Doug and Wayne were among friends drinking in a bar—not a bartender among customers, like Woody. Woody used his position as bartender—only selling while he was "working"—to minimize the contradictions of conducting business among friends. By removing himself socially (selling "exclusively, pretty much, while working") he was exempt from the normal social requirements of drug sales, and their high transaction costs in time and drugs used or given away. It was a hybrid model, with efficient elements of urban sales (a set price, no gifts or discounts, no time spent "partying") but the safety of suburban drug dealing (only selling to known people in relatively safe contexts).

Since Woody did not present himself as involved in the social use of cocaine, I was interested in his view of how that worked, and more specifically about the link between cocaine and sex that others discussed, so I asked him about this. He thought and said, "There were some girls, but primarily it was men." From Woody's perspective cocaine was "something you would bring on a date kind of thing. You know, you're going to go see a concert. . . . Alcohol, drugs, it's all kind of part of the package. . . . It's like. 'hey I have a concert ticket, I'll buy you a drink, we'll do this' . . . it's like anything you can do to add on to the package of how desirable you are. Depending on the girl. Whether it's dinner or blow. It depends on what she's into, what she considers a good time."

I asked whether this was tantamount to trading sex for cocaine, whether it was a kind of economic transaction. He replied, "In itself it wouldn't be a way to get women. If they were not into you then having some coke wouldn't do it. It's like taking a woman out to dinner, whatever you do to impress them, or not really impress them but . . . it's a courting ritual."

Woody pondered more and added, "Plus, no, there were definitely groups of girls who'd get their own, it's pretty common," and I quipped, "They didn't want to wait to go on a date?" Woody continued, unamused, "They knew what they were doing. They had money. Usually in groups, I would say. Men, almost never. It was like four . . . women would go in on it together. Men would have their own."[3]

Here I wondered if that gives women independence from men.

"Yeah, that's what I'm saying," Woody decides.

Still, I couldn't stop thinking about his own lack of socializing with coke, so I ask Woody about this again. The answer, again, was that for him there simply wasn't time.

"They'd walk up and say who's holding. I'd say, 'I am.' And that's that. . . . We could transfer money because I was already in that business, it wasn't raising eyebrows. If someone is handing you a stack of cash they can't tell if it's three dollars or three hundred. We all knew each other, but they would go hang out and talk. I didn't really like it. I don't like hanging out late night with a bunch of guys. It wasn't my social scene . . . it didn't interest me. Which a lot of people were into. They would like to sit around and listen to music and talk. It just didn't interest me."

I pondered whether this made Woody a better dealer, and here he laughs.

"Yeah, don't get high on your own supply! Definitely. I was working. You could do a little toot or something, but I was not off socializing. I was busy. There were 300 people yelling at you for drinks. You don't have a minute to yourself, really, until it's over. I guess that . . . the exception to selling to people we didn't know was the bands. The bands all want drugs when they traveled around. Different guys in the band. And you just kind of figured, I guess they weren't cops. Since you've seen their tour schedule and you're writing them checks and you know they're from out of state and all these other things. It would be a pretty elaborate sting if it was the police. They'd have a band that would go around to every bar."

We both thought this was pretty funny, and I joked "So it turned out the members of the band *Sublime* were FBI agents? They would have wanted more than a gram."

"Yeah, but most bands don't make a lot of money, either. Most guys aren't rock stars. They get gas money and a per diem. They'd crash ten of them in a condo. So, sure, they *wanted* stuff. . . . The more popular bands, people would buy them stuff, to hang out with them, but if you're just some dudes, nobody knows who you are, you're paying for it. People think you're a rock star and they want to be around you, whether it's guys buying them drugs or girls sleeping with them or whatever. It's

basically like entertaining . . . to make yourself popular . . . whether you
have a bunch of nice wine or whatever it is . . . you can have people over
to drink this Bordeaux I have or you can snort this eight ball I have. I
guess in a way you're paying, but it's like entertaining . . . providing."

From here Woody and I move to discussing gifts, what makes a gift.
To his assertion that some people would buy cocaine for the bands and
this is "providing" or "entertaining," I suggested "You don't go to dinner
at someone's house and leave somebody $25, you bring a bottle of wine."

His response is that "Yeah, it's more of a social thing than just handing them money. Maybe down at the base of it, that's true. But that's
based on gratitude, for hosting or whatever, having people over or whatever that might be. I guess that goes back to if you're a caveman and you
kill a buffalo or whatever and share it. The tribe likes you. You helped
them out. Same deal."

It seems to me that we have arrived at the sort of ambivalence that we
found with Art and Wayne. Dealers—or Americans in general, if they
stop to think about it—struggle with the idea of gifts, whether they are
"real," generous and altruistic, or instead intentional, self-interested, and
therefore false. I suggest to Woody that in his buffalo example it would
seem important to "share." It cannot be a quid pro quo, I'll give you this
meat but you give me your spear. The tribe won't like you if you're *selling*
it to them.

Woody says "Yeah, that's a butcher. He sells meat just like you sell
blow. The next person who shares that thing, after he bought it, that
changes from a straight up transaction to a social thing." Woody sells the
cocaine to people who are then going to share it. So for Woody there is a
stark difference between a "straight up transaction" (which is what he
was involved in) and "a social thing," but cocaine can easily cross that
boundary, transform from one kind of thing into the other. It is not the
substance itself that defines its status, nor even the apparent actions of
people, what they physically do with it.[4] Cocaine changes hands, but
what does it mean? It depends on the situation and intentions are key,
what people *mean* by what they do. Cocaine says something in every
context, but it readily changes contexts, and it can say different things at
the same time.

PETE'S PROBLEM

Wayne represents a relatively happy outcome. He never became addicted, in the sense of degrading his reputation or his health to get cocaine, and he never suffered any big social or legal problems from what
was a long and occasionally large cocaine dealing operation. Wayne is
astonishing in his ability to walk away from drugs, from alcohol, from
pretty much anything that he decided was no longer of interest. He has a

rare personal biochemistry that can withstand absurd quantities of drugs and alcohol, quantities that would kill an ordinary person, and he can stop using just about anything any time he wants. Woody maintained control a different way. By separating his dealing and his socializing, he was able to keep cocaine under control. None of this was true for Pete.

Pete grew up in Southern California in an ocean view house with two brothers, two parents, and a dog. An all American boy—surfer, athlete, lifeguard, star student—Pete retained his swagger (and all of his hair) into his fifties, when he sat down with me for a set of interviews. Still lean and garrulous, Pete was kind enough to show me around his world in Hawaii, where he has lived and worked since the early 1990s. He introduced me to his friends in bars, and his buddies from work and the beach. Pete received a small inheritance, and he built his own house; he does not struggle financially. He has a college education, but works in construction, and augments this with earnings from growing cannabis. Pete's cannabis farm is the topic of the next chapter. Here we focus on his earlier cocaine business.

Pete is deeply negative about cocaine, and the business of transacting it. He has avoided it for many years. Pete first smoked marijuana in 1978, "but it didn't do anything for me," he says. His dad was "OK with drugs," but told Pete not to smoke pot until he was sixteen "because of the brain," presumably meaning a concern for Pete's brain development. Pete claims that he was initially attracted to the money to be made from drugs rather than the drugs themselves and to make this point he told me a story of buying candy in third grade, breaking it into smaller units, and selling them to friends at school for a profit. It sounded something like my early hashish endeavor, but the point was the opposite: Pete wanted to make money. He was very concerned to show me that making money was the point of dealing, and that making money—in this or any other way—was fundamental to proper masculinity.

The precocious candy dealing set the stage for selling drugs later. "It was all about the economics," he said emphatically. "The way I got started was to make . . . money. I didn't even do drugs." Pete's family was from Texas and his values tend towards the right end of the American political spectrum, especially on economic issues. He deeply believes in the American dream, even if his version of it is not quite what they teach at the American Enterprise Institute. Making money is a moral good, an American thing to do. Drugs were perhaps not the ideal way to do it, but the positives of making money mattered more than the negatives of making it from drugs. Real men made money.

In high school the one clique Pete was not part of was "the stoners," but he set out to change this. He sold marijuana early in high school, then hallucinogenic mushrooms, and finally, by senior year, cocaine. Since he claimed this was all about profit, but he was from a prosperous family, I wondered why he needed cash so badly. At first he said "there was nothing I lacked in any way," which seemed to me to be agreeing with the premise that he had everything he needed, that there was no reason to go out and make money. But he shocked me by saying that drug money was different, it was "like driving a Porsche," and that his goal was not just to have money, but to be "nigger rich." What I take this to mean in this context is that drug money had cachet in his white, wealthy community, an audacious visibility that was cool in itself.[5] Pete wanted to be flagrantly profitable. Dealing involved conspicuous consumption (of drugs) and an equally conspicuous *production* (of money, identity, masculinity).[6]

When I pushed him further on this, asking why in his upscale community being conspicuously wealthy would matter, he was clear. It was about sex. "Getting pussy," as Pete phrased it, was the point of life as a young adult. In this he sounded very much like Wayne: "you want to be the man," Pete said repeatedly, using exactly the same words as Wayne. In those days the man with cocaine was *the* man (though, oddly, the police were also "the Man").

Still, I found Pete difficult to understand. He was very definite—totally sure—that his dealing was only about money, but it was equally clear that dealing was linked to sex and masculinity. Otherwise, what did "being the man" mean? It wasn't just money that was important, but money from high-risk behavior consolidated into a hard to get, sexy substance that people wanted. I suppose that in an environment where having money was common, having money in the form of cocaine was symbolically significant, more than mere cash. (Arthur had said this, too.) Cocaine represented a hip way to have money, a dangerous way, or a fashionable way to expend it. Another factor is probably that while Pete's family was very wealthy compared to the average American, they did not have the level of income of others in this exclusive beach community. So while Pete did not have to sell drugs to meet his financial needs, selling did provide the flashy cash necessary for a particular sort of masculinity. Drugs were involved in building the identity of a money-making man, one that Pete wanted to cultivate, at least for a while.

Pete's cocaine career was short and tumultuous. As he said, "in 1977 coke wasn't bad . . . everybody did it . . . as far as anybody could tell." I protested that he himself was not doing it in 1977, and he responded "no, but that is what you aspired to do." So he began dealing late in high school, as he says, to make money, but his involvement took off in the mid-1980s when he met a Venezuelan woman who was, in his words, "super-hot." Pete was smitten. Almost immediately the super-hot Venezuelan told Pete that her "father has diplomatic immunity" and that she regularly "flies into LAX with a suitcase full of cocaine and three pairs of underwear." Pete really wanted to get in those diplomatically trafficked, coca-scented panties.

However, while Pete was fixated on "getting pussy" (his words), he was also sleeping with men. He explained that he would make his way to Laguna Beach, in those days a gay mecca, and spend the afternoon in beachside bars. Young, fit, attractive, and horny: nobody in the bars asked Pete for ID, and generally he didn't spend a dime. Even back in college, when I first met Pete, he wondered aloud why others weren't doing what he was. I didn't record those conversations, but it went something like "you go into a bar, you sit down and guys buy *you* drinks. If you want, they give you great drugs in the bathroom, and then suck your cock. Why would anyone *not* do that?" At the time I didn't have an answer. It had simply not occurred to me to have sex with men, and I was fairly sure that the sex of a person in front of me would influence my level of arousal. Pete found this absurd.

The sex of his partners matters to Pete in ways that are complicated. When Pete says "why I was doing what I was doing as a teenager . . . the whole thing was basically to get laid," he means "getting laid" specifically by women. From his perspective, it is difficult to have sex with women, but men are easy. All he had to do was show up where men congregated and present himself as available. But women were different. They were hard work. They do not readily agree to sex, especially anonymous sex, and they certainly do not provide you with alcohol and drugs before having sex with you. That's what men do. So, to be a man, you have to have the money (and the drugs) to perform proper masculinity, to woo or seduce people (women or men) in culturally sensible ways. To Pete, proper masculinity is more or less the same whether the sex is homosexual or straight. If you want to get laid by someone you consider desirable, you must be prepared to attract them—chemically and financially, in addition to everything else. The traditional masculine role is to pursue, and drugs are for pursuit. If you are the object of desire, the one being sought, people use drugs to pursue you. It was pretty straightforward from his perspective.[7]

At the point that the Venezuelan came on the scene Pete had developed a serious relationship with a man. Fortunately for Pete, this fit the Venezuelan's tastes. She admitted that she liked to watch men have sex, and Pete readily agreed to this. "We got together because she watched me and my boyfriend have sex," he said. And while not exactly a Hollywood romance, these initial drug-fueled sex events evolved into a deeper passion. The Venezuelan eventually left her boyfriend for Pete and Pete left his boyfriend for the Venezuelan. Now when she flew in to LAX with a suitcase full of cocaine it was Pete who met her at the gate. You could still greet passengers at the boarding gates in those halcyon days.

The Venezuelan girlfriend made the case that cocaine in itself was never a problem. Problems, according to her, came from money. This concerned Pete because, as we noted, money is fundamentally positive for him. But the Venezuelan asserted to Pete that cocaine is "only bad if you buy it" and Pete agrees that she has a point, that "technically it worked pretty well for me for a time. I did it, I didn't buy it, and it wasn't bad." Really, though, it wasn't bad *yet*. Pete had so much cocaine at such reduced prices that he made far more money off the drug than he and his partner could ever spend on it. And he ingested more of it than any reasonable person should ever consider. But the girlfriend intends more than this with her statement. According to Pete, she "used the term 'buy it' but also meant that *you didn't want it enough to buy it*." Unfortunately, Pete did "want it enough to buy it." For him, at least, cocaine seized control. It became bad because he wanted it very, very much.

Gradually, I came to understand that Pete's ambivalence was not limited to the material substance of cocaine. It extends to the economics. Pete explained at agonizing length, and in a number of different ways, that he was a lousy businessman, bad at the clear-sighted calculation necessary to make real money, incapable of effectively focusing on his self-interest. For instance, he "passed on" his Venezuelan contact rather than jealously guarding it. Pete put his main customer in touch with his Venezuelan girlfriend, in other words, thus depriving himself of the ability to make a profit by buying from the one and selling to the other. He lost his source of revenue, and eventually he lost the girlfriend this way, too. He says, "I introduced the two of them and that was it for me. I was out of the loop."

While money was the main point of dealing ("the way I got started in it was to make fucking money") looking back Pete says bitterly that "I don't think I have leveraged . . . my da kine, da kine," or in other words, he has not leveraged his advantages as he should have. He "failed" (his word, repeatedly used) at "capitalizing" (also his word). Primarily this is because "You gotta have the ability to fuck somebody over to make money in this business." He pauses here, which is rare for Pete. Of all of the emotionally difficult things we discussed, this was the moment he seemed saddest. "I destroyed my business by giving it away." Why? I ask, and he does not hesitate: "Because I'm dumb." He dwelt on this for some time. To Pete's way of thinking a smart dealer—a real man—would have taken better advantage of his opportunities. Ultimately Pete says "my cool gene just doesn't fucking exist." No matter how hard he tried to do the cool thing, the right thing business-wise, the manly thing, it was never going to work. For him, then, growing marijuana makes more sense than dealing because the demands—the practice of it—better suits his character. We explore this in the next chapter.

CONCLUSION

Drugs and sex go together—with rock and roll, as the saying goes. But the cultural context of sex has as much to do with how this works as the chemical composition of the drugs. It also seems strikingly personal.

Some people find cannabis to be an aphrodisiac, for instance, while others are left with only a dry mouth (and other mucous membranes) and a lust for ice cream. Cocaine has been the main topic of this chapter since, in the era that concerns us, it was by far the most sought after drug and the one most closely associated with sex. Cocaine is a stimulant. One thing it was thought to stimulate was passion. It is also connected to masculinity, partly because of its association with money (and money with power) and the way that male sexuality in particular is dependent on money and power. Whatever cocaine does physically to the body, its cultural meaning was closely tied to desire.

However, the relationship between sex and cocaine has varied over time. It seems more correct to say that cocaine *had* a reputation for being sexy, a reputation that has dwindled over the years. Indeed, it dwindles in the space of one song—"Life in the Fast Lane," by the Eagles, but it also changed over decades. Younger dealers do not associate cocaine with money, power, and sex the way older ones did. It is also quite variable from person to person. Doug was monogamous despite his dealing business. Arthur never mentioned it. But Wayne, Woody, and Pete explained in clear terms how they saw cocaine, and cocaine sales, as connected to manhood. It is important to note that while the cocaine-sex linkage might have been the dominant view of things at the time, a wide variety of experiences and attitudes existed.

However young men conceptualized cocaine in its prime cultural moment, this was fading fast by the late 1980s. Some moved on—out of college, in Art's case, on to legitimate business in Wayne's, into sobriety for Doug. Others, like Pete, moved on to different sorts of illegal business—like growing cannabis. For Pete the money was clearly "the super easy thing that got me really hooked . . . hooked on the lifestyle." But the "lifestyle" had all sorts of elements that Pete struggles to sort out, even thirty years beyond his coke dealing years. This is the focus of the next chapter and it serves as a way to investigate how production of an illegal substance is different than distribution.

NOTES

1. Hugo Scwyzer, "Turns Out Women Have Really, Really Strong Sex Drives: and Men Handle It," The Atlantic, published June 6, 2013, accessed on June 6, 2018, https://www.theatlantic.com/sexes/archive/2013/06/turns-out-women-have-really-really-strong-sex-drives-can-men-handle-it/276598/.

2. Often framed as "toxic masculinity" today, this notion of masculinity as essentially "cynical, self-serving marauders ceaselessly exploiting" others is longstanding, and hardly confined to the suburbs (Liebow 1967:89).

3. Woody is careful not to succumb to easy gender stereotypes, which is important, see Morningstar and Chitwood (1987).

4. See Pyyhtinen (2014) for a rebuttal to this conceptual linkage of relationships to gifts, and its inattention to the materiality of the gift-object.

5. This is almost certainly what Mohamed and Fritzvold call "warding off the emasculating force of privilege," which is one of the motivations of middle class drug dealers (2010:58).

6. The notion of "conspicuous consumption" comes from Thorstein Veblen's 1899 book *The Theory of the Leisure Class* (republished in 2016).

7. Some reviewers wanted more on the sexual politics of cocaine, especially in the gay context, but I do not feel qualified to say much more than I have. I am not a researcher in sexuality, and I asked few questions about it. I took what Pete had to say at face value, and repeat it here.

SIX

The Culture of Cultivation

This chapter examines cannabis cultivation. Unlike cocaine and most other illegal drugs enjoyed by suburbanites, marijuana is produced in the United States, both indoors and out, clandestinely in some places and legally in others. Since it need not be imported, there is less need for large-scale capital investment (for transport, international connections, protection of supply routes, and so forth). So while large and sometimes dangerous organizations are devoted to growing cannabis domestically and pot is still imported by such organizations, small-scale growers can, and do, survive in the industry. These growers are sometimes from the suburbs, and sell primarily in the suburban way.

On an economic level, cultivating is different from selling. Growing is a relatively slow, continuous, and labor-intensive process while dealing is a fast, stochastic, and capital intensive activity. The two types of businesses attract different sorts of practitioners. Marijuana production can be a good fit for people anxious about drug sales generally, or, like Pete, who want to avoid cocaine specifically. This chapter contrasts two suburban growers, Mary, who raises plants indoors under lights, and Pete, whom we already met as a coke dealer. Pete sought to escape the demands of cocaine dealing by growing marijuana. He finds this a much better fit with his skills and personality.

PETE AND POT

Pete came to growing cannabis, at least in part, as an escape from cocaine. As we saw previously he was initially a marijuana and psychedelic mushroom dealer in Southern California, and then he got seriously into cocaine sales and abuse. Coke caused Pete enough trouble that he moved away from his circle of friends several times trying to avoid it. He eventually fled to the Hawaiian Islands, where he had no contacts for cocaine. In fact, he did not know anyone at all, which he saw as a virtue. It was a clean slate. He settled into working construction, and slowly came to be self-employed.

Pete first encountered his pot-growing partner in 1997, some years after he arrived in the Islands. Despite quitting harder drugs, Pete contin-ued to smoke marijuana more or less constantly and this habitual canna-bis use made him keenly interested in having a reliable supply. He was thus an excellent customer to his main supplier (who was a grower) and not very long after meeting, the two decided to work together as growers. It is worth remembering here that Pete conceptualized his decision to "share" (or "give away") his cocaine connections in Southern California as being "dumb," and presumably this would make Pete's pot-growing connection "dumb" for agreeing to split the work and profits with Pete. But that is what happened. Perhaps this shared fault is why they were still working together at the time of our interview, eighteen years after they began. It is "probably the longest partnership in drug history," Pete jokes, and while he and his partner have little social interaction other than growing, they work well together on that.

Their typical pattern is to plant on public land, of which there is much on their island. But this is tricky. Land that is officially and legally "pub-lic" often carries invisible claims by individuals or families who have long cultivated an area and consider themselves to have a right to it. Land politics in the Hawaiian Islands are often fraught and can be vio-lent. From Pete's perspective, even law enforcement officials tacitly understand this; there is real danger in transgressing undocumented property lines and claims. For instance, early in their collaboration Pete and his partner planted in a forested area a few miles from his house that seemed to them "wild." The area looked utterly abandoned. They knew they might have to deal with feral pigs, but the growing area was impos-sible to access other than by foot, and even that was torturous; there was no human habitation anywhere nearby. They assumed the spot was un-claimed and would make an ideal growing site.

As Pete tells it, their plants were almost ready to harvest when a police helicopter roared up, circled his house several times, and flew off towards the evidently not-so-secret plantation. Pete scrambled through the dense bush to check the plants, but the police got there first. He returned home dejected. Hours later, with the destroyed plants swaying pendulously in a cargo net beneath it, the helicopter returned, circled Pete's house again, and sped off. Pete's interpretation was that the unoffi-cial "owner" of the land called the police and told them where the plants were and who was growing them. The police didn't want to deal with a court case, or tip anyone off about their own role in policing unauthor-ized plantations, so they ostentatiously stole the pot and left it at that. Pete understood it as a warning—from other growers, not the police directly: "don't grow here," was the message he heard. And he never did again.

Luckily, Pete's partner gained access to a different growing area on another part of the island. This area was tacitly acknowledged by other growers—the land bordering their plot was also used for marijuana cultivation, but not by anyone who begrudged Pete's plants. The location was even less accessible than the first—a forbidding tangle of rock and thorny underbrush. The only way in to the growing site was to crawl, and that's what Pete did. Wearing thick clothes, knee pads, boots, and leather gloves, Pete and his partner would go late at night and clamber through the dark strapped with the plants, pots, and soil. They dug pits into the rock and briers, put the pots and plants and soil into them, and then built a watering system. This was the most important part because the area has abundant sunshine, but inconsistent rain.

The irrigation system involves burying a fifty-foot section of tubing in the ground, then moving several yards away from the end of a pipe and installing another section of tubing heading off in another direction. The pipe could not be laid in a clear line, and the sections could not be permanently connected, because it would be too easy for thieves to follow. (If the piping went directly from a water source to the plants, law enforcement or thieves could stumble upon one section and easily follow the tubing to the plantation.) On nights they plan to water, one person crawls into the brush and uses temporary hoses to connect all the gaps between the sections of underground pipe, and then signals the other. The second person arrives with a truck full of water at a place where a dirt road intersects the irrigation system and then pumps water into the end of the piping. Once all the plants are watered, the first person removes the connecting tubing and leaves the buried pipe sections in the ground. Using this technique Pete and his partner have never been robbed, and have never (again) had trouble with other growers or the police.

Pete and his partner are specialists. The cannabis variety they grow is called Neville's Haze, and they grow hundreds of plants at a time. This is a classic cultivar said to be 75 percent *sativa* and 25 percent *indica*. Winner of *High Times* magazine's "Cannabis Cup" in 1998, it even has its own website (nevilleshaze.com, "An Ode to the King of Cannabis & the Father of Haze"). The variety is well suited to their locale. It needs a great deal of sun, grows tall outdoors, and has a high THC content. The strain has enthusiastic fans, and Pete caters to them. Pete usually works from clones, that is, he removes small cuttings from his plants and induces these daughter plants to root and grow. When the mother plants flower and are harvested, Pete replaces them with new, genetically identical daughters. In this way he has a permanent supply of consistent, high-potency cannabis.

Some of the things that Pete critiqued about himself as a drug *dealer* have turned out to be assets as a drug *grower*. For instance, his lack of ambition ("I never wanted to be a drug dealer") has been key to the stability of his partnership. Pete explains "I never wanted to jump up a rung on the ladder. I'm perfectly happy being his [the drug growing partner's] helper. I've never taken his things. I never started my own operation." The partner is the one who secured rights to the growing area, and Pete is content to play his role in the production without trying to improve his cut or take over the position of the primary grower. As we saw earlier, the refusal to be properly entrepreneurial as a cocaine dealer was portrayed as a character fault, in Pete's telling, but what is a fault in one domain has stabilized his new friendship, and allowed his growing operation to continue.

For Pete this sometimes disgraceful humility, or willingness to value the long term partnership over a short term economic gain, fits with the social nature of marijuana production. Pete argues that cannabis has "up to 100 percent price difference depending on who you are." In other words, the better friend you are, the better price you get. I ask why this should be true for growing when it was not (for him, anyway) true for selling cocaine. Pete explains that in growing you "put a price on your time, your effort, and what you're willing to valuate it for. So for some people I'd gladly hike four miles—on a nice day—and so here you go [mimicking handing me a bag of marijuana], this is no worries, but for other people hiking four miles is horrible and you've got to frickin take advantage." This "taking advantage" is precisely what Pete thinks people *ought* to do. He is consistently critical of himself for his failure to do this. In another interview, however, he admits that nearly all his customers get "the bro price," or the cheapest deal he can allow himself to give. It may be that you *should* "frickin take advantage," but as a grower you don't actually have to. A sensible man might sacrifice his time, but not his capital. Since Pete can't seem to "take advantage," growing makes more sense than selling.

In a third interview Pete expands on this line of thought. "You can place a value on your own labor more easily [in pot growing] than if you buy a quarter pound of coke for x amount of money and sell it for y amount of money. The in-between time, that profit . . . comes from your labor but it's not like if . . . you pick it up in Fresno and drive it to Connecticut you're . . . going to charge a gazillion percent more than if you pick it up on A Street in Fresno and drop it off on C Street. Your effort could change dramatically but your income is not going to change dramatically."

I am not certain I understand his point here, but it seems that in selling (cocaine, in this example) material costs and prices are relatively fixed and are unrelated to the cost of labor. The price of acquiring the commodity wholesale is inelastic, in economic terms, and this reduces your ability to value it as you wish, to sell it cheaply or give it away. (Note, however, that for Doug, Wayne, Arthur, and at some points Pete himself, access to incredibly cheap cocaine changed this dynamic.) In growing, by contrast, the majority of the "cost" is time and effort. For Pete, then, discounts of marijuana are ultimately gifts of his time. He does not begrudge himself (as much) for giving away his time as he does for giving away money. Cocaine operates as crystalized money. Cannabis is congealed labor and time. Gifts of labor-time are culturally sensible. Gifts of capital are not.

GROWING INDOORS

Mary is a spare, energetic woman with cropped hair, a loping gait, and a wicked sense of humor. She wears blue jeans exclusively (she hangs them on artisanal nails along her bedroom wall) and, the day I met her, she sported a white, sleeveless tee that showed off her tan arms. Mary lives in a modest home in a medium sized town in Northern California. She was forty-eight years old in 2014, when she invited me to see her pot growing operation, which she has operated continuously since 1996. When she started out Mary was not the sort of person who ever thought she'd become a cannabis producer. She smoked rarely, and still does not use marijuana very often; she had no background in botany or farming, and wasn't sympathetic to drug culture. Her current profession happened more or less by accident.

As she says, "I was working two jobs screen printing, the first one on my own, a private business in my garage and as a full time job for someone else. My girlfriend at the time had driven half way across the country with this . . . hippie dude that she met through friends. They really hit it off and he was a grower and she came home all excited, 'he's going to set us up and we're gonna grow. And we're gonna make all this money.' I was hesitant because I grew up military. I told the girlfriend 'no, we're not going to do that. We're not doing that. That's not going to happen.' Then the hippie offered . . . to set it all up. He was going to pay for everything. He was going to come and take everything. He was going to show us how to do it in exchange for half of the first two harvests. And that was going to be the deal. And we weren't going to lose money. Our contribution was basically going to be our house. I'm like, 'OK, we'll try it.' Because at that point I was sick of my job." The decision was not easy for Mary. "I first hated it because of what it was. It was *illegal*. I grew up in a military family, a Republican family. I was like, holy shit, this is illegal. We don't litter. We don't do marijuana. We put our flag out. I was . . . freaked out."

But for Mary, too, the positive valuation of profit outweighed the ethics of gaining it via dope. Mary went along with the plan of the girlfriend, and the hippie "set us up, in a bedroom, in our house, and I remember walking in going 'holy fuck, no way. This is too big, this is too huge.' And I remember any time I ever walked my dog and I came home and I saw any lights or any sirens or any action on my street, I freaked out." Initially Mary found growing to be very stressful.

The system Mary showed me is substantially the same as the "hippie" originally set up for her, and a quick Internet search shows that the basic components are shared by many indoor growers. The centerpiece is a rack of special lights (fluorescent can be used, but metal halide and high pressure sodium are preferred; LED is becoming more popular). These need to be raised as the plants grow beneath them so as to keep the maximum amount of light on the plants without burning the leaves. Cannabis thrives in bright sun. The plants themselves can be grown from seeds or clones. Clones are more work, but cloning female plants has the advantage of ensuring that no male inadvertently fertilizes the crop and causes them to go to seed and lose value. As Pete explained earlier, it also ensures consistency of product. To clone a plant you take a cutting, induce it to root, and then plant it as you did the parent. There are a variety of products and devices available to facilitate this process. Seeds can be purchased for top strains, too, but growing seeds to sell is separate from growing flowers for consumption. Cloning allows growers to maintain specific genetic varieties consistently, and market them as such.

The plants are set in plastic lined boxes or pots with soil, or some people prefer to grow hydroponically, in a liquid nutrient solution, or even with spray nutrient devices. Reflective material taped on the walls seals light in the growing area. There is an air intake vent (in Mary's case this takes air from the garage, where nobody can see it) and a carbon filtered exhaust vent. The fan has to be strong enough to remove all the air in the growing area every few minutes, both to refresh the supply of carbon dioxide for the plants and to ventilate the often intense heat of the lights. The carbon filter removes the marijuana smell from the exhaust air. Other fans blow directly on the plants, circulating air under the leaf canopy and preventing mold and mildew. In Mary's case a drip irrigation system delivers the water, while an electrical timer controls the lights. It is important that lights mimic the long days of summer during the growing phase; these are shortened to induce flowering (except in varieties bred to flower spontaneously). The female flowers, or "buds," are generally what people consume and are by far the most valuable part of the plant. A ballast controls the electricity for the lights, and a surge protector keeps the whole system from overloading.

At the time Mary began growing, a pound of very high quality marijuana might fetch $5,000 in California and the system she ran produced about three to five pounds in a three month growth cycle. This helped Mary to overcome her skepticism. Still, "the whole first round of three months I was like 'oh my god, we've got to get this out, get this out.' Finally one night we all sat down and trimmed it together, and put it in garbage bags as we trimmed it." After growing, the buds are cured and, as Mary notes, tidied up for marketing purposes. I asked whether the hippie was teaching the two women how to do it and Mary responds, "Yeah, he taught us how to do it. . . . He bagged up the garbage bags. He put them up in our rafters. He came back three days later and he grabbed it all, put it in one big bag, left. And three days later he came back with this big lunch bag full of money and he handed it to us. It was fifteen grand. I remember opening it and going 'holy shit. I've never seen this much money in my life' and laying it out in my bed. In fives and tens and twenties and hundreds . . . and just laying down in it. I couldn't believe it."

"It was more money than I ever saw. We went and bought a convertible. We went and bought a television. We went and bought a couch. We went and bought a stereo. And that was the last of buying anything, because then we pulled it together and decided 'no, we're going to make this work for us. We're going to save money and pay our rent, buy houses, and that's what we're going to do.' And that's what we did. From then on we did the same thing. So we had to do two deals with him, and he took half. And that first half we got fifteen thousand, so he obviously got fifteen thousand, so it was a thirty thousand dollar deal. The second one was the same. The third one, we got all the money. So it was about twenty-five or thirty thousand. And we tucked it away and we just started buying houses." Mary has good carpentry skills, so she and her partner bought run-down houses, put grow rooms in, and used the money to fix up the houses and sell them. It was a good way to turn the cash from cannabis into legitimate investments, and to quit her regular job.

While the business started as an opportunity to earn money, Mary's motivation and understanding of growing changed over time. "When I got paid for it I thought this is more money than I've ever seen, more money than I'm ever going to make clocking in at my job. And I ended up quitting that job because growing was more money. But then I started to really love doing it. I started to love the plants. I started to love the process. I really got into it. Now it's not about the profit. Now . . . I just love the process. It's like raising kids to me. I plant them, they're little clones, they're little girls. And I plant them and they're babies. And then they're teenagers, and they're a little more antagonistic and I add extra things and I'm like, come on, we've got to, you know, work this. And then they're adults and I'm like, this is what you need for this. Then they're ready to go to college, and I'm ready to cut them. And I cut 'em, I cure 'em, and I sell 'em, and they're off, they're out. It's like raising a kid in three months. That's what it is to me."

So, for Mary there is joy in the process of growing the plants, but it seems to me that she also enjoys the social aspect—not necessarily of smoking, since she rarely does that, but of the transactions made possible by being a producer. For instance, at one point Mary discusses how cannabis circulates without money. She says "I trade for haircuts, I trade for wine, I trade for a lot of stuff. So that's kind of a nice . . . it's like back to the old school. You trade for shit." It is not that this is purely altruistic, or divorced from economic calculation, but it feels different—more humane—to her. Mary has a clear understanding of the economic value of different elements of her product, but other values are mixed in. She says "When I process my stuff I have, quote unquote, top shelf. And that's my solid huge buzz. And then I have what falls through the screen. And then I have what I scrape through my screen. So I have cooking grade. Smoking grade. Well, it's all smoking grade . . . but I have cooking grade, top shelf, huge bud, which I never understood because they all break it down. So you have top grade, huge bud . . . this, that, that. . . ."

She sums up her framework this way: "basically to me that means: what I sell, what I give away, what I trade. There are a bunch of different levels. I have several baggies in that bar right there [she points]. My top grade, that's what I sell. Here's what I trade for wine. Here's what I trade for my haircut. Here's what I trade for this, here's what I give away. It's all good." It's all good, as Mary says, but also specific—different parts of the plant are more like apples and oranges than different prices of apples. Mary sells the most popular, profitable elements (her "solid huge buzz"), but there is much else to trade and gift, and these parts of the production are important in their own distinctive ways. For Mary cultivating marijuana is like raising children, but it is also a way to cultivate friends. And just like an apple might be an appropriate gift for an elementary school teacher and a potato salad for a barbeque, the distinct elements of Mary's production are transacted in precise ways.

Even when Mary does sell her product, there is a connection to it and to the customer that is different from the mainstream economy. For instance, Mary sometimes grows for particular tastes, as she explained when I asked her why she grows multiple varieties at once instead of specializing in a single one. Mary says she diversifies "because everybody wants something different. It's like beer drinkers. People like IPA. People like Coors Light. People like the cheap. People like the expensive. So I try to cover all of it. So I grow like five different types of plants at a time."

She has one buyer in particular. "He likes to sell ounces to all his friends, that's why I grow different blends. He wants a bunch of different ounces like he's at the legal cannabis dispensary. So I do like five, seven varieties. . . . I just sold him a pound four days ago and gave him seven different varieties. And that's what he likes. So that's who I basically grow for. That one dude that buys multiple varieties every month." This customer could, in fact, go to a legal dispensary, but he prefers not to. Mary fills a small, micro-niche in the market, getting this man the specific varieties he and his friends prefer, and doing so clandestinely without using the dispensaries then available for medical cannabis. By the time of writing, of course, recreational cannabis had become legal in California, but that had not changed the problem of federal jurisdiction.

When Mary talks about "varieties" what she means are different strains of marijuana that have different effects. Some stimulate appetite and some don't, some are said to be good for insomnia or anxiety while others keep you alert, some are advertised to have anti-inflammatory qualities or are good for pain relief. Varieties are promoted through cannabis dispensaries, which have their own experts, but there are many websites that do the same thing. Some sites review varieties without much pretension to health benefits (the varieties are discussed in terms of the distinct quality of the "high" they produce) while others focus on the purported medical properties. Some strains are promoted via pop culture, for instance in music. Mary asserts that, "Rappers are paid to rap about a certain strain. There's a song 'Girl Scout Cookie.' That's a strain of marijuana. I just grew that in my last round. . . . So there's a song 'Girl Scout Cookie' and that shit gets out there and apparently, what I hear, is that dude was friends with a grower who was doing Girl Scout Cookie and he wrote a song that made it hugely popular. There's nothing that significant about that strain [i.e. it is just marketing]. If you go back and listen to rap music it's always referencing O. G. . . . O. G. Kush, O. G. Kush. . . ." Whether artists prefer a certain strain and promote it for that reason, or whether there is a more coordinated marketing effort going on, the specific effects of different varieties are a big part of the twenty-first century cannabis business.

Clearly, some of Mary's decisions involve straightforward business sense (giving the customers what they want), but that is not all there is to it. Mary has chosen to wholly please a few people rather than grow the maximum quantity for the greatest profit. Like Pete, Mary says that the price of marijuana is "totally contingent upon the relationship with the person. Some stuff is free, and friends definitely get a different price. For sure. It's all contingent. I have a bottom line of what it costs me to run the growing operation per month and then. . . . There's a line, like $200 an ounce. That's a high end. I can drop mine to like $120 and still make a profit." Mary remains committed to the idea of "profit," but she is flexible in terms of what she counts in that category. She is certainly not looking to "maximize" profit, as economic orthodoxy might recommend.

"LEGALIZATION" AND ITS DISCONTENTS: WHAT'S CHANGED?

Cannabis laws are rapidly changing. As of this writing, twenty-five states have legalized cannabis for medical use (it was seventeen when I first drafted this chapter). Sometimes the medical requirements to get the drug are quite lenient ("pain" in California, before it was legalized for recreational purposes) and others quite strict (only a few conditions, like glaucoma and chemotherapy, in Connecticut at the time of writing.) This means that the availability of the drug varies greatly even within states that have decriminalized it to some degree. Obviously places like Colorado that have moved forward with full legalization have made far more pot, and far more types of it, available.

Sometimes this impacts the economics of dealing in straightforward ways. For instance, a grower I met in Colorado had been at his business for decades, always in the same small town. Hiding his source of income was difficult in such an intimate community, and while this community was always politically liberal (or more like libertarian), it still made things difficult for him as a parent. "What does your dad do for a living" was a question the grower's children were trained to avoid. Now, however, he has taken his skills mainstream. He runs both a medical outlet and a recreational pot store, and instead of fearing the police, and worrying about the impact of his business on his kids, he has become a proud leader of his town's chamber of commerce. The grower now pays his taxes (which are much higher on the recreational side of the business), begrudges this publicly, and finds he has much in common with the other legitimate businessmen in town. This was surely what many expected with legalization, and there are some obvious advantages.

In California, Mary, too, adapted to the changes in the law. First of all, she got her medical grower's license so at the time of our interview she could legally grow thirty plants. (She grew twenty-eight, because, as she said, "cops can't count.") She emphasized again and again that while she used to fear the police, she no longer does and she is now only concerned with home invasion and robbery. If she was being robbed, Mary says she would call the authorities immediately, and this was not the case in the past. She feels much safer, and in this sense Mary is ardently pro-legalization. She has also secured a day job with a large, legal, medical cannabis growing facility.

Mary is the quality control director for this cannabis company, a job she's well-qualified to handle, and she oversees a dozen or more employees. She is proud that her employer emphasizes the medical aspects of the plant. As she explains, "what's cool about the dispensary I work with now is they're growing strains that have less THC, so it won't get you high. That's what they're really promoting in this medical field. I work for a *medicinal* cannabis company and . . . what they're trying to do is pull the THC off the plants and produce it as a . . . pain blocker and a blocker for seizures, and make it legitimate."

In our discussion, I am a little surprised at this line of research because hemp is cannabis that already lacks THC. Evidently the point is to maximize some of the other cannabinoids without the THC. It was unclear in the interview why making pot into a non-intoxicant should be important to Mary, but it is. Maybe it comes from her background. She says "I believe in what they're trying to do [i.e. make cannabis medical and less intoxicating], but also there is the other side of it. I mean, everyone I work with is a fucking stoner. They're medicating beyond the point of medication. The whole thing is a little bit sketch [i.e. sketchy, problematic]. I mean, I totally believe that it has medicinal value, but judging from where I work, I don't see it. All I see is a bunch of fucking stoners." She describes her frustration supervising employees who are incapacitated on cannabis. She calls it "like herding kittens" to manage them. Her workers are young and idealistic—and very stoned—and Mary constantly has to shoo them back to their stations to do their work.

That is not the only dilemma, from Mary's perspective. "I've got one buyer in San Francisco, who is HIV positive. He could go to a dispensary and spend $400 on an ounce. A friend of mine turned me on to him and said 'hey, bring him samples' and let him test your stuff, because he buys a lot of weed.' He's a gay dude in San Francisco, has a lot of money, but he and his partner didn't want to get licenses because of their job positions. They didn't want to be compromised. . . . Cannabis is only legal in California. The Federal government trumps it. So at any point of time . . . you could get tramped down by the Federal government. I doubt they would over my thirty plants but you never know." This is the man for whom Mary grows several varieties. The point she makes is that legalization is incomplete and incoherent in a juridical sense. Many Californians got medical marijuana cards who might not necessarily need them, at least before full recreational legalization (in Mary's view, anyway, the "fucking stoners"), but some people who have a legitimate medical need avoid the legal market because they want to avoid the potential exposure. They fear being punished under federal statutes, or they fear visibility socially or politically. Someone with a high profile in politics, or perhaps a federal job, might want to avoid being identified as a cannabis user. Legalization is a long way from complete, from Mary's perspective, and cannabis has some ways to go before it is socially acceptable.

And there is more to the shifting economic dynamics than changes in the law. Legalization was important to a recent drop in prices (an unfortunate drop, in Mary's view) but "it was a combination. It was a combination of that and 9/11 and the shutting down of the border. Drugs were crossing the border pretty freely and then the government shut that shit down. So drugs weren't crossing the border. It was easier for people to cross the border and grow here rather than bring drugs across the border. It's easier for people to go through the desert and cross over and tend gardens than it is to cross with a van full of drugs. So they just grow them here." This visibly agitates Mary. "Now they don't smuggle drugs across the border from Mexico, they smuggle people. They smuggle people to run their farms. These are in the mountains of California on other people's land. Thousands and thousands of acres of illegal weed that they sell for cheap."

I ask if by "other people's" Mary means public land (she does) and if the reason these large, Mexican-financed farms produce cheaply is because they have lower overhead. "Right. But they have armed guards. They'll shoot you. So any legitimate grower who has a license hates those people. It's a real battle. Because they're really undercutting the market with an inferior product, because they're using pesticides, they're not growing organic and all that. And so there's a real classist issue, like their shit is shit and our shit is good. You know, you want them to get busted. They're using public land. Their littering and they're ruining creeks. They're polluting it. They're running battery acid in the creeks, they're killing deer, they're poisoning, they're using pesticides that aren't even legal here, they are bringing it in from Mexico. . . . It's a battle. Diverting water from where it's supposed to go. So the battle is pretty intense."

They also operate at an economy of scale that Mary cannot match. "They will have 40,000 plants and it will be inferior quality, but they sell it for $800 a pound; I will grow thirty plants and try to sell it for $2,100 a pound. They're flooding the market, and they're outdoor. I'm indoor. So I go all year long, every three months. I have overhead. They're paying two guys to sit at their campsite for the summer. . . . So, yeah, I hate them. They're the enemy." From Mary's perspective decriminalization has done nothing to eliminate the black market economy in cannabis; it has made growing safer (which she appreciates), but it has not brought the anticipated transformation of the industry.

Pete, too, has suffered from the drop in prices. As somebody who grows outdoors on public land he does not have the same antagonism towards the "Mexican" technique that we heard from Mary, or at least he thinks of himself as an American, and thus having rights to the public land. He certainly has no problem with "fucking stoners," and in fact considers himself one. But the drop in prices has reverberated through the Hawaiian underground. At the time of our interview Pete had "four pounds in the freezer. And it will be there next month. And the month after that." If he could get $2,000 a pound, that is $8,000 sitting around getting stale. The market is flooded.

Pete credits this drop in prices with a new malaise among the socially marginal on his island. Heroin and crystal methamphetamine are becoming more popular because people "can't afford coke anymore," and while Pete has a low opinion of cocaine, he credits heroin and meth with far more destructive power. The market for Hawaiian pot on the West Coast has clearly diminished (Washington, Oregon, and California had all loosened marijuana laws at the time of writing, so there was less incentive to import it from Hawaii) and that has caused a sharp drop in income for the Hawaiian drug-growing and drug-dealing community. In the past, rates of unemployment might have been terrible, and a person might lack marketable skills, but Hawaiians with time on their hands could always cultivate a few plants and make a little cash. Now this is less possible.

Visiting with Pete I sensed a grim desperation in many of the social interactions I witnessed, a surface conviviality that did little to hide ominous undercurrents. From Pete's perspective, it was not always like this.

Still, Pete does not look to structural economic explanations for his own—or anybody's—position. For him, as for most people with his brand of libertarian political sensibilities, a person's situation is the result of that person's decisions, which in turn spring from one's moral composition. Thus Pete explains his unhappiness this way: "My problem is . . . that I don't take control of situations and don't make myself profit by situations . . . I continue to do people favors and don't personally profit. That's why I can't make any money selling my pot. You've gotta have the ability to fuck somebody over to make money in this business." It was a refrain, a self-indictment.

Because of his relatively affluent situation (family money helped him buy a small house, for instance) Pete does not actually need to make much money. Still, money matters to him on a moral level, on the level of identity. Pete considers himself a failure, a "loser" for his inability to meet the expectations he set for himself (in his view) or his culture set for him (in my view). Pete is pained by what he sees as his lack of ambition and his inability to properly profit off of his business. He would like to be competitive, aggressive, and materially successful. He cannot seem to do it. So he grows pot, smokes lots of it, and gives bags and bags away to friends with dubious loyalty. He sells what he can.

SEVEN

Ambivalence Renounced

Growing up and Out of Dealing

In this chapter we turn to the question of why suburban dealers quit selling drugs, especially cocaine. Most of the dealers we have met do not take drugs any more, at least hard drugs, and they certainly don't sell them. Some continue to use or grow cannabis, but cocaine was always a young man's game. To explore this, we will return to the story of Woody, who sold coke in the context of the bar, and we will meet Simon. Woody is older, born in the late 1960s. Simon is younger, born after 1990. Woody discusses his entry into and exit from cocaine dealing and Simon will reveal how he got involved with and exited marijuana dealing, and why he never touched cocaine in the first place. Woody shows how normal cocaine dealing was at one time, and how in his community it became untenable after a certain point in one's life. Simon explains how differently cocaine came to be thought of in America more recently.[1] Both men emphasize the life cycle, the biological and cultural process of "growing up," and how in suburban America "growing up" means changing the way we engage psychoactive substances. Given the intractable drug problem in the United States, understanding why some people transition out of drug culture is urgent.

GETTING OUT I: WOODY

One of the main things I wanted Woody to discuss was how and why he got out of the business. After all, he sold for a decade, he never had problems with the police, he was making great money, and he seemed to be able to separate his social life from his cocaine business—despite the fact that he only sold to friends. There was no talk that quality of the drugs was getting worse (as for Wayne) or addiction (like Doug, Brad, and Pete). He did not graduate from college and lose his customer base (like Art). So why quit? Other people had obvious reasons, but for Woody it was economically sensible to sell cocaine for more than a decade. What changed?

Woody explains, "I worked at a night club.[2] I would go in at ten or eleven at night and get off around three in the morning. Cocaine was in high demand at that time of day." Importantly, this "high demand" occurred *after* the general period of cocaine's popularity. Woody sold from the early 1990s to early 2000s, and the image of the drug had already changed in popular culture. The use of cocaine by Americans had subsided dramatically, by as much as 50 percent.[3] However, in some contexts—the middle of the night at a rock club—it was still widely used. So, again, why get out?

"I would say it was just my age group. Once I was in my mid-thirties I was married and had kids, I wasn't out at night when people wanted to do that stuff. I didn't want to get in trouble. You got a kid, you're up at six in the morning changing diapers, you're not out partying all night. I think any time you go from twenty-two to thirty-two to forty-two, you know . . . you drive slower. You're taking less risks, you know, you're not doing stupid things . . . you would hope . . . you'd stop doing things that are going to get you in trouble . . . so I don't think it's drug related or career, it's everything . . . you settle down."

Woody thinks some more about this and continues, "But, yeah, it's risk. It's not that it got unprofitable or anything like that. . . . It wasn't worth the consequences. But when you're twenty-two, who cares? I got a job with government clearance. I couldn't have any arrests. As far as the age stuff, it had do with my peers. We were the same age. When you're in your twenties you had a little discretionary income . . . people aren't buying houses or anything like that, or buying diapers, they're going to concerts and stuff like that."

So it seems pretty clear that in Woody's estimation cocaine and child rearing do not go together. There is a kind of social moment (the transition to the category "parent") combined with a biological change ("you drive slower," you are less tolerant of risk). But there is also the overall shift in how cocaine was seen in the culture, and how it was seen as appropriate, or not, for people of different ages. Again, Woody was a dealer after coke had become "bad," after the crack epidemic and the onset of draconian sentencing laws. The place of cocaine in the wider culture did not seem to matter to Woody when he was young. It most definitely did when he got older. This is not just an increased sensitivity to risk; it is also a concern with reputation and the onset of a new, self-consciously mature identity.

He continues, there are "lifestyle changes around the mid-thirties, people are settling down, getting ready to have kids. Coke wasn't really conducive to that. Obviously not everybody, some people are still going strong, but I'd say the majority of them are on about the same timeline as me. That drug in particular is probably looked down upon in our community, like if you did get in trouble. I mean, growing pot, I don't think people really care. Across the board. There's a negative connotation to cocaine. . . . It's a cultural thing. Where I live marijuana is totally socially acceptable. It's legal. It was voted in to be legal by 89 percent of the community, even if they don't do it. . . . I would say that it wouldn't be the same for other drug use. So say if you lived in Utah, or someplace pretty conservative, marijuana wouldn't be acceptable, so people would think twice if you got caught growing some plants."

The negative connotation of cocaine did not surprise me, but surely that had been there when Woody started. So I asked when the negativity began. "All the way across, but you were just young and who cares what the old people think? They weren't my peers. The earlier generation saw a lot of lives destroyed, especially because I was living in a resort community. People might have partied more than in other . . . occupations. I mean, we saw people older than us screw up their lives, too. But same deal. They were hitting that age, having kids. They would still pop out once in a while for a bindle, but you know, generally you're home at ten o'clock at night. And that was just my generation, it was the next to come in. I think the generation behind me, probably other drugs became more popular, like ecstasy, that kind of thing. But basically the same thing. Buying powders. Taking them."

I asked him to continue to talk about the history, about the generational change.

"So this town, the older generation was sort of based on drug dealing. It's hiding drugs for another resort town. It's in songs and stuff. You would hide it up in my town and ship it over there. Those guys that came back from Vietnam, and then they lived here in the 1970s, they were doing it. By the time they got old, in the eighties and nineties they were kind of burned out, they had problems doing it. But they're definitely around. The negative end was there to see, for everybody. Consequences. . . ."

As for the current state of affairs? "I believe now . . . it's half the cost of what it used to be, fifty or sixty dollars a gram. There became a big Latino population that came up to work with the booming housing industry and everything else. I think they carried a lot of blow up with them. They brought connections, and they were young, twenty-year-old guys who had nothing to lose because they were just getting shipped back out of the country. They really didn't care, so it kind of flooded the market, became cheaper, but that was pretty much when I was done."

These days Woody takes seriously his role as a husband, he works at raising his kids and keeping his government clearance. A new generation of dealers, comfortable with risk and impervious to what "old people think" has come in to take over the business.

GETTING OUT II: SIMON

Simon is part of this new generation. He only sold marijuana, and quit that by the time he was twenty-four, when I interviewed him. Many things about Simon's experience are peculiar to him, but he also demonstrates a generational shift. Woody seems to suggest that the pattern of drug sales is being continuously revitalized by young, new dealers. Simon suggests that, for some at least, things are changing in deeper ways. Business runs differently now, laws are mutating, there are new economic opportunities and constraints, but there are also new ways of thinking about specific drugs. We will explore this at length in the next chapter, but what we see here in Simon's story is the ambivalence inherent to business with friends, and the decreasing tolerance for risk as people age.

Simon describes himself as starting life in the "lower middle class" but his mother remarried and from then on he was part of the "upper middle class." This means that he and his siblings share a large house in a wealthy suburb of Connecticut. They were sent to private schools and drove late model cars when they reached the legal age for a license.

Simon began selling marijuana in his freshman year of high school, but his dealing accelerated during his sophomore year, when he got a car. This is how he describes his entry into the business: "At first . . . they'd call it 'smoke for free.' I'd get an eighth and make ten or fifteen dollars off it. Or you just smoke the excess. That's what a lot of people would do. And then you're fronted an ounce. And then your clientele expands. It starts from friends and then friends of friends. It was usually done by text message. They would send me a text and I'd go meet them. Or they'd come by my house and I'd go outside."

Simon never experimented with cocaine. "I grew up with it being violent . . . a violent industry. Very violent. Heroin was dangerous . . . violent . . . similar to cocaine . . . I kind of lump those two together . . . And meth, because of how addictive they are . . . how much they can destroy your body and everything like that. And how much money is in it if you're on the selling side. That's why it's so dangerous. I stayed away from that stuff based on what I'd hear and what I know. Alcohol, weed, cocaine: that was the progression. After cocaine, prescription medicine and after that heroin, and heroin is either death or recovery. I have a lot of friends that followed that path . . . and during the cocaine/prescription pill thing . . . they changed. They severely changed . . . who they thought they were."

Avoiding this path, but with his car and a good marijuana source, Simon's business grew quickly. "I had known about drugs because of my older siblings. I had always been privy to what goes on in high school. I wasn't completely naive, but I didn't have an 'in.' But my friend, he had a connection from LA. He had an agreement about shipping and receiving, and for very good prices. We made an agreement that he would get the weight, and then he would give me the weight on loan and I would sell it amongst friends."

Unlike the cocaine dealers we have met, Simon makes a conscious decision to "move up," to follow the drugs to the source. "The higher you go, the more you're pushing, and the more risk, but the bigger the reward. That's always what people told me. The more you sell, the more risk. Around here, there wasn't a lot of people who got caught for slinging dubs, or got in trouble." I didn't know what a "dub" was, so Simon explained. "A dub is twenty dollars' worth, so that's one gram. Then you go $50 for an eighth, that's 3.5 grams. Most of my competitors would sell quarters, which is seven grams, for $100. I did them for eighty dollars and I sold them quicker. I didn't make any money off it, but I gained the respect and trust of the guy I was picking up from. So he introduced me to his LA connect and then instead of him going through my friend, he was going to both of us. My friend had moved to New York. So I no longer had to pick up from him. I started funneling directly from LA."

Simon was clear about his motives. "I made the sacrifice because, for me, getting into it, at first it was money," and to make money you needed to move up. My next question, as it had been for Pete, was why he needed money. Simon was not poor, and he lived at home. He didn't pay rent (like Doug) or even need money to "party" (like José). Pete had had money, too, and his goal was to "be cool," to be part of what was hip, to seduce women, but this did not seem to be the case for Simon. For Art the motivation had been to "reciprocate" with specific friends, but I did not hear this from Simon either. Instead, in Simon's case, as in Brad's, the motivation was remarkably conventional: to be independent from his parents. "Independence" meant having your own money.

He explained that when his mother remarried and had a daughter with her new husband, the children from the previous relationships were in an ambiguous position. The new half-sister was "the focus of their family unit" and Simon didn't want to ask his stepdad for money. It "felt awkward," he said. "I always wanted to be financially independent from him. It wasn't a need, but a desire to be financially independent. I always felt a lot of pressure, guilt, my stepfather did so much and I appreciated it, but I always wanted to sever that tie. In hindsight that's what all this allowed me to do because . . . I really didn't like to work." Here Simon laughs, presumably because for Americans "working" is important for reasons beyond money, especially in his social class.[4] Simon considered drug dealing a way to develop "choices, opportunities" and he considered the next level of selling a real "business enterprise." Ultimately he started to think about how to "really, really, really make money with drug dealing, and turn it into a lifestyle . . . to get enough tax free money that you can eventually use to start a business and go legit, as they would say." Starting a legitimate business does not seem like an unusual goal for young men in a leafy suburb of Connecticut. Simon just goes about it differently than most.

What kept Simon from getting to the level where he might "go legit" was not problems with the law, or even the risk, but the way business felt incompatible with friendship. All the while Simon told me about his business enterprise he was also talking about the relationships that were necessary to keeping it going. So, for instance, he discussed having an "initial six friends who allowed me to get my product moving" and this moved on to "friends of friends" until ultimately "two of these became friends." He spoke at length about the need to smoke with people, to engage socially to do business. "It's a social relationship. I'm not going to do anything shady. And I think my friends helped spread that message."

At the same time, he was getting large quantities of pot from Los Angeles and he needed to market it. He discussed how he wanted "positive reviews" and the importance of being considered "trustworthy." He always used a scale, for instance, and often weighed the pot in front of the customers. "A big thing in [this affluent suburb] is that it is a very privileged, haughty environment, and a lot of the kids just feel entitled and if they would get even a little bit shaved off of the stated weight they wouldn't pick up from you again. They'd have a big conniption about it. So I got a scale immediately. Sometimes I would give a little bit more, just in case my scale was wrong. I always wanted to be known for giving the proper amounts." Beyond this he started getting marketing advice from his LA source. "He would give me selling points, like 'this is Amnesia Haze from Humboldt County. It's a daughter cross-hybrid of Purple Kush and Afghani Kush and it makes this other kind of kush. He'd give me all these fancy names, the history of it, and it really worked. It's like the placebo effect. If you sound articulate, and you know what you're talking about, and it's not bullshit, then it's going to be better . . . in a way. He did a very good job of giving me good selling points. And it would always change, month to month." This increased sales, "at first it was two ounces and eventually a pound." Sixteen ounces at a time was being shipped east.

Inevitably, however, it did get "shadier." Simon "started dealing with people in New York and Bridgeport," where José had sold crack. Simon noted that "I no longer sold to my friends. I would get a pound and split it up into quarters or halves and I would give it to certain people. I would front it to them. I became what my friend had been to me. The fronting is actually really tricky. Building the relationship, the trust where they'll come back to you, because . . . I'm a little white dude. I'm not threatening.

There is nothing stopping them from just robbing me. Which did happen a couple of times because you get to know people, you think you trust them, but they turn out to be . . . not that. But as you start expanding you have to deal with other people, not just immediate circles. That was a bigger issue."

I asked Simon to tell me how he expanded his circle of contacts, and about the ritual of the sale. To this he said that the way a sale happened "depended on who they were." It could be "awkward" and you didn't want to move too fast or too slow, he "didn't like to act sketchy." Interestingly, he gave the same exact amount of time that one should spend on a marijuana sale that others had outlined for cocaine: thirty minutes. "Thirty minutes was a solid time, it didn't make people feel stressed." For new customers "I would always weigh it out in front of them the first time." And there was a racial component. Of the tension in a first-time sale Simon says "I think it's more of a white thing. I'm not trying to be a racist here, but there was a clear difference between selling to black people and selling to white people. I mean the white people were always antsy and nervous . . . regardless of where they were from. A deer in the headlights kind of attitude." Black customers were more relaxed, and eventually Simon was introduced to a kind of secret handshake, and this created an even more amenable selling environment around his black business associates. "It was ritualized, the process, it was pretty friendly. There weren't a lot of scary calls. I wasn't in it for violence or crime. The only time there was violence was because there were other drugs in those circles. There are violent drugs and nonviolent drugs. I consider marijuana a nonviolent drug."

Meanwhile, Simon's parents are expecting him to pursue the path of young men in his social class. He says, I "got a scholarship to college, my parents were pushing, there was pressure but all the while I was making plans to go to college for a year and then drop out and move to California, where my connect was really from." This is what Simon did.

"I got a job at [a famous Los Angeles cannabis dispensary] where there were patients with glaucoma, cancer, things like that, and a few celebrities." At this point cannabis was not legal for recreational purposes. "Celebrities that would call with these massive orders and I was the delivery guy. You'd have to go out at like two in the morning to Beverly Hills, type in these confusing codes to get in these huge gates. This one time . . . I still don't know who it was, my boss wouldn't tell me. I was delivering lollipops, cereal, drinks, brownies, all sorts of . . . cannabis-infused products. And there was this huge bag, and they'd call in the order once a month to get this big order. I think he was a writer."

Working as a delivery person for a dispensary is no way to make real money, however, so Simon "started getting into smuggling . . . not smuggling exactly, it's shipping . . ." in other words, mailing other people's pot. "I knew how to send it with a very high success rate," he says.

"Other people had crazy ways of sending it, but all you need are packing peanuts and $300 for a good vacuum sealer." According to Simon, the trick was to use a different post office for each package, a fake return address, and "you only send up to a pound at a time." He admits to having "something like five packages" intercepted, but there were "no repercussions for the receiver" because the government "doesn't care about who gets it." Presumably, they care about the source and not the destination, or maybe he was just lucky. Simon estimated with telling precision that he had a "93 percent success rate," and you only had to worry about "random checks." It was very lucrative.

"Let's say you sell a pound, that's $1,500 in LA. You sell that in the East whole, if it's good, for up to four thousand, even higher in places like [my affluent suburb]. People will pay $20 for a gram when that's usually only ten or even five dollars. So the fact that it was so cheap in LA and you could send it out to Connecticut and mark up the price . . . you can take a pretty hefty middleman fee. So, if it was a pound, I would take $250. If it was less than a pound, I'd take like a hundred bucks. At most I was sending three packages a week and just taking a little fee off it. For me it was stress free, $250 a package, four times a week. It took me maybe an hour to do that. It was simple and I made a lot of money. . . . I had $20,000 saved. It was also my salvation, my way out . . . because I was no longer drug dealing. I wasn't smoking it as much because I wasn't around the environment." Notably, drug dealing in Simon's telling still requires drug taking.

In addition to using cell phones to set up connections, Simon developed a system using the online game *World of Warcraft*. "That was how we communicated for transporting and selling. I started doing it more and more. I thought OK, I want to be a little more coded about this. So I had a character on Warcraft and there was another character over there. I paid for both accounts. It was only ten bucks a month. It was easy to do with the income I was making. And you can exchange currency that is . . . you can sell in game currency for real currency in the world, or vice versa. There is so much chatter in there, so much data . . . it's like who's going to sift through that? So you could transfer money as . . . collateral. So if it didn't arrive there was something that compensated a little bit."

At first I thought Simon meant that people actually paid for pounds of cannabis with *World of Warcraft* money, but that was wrong.

"No, you didn't entirely pay for it but you could talk openly about weights and stuff. You just throw in a little game lingo. People would say 'LFG' for 'looking for a group' but you could say 'LFG' as looking for a grand, where a grand was like a half pound or something. That was fun. In the game, the character, I bought . . . a hat for him, dirty ass clothes. I made him look like some gross drug dealer. I had some fun with it. But it was more like a safe channel for communication. The market in that game is mimetic to the real world. The economics in that game are crazy. . . . Making the character a dope dealer. That was my shining moment." It is notable to me that Simon makes his virtual doppelganger his cultural opposite: a "drug dealer" as they are conventionally viewed, "gross" with "dirty ass clothes."

If for Woody it was marriage and children that signaled that it was time to "grow up," for Simon it was the sense that he should go back to school. "In LA I was hit with some hard truths" he says. "I was becoming someone I didn't want to be. I was surrounded by disingenuinity [sic], I felt alone, I felt isolated." For Simon it seemed like it went from an "honest underground black market to . . . the same thing as capitalism in the world . . . it's just another business where greed perpetuates through it. My boss at the dispensary would fire people for smoking on the job. Which I understand, but I'd see her smoking in the backroom while she was counting out the money. It's hypocritical." On one hand, building relationships had been crucial to his drug dealing business, but on the other hand "I realized that none of the relationships I was making were genuine."

I thought this was interesting, so I asked Simon to elaborate on what counted as genuine, in his terms the difference between what he called "mutually beneficial relationships" and "friendship." Simon responded, "I'll use an example, the kid I went out there with . . . the reason I call that a mutually beneficial relationship, or why most of the dealings, as the money rose, were just mutually beneficial relationships. There were times out in LA when I paid for the rent. . . . It's fine, he's had a hard life, it's fine, he'll pay me back eventually, or really, I wasn't even so concerned with that. It was just like a no-brainer for me. But then when it came time for him to reciprocate the gesture . . . when I was going away for six months and I needed him to take care of my bird. And I loved that bird and he knew that, and I find out . . . I can't even believe the bird survived. I don't know. That was the first thing. And them from there I'm focusing on 'what is it that people really care about in a friendship?'"

"I realized when I was out there he didn't really care about me. It was just a mutually beneficial relationship. For me, I'm kind of extreme when it comes to friendship. To call someone a friend, to view someone as a friend, you have to at some level love them. . . . You will put suffering on yourself before you let it get to them. That's what I mean, there's relationships where people get along, and they elevate each other but . . . is their personal agenda more important than maintaining trust . . . and a good relationship? Nobody really cared about me. I had to be a little selfish then. I kind of had to question my identity. I got my shit together. One day I quit my job in the dispensary. My lease was up. I just packed my shit up and drove home. I was like, 'hey mom, I'm back. I'm going to go to school.' [In his mother's voice, 'nice!']. I cut it out completely. Something had changed in me. I went from a more lackadaisical, not giving a shit, not caring about the future, not caring about my health to . . . more serious, taking things more seriously."

After three years of selling in high school and two years in Los Angeles Simon decided to quit. Luckily he could do that. His parents had space for him to move back home, they paid for him to return to college. There were no repercussions from either his selling or his transshipment business. And while it sounded like Simon's original goal was to make money and achieve "financial independence," in the end the process seemed to be more about finding himself, figuring out who he was as a person and how "friendship" fit into that. For him friendship and drug dealing did not go together, at least not the way he originally thought. "Mutually beneficial relationships" were common, but true friendship remained elusive.

DENOUEMENTS

At the very beginning of the book we saw how José was pressed out of drug sales. He was a social pot smoker, and his marijuana sales were meant to sustain this. But it was difficult to make any profit selling pot so he tried to be entrepreneurial and move into crack cocaine. That ended quickly, and brutally, at the hands of the police. José continued to sell marijuana through social networks in the suburban style, but this too ended poorly when he agreed to a single anonymous sale and ended up on the wrong end of a gun. "I was crying, I was scared. It was worse than jail. I was four-foot-eleven," he said, and terrified. He wasn't "cut out for the life." As for drugs in general, José still considers himself addicted, but only to marijuana. As he said, "I tried cocaine a dozen times but I did NOT like it. It would make my heart pound. It wasn't for me. I didn't have any interest in it at all. But I love marijuana. Still to this day." José spoke ruefully about the tribulations of everyday life. Conflicts with his wife and boss, for instance, are much easier to handle if he smokes cannabis. Yet he avoids it. "It's a huge struggle. It's tough to be around it." But he feels his life is best drug-free and he works hard to keep it that way.

Doug's explanation is similar. We can recall that he blamed his addiction to cocaine for his inability to make money, and his inability to make money as the reason he had to quit selling (and doing) most drugs. Doug still smokes cannabis. Pete was another dealer who went fairly crazy, doing large amounts of coke and then struggling to get away from it. It was not the sales or the relationships that were the issue for him, but the desire to ingest dangerously large amounts . . . and then go searching for more. Pete had to physically move to get away, finally ending up in the middle of the Pacific Ocean. There is pride in his voice when he says, "when I moved here I became a 100 percent pure consumer"—and only of cannabis.

As we heard earlier, Wayne did not struggle with the substances themselves. He acknowledged that "some people get addicted to the point that they'll turn to stealing from you . . . just blatantly robbing you," but he claims to have kept his friends and his customers separate. According to him, his friends were there before, during, and after the drug dealing. Wayne did not experience the same loss of social standing as Doug. For Wayne it was the arrival of a child and a drop in quality that made the cocaine business less attractive. As we heard, "It got harder and harder to get, and the quality got worse and worse. That had a lot to do with it. The networks change, move, go away, die, go to jail and/or the shit just gets so bad it's not worth doing." Wayne drifted out of dealing over a long period of time and now he takes no drugs whatsoever. This was not related to the law. "We've had cops take it away from us and put us in jail and not press charges. Just to get us off the street. You know, when we're out partying. . . . And when you do get busted, 99 percent of the time it's going to be doing some sort of drug diversion class. And you're probably going to drug diversion class high." Wayne, too, cited fatherhood as the transformative event that led him away from dealing.

Even Art, who was relentlessly positive about drugs in general, admitted that cocaine "junkies" could be an issue. He told me stories of lying to avoid them (saying that he had no coke for sale when he did) and of the way a lust for drugs ruined people's sense of decorum. One time, for instance, someone bought some coke from him and Art provided the customary line of free cocaine on a mirror. The customer inhaled the drug, but then ran his finger across the mirror to get the last of it. This is not necessarily uncommon, but Art was outraged. To him this suggested that the original offering was not generous enough, and smudging the mirror suggested that they were done consuming, that Art was not going to share any more of the pile on the mirror. To Art, it meant he was being stingy, or to use his favorite term of derision, chintzy. To emphasize that it was about honor and not money, Art tipped the mirror upside down and dumped the rest of the communal drugs into the carpet. He told me this story with pride, as it emphasized the importance of character. So, even though Art insists that nobody in his three-person cocaine collective ever became grasping or "addicted," he recognized that cocaine-related bad behavior was common. He did not seem especially sorry to walk away from dealing as he walked off the stage with his college diploma. It was time to move on.

By the time we arrived in the new millennium, cocaine had changed. For young men like Brad, Woody, and Simon, cocaine had a bad reputation. This did not in itself keep Brad from doing it, and initially he liked the impact it had on parties, on the quality of social relationships, but almost from the beginning of doing it, he was trying to not do it. Despite the fact that Brad was selling many thousands of dollars' worth of cannabis (as well as LSD and other drugs) what he feared most was exposure as a cocaine dealer. This is perhaps one reason why he never came to specialize in that drug, and why he used it socially more than for making money.

Cocaine's bad reputation did not keep Woody from dealing, either. He made plenty of money off of it for over a decade, but he managed this by separating his recreational drug use from his business. In some ways he seems to have had the most successful model, a way of combining the efficiency of quick, anonymous sales with the safety of friend-to-friend suburban dealing. Once he reached a certain age, even this became untenable. Woody came to care more about the opinions of his townsfolk and his wife, and he saw cocaine as incompatible with family life. Simon, of course, never touched it in the first place. From being "what everybody aspired to do" (in Pete's words) cocaine had become "like heroin and methamphetamine" to Simon—drugs so dangerous that it was not worth having anything to do with them, even for a dealer.

How to make sense of all this? The fact that nearly everyone starts dealing during late adolescence and quits in early adulthood suggests that there is something deeper than culture going on. Young people, and young men in particular, lose their aversion to risk about the time they start to grow body hair, and then seem to gain some sense back once they are physically mature. This suggests a kind of biological clock at work in patterns of drug sales and use, but that does not mean culture has nothing to do with the process. What sorts of risks are worth taking? What sorts of rationales make sense of those risks? Culture—not biology—provides those answers. Even transgressing cultural norms involves boundaries, cultural understandings, a collective (which is to say cultural) framework. Young men are not randomly deviant, in other words. Their behavior—good and bad—is focused and meaningful . . . to them and their friends at least.

I think this is usefully approached through an integrated biosocial model, one focused on "ontogeny" as a term that links multiple processes. I borrow this from the anthropologist A.F. Robertson (1996).[5] He asks us to remember that human beings are always becoming—both in a biological and a social sense. There is no one moment when a person is completed; instead, each of us is in a continual process of becoming. Who we *are* changes over a lifetime. We do not necessarily perceive this consciously, but, for instance, my body is currently, and always has been, in flux. Few of the molecules of which I'm now comprised were part of me a decade ago. I am literally a different sack of stuff, a different material thing than I used to be. The integral and transcendent "me" I feel is an illusion, a sense of a me that started small, grew large, and is now in a regrettable state of growing too large even as it proceeds towards dissolution. At the same time, my social-self emerged slowly, first inchoate and dependent. This me grew through childhood and various stages of responsibility to independence. My social self is now focused on nurturing dependent others (children, primarily, but also parents). Eventually I will become dependent again, as I remind my children, to their horror.

Culture, too, is a *process*—not a thing—and it is interrelated with our biological and social processes. Meanings emerge over time and change. Ideas, goals, and actions that feel profound and sensible at one moment are plainly insane at another. Selling and using illegal drugs fits into the human biosocial trajectory, and is rendered sensible in American cultural terms. Young people use drugs socially in adolescence as they strive to expand their social circles and bid for independence and status. Drugs are tools for engaging others, they are useful to young people working on adult versions of themselves. But this phase ends in early adulthood. It stops making sense. People aim to "settle down," and drugs do not readily fit with this. Instead of expanding social opportunities broadly, people start to prune their social networks and focus energy on primary relationships. For many, parenting becomes the most primary, but even in cases where this is not so (Art and Pete, for instance) there is a marked turn towards "growing up" and building an adult identity. This does not work exactly the same way for cocaine and cannabis. The former has come to be demarcated as appropriate only for relative youngsters, while cannabis use often continues, at least sporadically. The role that these drugs play in the lifecycle are influenced by their meanings in the larger culture, meanings that have changed quite profoundly in the last thirty years. This is the topic of the next chapter. But it is worth remembering that privilege is what makes possible the choice of whether and how to respond to shifting meanings. Ultimately, white suburbanites get out of dealing because they can, because dealing is one option among many. Suburban men have more control over their interlinked biological, social, and cultural processes of becoming than do less fortunate others.

NOTES

1. While there is clearly a historical shift, we should not overlook "intracultural variation" in the meaning of substances (Cleckner 1976).

2. See Kelly and Parsons (2009) for a discussion of cocaine use in particular locales and subcultures.

3. See Johnston et al. (2016:20).

4. See Terkel (1972).

5. See also Singer (2009) for a "biocultural and political economic" approach.

EIGHT

The Rise and Demise of Cocaine Culture

The older people in this book first encountered cocaine about the time that the United States in general was rediscovering its allure—the late 1970s. Wayne was first, then Doug and Art and Pete. Brad—our most privileged dealer, and the one who sold the widest variety of drugs—is younger than the others, and came to cocaine later. While Brad had a voracious appetite for chemicals in general, he was wary of cocaine from the beginning. In this he was in tune with his era. By the time Brad started dealing seriously, in the 1990s, the whole country had soured on cocaine and everything associated with it. José, who is approximately the same age as Brad, never tried the crack he sold. He clearly thought of it as too dangerous (and too expensive) to indulge, and he never liked powder cocaine or found it alluring. Simon specifically avoided it.

So in the United States cocaine was widely popular and commercially available 150 years ago, then was rendered illegal and languished in obscurity for more than half a century. Then it re-emerged as an intoxicant rather than a medicine, and became de rigueur to sniff (as opposed to drink or take as a pill). And finally, after the media frenzy around the "crack epidemic" in the mid-1980s, cocaine was once again disreputable. Our story has been mostly about the wildly popular phase and its aftermath. It is this cultural moment that set the pattern for the suburban drug dealing that continues today.

What happened? As we saw in the previous chapter there is striking conformity in the stories our dealers tell. All started to experiment with drugs for the same reasons (it was normal, culturally desirable, and a way to make money and be independent). All began in their teens and all stopped dealing in their twenties or early thirties. Quitting was almost never related to interventions by the criminal justice system or to explicit external threats or pressure. Generally, it was "time to grow up," it was a "young man's game," they were "using too much," or they were just "tired of it." So there appears to be a pattern: experimentation in a context of social pressure, acceptance of risk when young, an identity and social connections formed around dealing as they get older, and a diminished tolerance for risk and a sense that it was time to "get serious" about life sometime before age thirty. Drug use appears to map straightforwardly on to lifecycle trajectories.

But if there is a pattern to the stories of individual dealers, it is much less clear why and how the broader culture changed. Historically cocaine went from being a commonplace and vaguely medicinal ingredient to something dangerous and repressed, then to something sexy and exclusive (when Wayne first started dealing, for instance), and then into a dangerous and dirty commodity (by the time Brad and José got involved). This did not stop Brad from doing it or José from selling it, but the meanings that cocaine held for them, and the way cocaine operated socially, had changed in important ways. The term "culture" is widely used to mean the shared understandings we have of proper and desirable behavior. Different cultures are understood to exist, and to have different values. What is less clear is how and why cultures change.

As the dealers tell it, three main themes emerge in the culture of cocaine use. First, for the older dealers, there was a sense that cocaine was "everywhere" and yet it was simultaneously hard to get. Ubiquitous *and* elusive, access to cocaine demonstrated privilege and prestige, a sense of being in line with the times and having access to important people. Cocaine was the thing to do, but you needed to know people to do it. Money was not enough. You needed contacts, people, and access.

This privilege could be shared or withheld for a variety of ends. This is the second theme: cocaine was used *socially* in a double sense. The drug was generally consumed in small groups, and its consumption indicated membership in those groups. But it also emerges as a strategic mechanism of sociality. Because it was expensive and unavailable to the general public, cocaine was a powerful tool for registering friendship, sexual interest, and status, among other things. What the dealers in this book seem to be saying is that they wanted to be acknowledged in the social world, they wanted to be part of what was going on. The way to do that, in some times and places, was to sell cocaine.

Finally, cocaine's very desirability contained the seeds of its downfall. "Addicted" people were unreliable, dishonorable, desperate, and annoying. They were the opposite of cool. While the dealers interviewed understood the addictive potential of cocaine differently, all understood the drug could be troublesome, and it was obvious to everyone that it often ended up that way. There is a general drift over time towards seeing cocaine as a problem.[1] In the early 1980s dealers classified it with marijuana and psychedelic mushrooms. By the 1990s it was thought to be in league with heroin and methamphetamine—far more problematic substances in almost any context in which they appear.

POPULARITY/EXCLUSIVITY

However it happened that cocaine initially eased back into American respectability, by 1980 the drug was established as desirable and commonplace in the suburbs. As Doug told us, "There was a great need for it. It was everywhere. Everybody was selling coke. Everybody was doing coke. So I jumped in and started making money." Wayne echoed this. For instance, when I asked him how he found customers he just laughed. "That's the easy part! Shit, especially back in the '80s you couldn't go in a bathroom in a bar without hearing [sniffing noise] in every stall." The difficulty instead was in finding a supply of the popular commodity. Doug, Wayne, and perhaps especially Woody, had great luck finding suppliers, and so became successful dealers easily.

Arthur too conveyed this sense that coke was desirable for cultural reasons. About his introduction to cocaine he said "I think it was kind of a normal evolution. Obviously when we were in high school and someone was like 'hey I've got some coke' we were like 'absolutely.' We all wanted to try it. It was just one of those things where it wasn't that readily available." The "obviously," "normal," and "absolutely" make it clear that he did not see himself as an outlier, as taking special risks or acting exotically. Later, in college, when cocaine was readily available to him, there was no real debate about whether or not to procure it. Cocaine's desirability was taken for granted. Pete felt the same way. As he said, "coke wasn't bad . . . everybody did it." Long before he himself became a user it was clear to him that cocaine was "what everyone aspired to do." While Pete initially claimed that his interest in drugs was only to make money, having cocaine was clearly aspirational in itself. For Pete it was associated with the potential for sex with women, with prestige, with an enviable life. As time goes on Pete has the most negative experience with cocaine of the dealers I interviewed, and his is the most forceful denunciation of it. But even for him it did not start that way.

Later, by the 1990s, Pete has left California, at least in part to escape from the availability of cocaine. He has come to see it as profoundly negative. Doug has retired, Art finished school and quit dealing, Wayne is drifting out of the business, while Woody has figured out how to sell it without the social and physical toll others experienced. Meanwhile, Brad is in high school and is just being introduced to the drug. Brad's experience is interestingly different from the older men. Like them, he had done other drugs first. But unlike them, cocaine is not obvious in this era, "everyone" is *not* doing it, at least in Brad's milieu, and there is a great deal more ambivalence associated with coke than there had been in the earlier period.

In one interview Brad says, "it was a weird thing, nobody knew who did coke and who didn't. People who did coke didn't tell anybody." Perhaps cocaine's relative invisibility is because he was still in high school and many of the dealers did not encounter cocaine until they were a bit older. Brad's circle of friends seem willing to ingest almost anything, however, so it is striking that "people who did coke didn't tell anybody." By the 1990s cocaine has lost its "everybody is doing it" cultural approval. It was no longer "what everyone aspired to do," as Pete had told us. It was still ingested, but its meaning had become deeply ambivalent.

Brad continued, "People in the grade above us didn't really do it, I didn't really know much about it, and I think, there were a couple guys who had graduated and had sort of stuck around town and had rented a big . . . house on the river. I think they were doing coke. I think Elliot had tried it but I don't think I knew that he had tried it." Again, this is revealing. Elliot was Brad's closest friend, his business partner in many of his drug enterprises, and even Elliot initially kept his cocaine experimentation a secret.

Finally, Brad begins to use the drug himself, though with some reluctance. "I vaguely remember that one of the first times doing it was at this girl's house, she would have parties a lot, her parents would let her have parties. And I remember just doing coke in the bathroom upstairs. . . . I remember basketball season having done coke, you know, the night before a game and the next day I had like no legs and I just, it was a whole different beast than having drunk a bunch. . . . You could sort of lumber through drinking, you could lumber through with a hangover but you couldn't like . . . the toll that staying up until five in the morning high on coke was of a whole different order. I remember I hadn't really realized that until I had a game the next day." There is none of the enthusiasm for cocaine that we heard from Wayne or Art, or the inevitability we encountered with Pete or Doug. The drug is ingested, but its costs are immediately apparent, not hidden behind an ideology of normalcy. From the beginning Brad is more self-conscious about cocaine than the dealers who came before him. This is a significant cultural shift.

Interestingly, not one person discussed their initiation into cocaine use in terms of its physical effects, other than Brad talking about its negative impact on his sports performance. Nobody talked about the corporal experience of the chemical, the exhilaration, the high. *Every dealer focused first and foremost on the social context that gave rise to their use.* Some were excited about using the drug (Art, and to a lesser degree Wayne), some seemed resigned to it (Pete), and some were interested in the money (Pete and Doug). But none of them seemed very concerned with the drug's impact on the brain, or at least they did not think to mention it. All of them were doing the drug with other people, because other people were doing it, as a way of engaging other people. If celebrities are people who are famous for being famous, cocaine seems to have been a desirable drug because it was thought to be desirable. This points again to our difficulty with "cultural" explanations: if people wanted to do it because it was the cultural thing to do, how did cocaine cease being a desirable cultural thing to do? Culture is a word we use to describe trends, ways of thinking or behaving that are "normal," shared by a group. So the concept of culture in this context is, at best, descriptive rather than explanatory.

COCAINE AS A SOCIAL TOOL

It sounds odd to describe cocaine as a tool, but it is illuminating to think of it that way. People use the drug to alter their brain chemistry, and that is one obvious way it is a tool or mechanism. People also use and sell it to achieve specific goals and aims, and this is a sort of tool too, a way to change a situation, and in particular to improve an economic situation. For suburban dealers there are two main social spaces where cocaine was used—living rooms and bars. Both domains had particular rituals and formalities, culturally appropriate ways of using the tool and culturally sensible ends one might use it to achieve. Dealers had to conform to the expectations of customers, and vice versa.

Norms and values are not always straightforward. Woody and Doug demonstrated how differently cocaine sales could work depending on whether you were selling cocaine from behind the bar or on the other side of it. Social context matters to how you use and to how you sell. Tools only work in their appropriate context. Spoons are terrible for chopping down trees, but chainsaws make a mess of breakfast cereal. Still, you *could* use any tool in any way you want. Tools provide options, but culture influences what you consider a tool, and which you choose to do what.

Doug explained the apartment dealing scenario in these terms: "It's etiquette. It's rude to just show up, buy drugs, and leave." His idea is that the transaction requires a larger, shared experience. Customers were expected to spend about a half an hour chatting, sampling the drugs, and perhaps reciprocating. They were supposed to act like guests, and then, like guests, they were supposed to leave at a socially appropriate time. As Doug said, "It looks good, you've been there for a little while, now it's time for you to go." Doug was clear that he expected to provide drugs to his guests. He also expected to supply those he considered his genuine friends free of charge (as opposed to customers/guests), the people he called "family." He quips, "Oh yeah, that's me, Mr. Generosity," but he turns solemn to make his point that if one was considered family "You were *never* expected to leave." Giving away drugs to customers/guests was part of his business, a required social performance, but giving away drugs to "family" was meant to demonstrate that they were family. There seemed a complicated group of people drifting through Doug's living room, all of whom were assessing their status via the drugs on offer, drugs being purchased, drugs that were taken away after being purchased, and drugs that were being offered up as reciprocation after they were purchased. The few who need not leave—"family," in Doug's terms—were meant to understand cocaine as a marker of familial intimacy. Guests were meant to understand it as something else. The cocaine in Doug's living room was a multifaceted tool.

For Doug, selling in bars was different. He clearly liked it, but it also appeared to be shallower, less conducive of real friendship. Doug says, "There was a total social payoff. It was like a win-win situation. We went to a place called [Bud's]. Tuesday night twenty-five-cent beers. I'd walk out of there with $500 in my pocket drunk on three bucks. It was killer . . . as soon as you get there everyone wants to see you, see if you're doing OK. Everybody wants to talk to you, that's for sure." At this point, riffing on his "Mr. Generosity" theme I asked "So it makes you Mr. Popularity?" He replies, "Yeah, I was never Mr. Popular in high school, so that's what it felt like." So it seems that Doug uses cocaine to show his affection (to demonstrate that some people are "family"), as a form of etiquette (to show guests that they are welcome), and as a way of building a wider if shallower array of friendships (the "total social payoff"), of making money and ensuring a range of people "wanted to talk to you." As the person bringing the cocaine, Doug was the center of attention, the man everyone was waiting to see. This is not "doing coke because everybody is doing it." The drug is deployed to diverse but specific ends.

We saw Wayne use cocaine to cultivate sexual relationships, and others used cocaine to initiate sexual assignations with Pete. Woody used selling as a bartender to avoid—rather than nurture—the social standing Doug sought. By contrast, Art was not explicitly interested in generating sexual relationships, or the broad array of friends like Doug made in the bar. He focuses more on close and trusting friendships, what Doug earlier termed "family." For Art, cocaine was an important tool for developing this deep solidarity. Above all he viewed his immersion into cocaine culture in terms of a "natural" progression," or a "normal evolution" (his words) with the only caveat being that "it wasn't that readily available." But then it was: "And then I get to college and I meet these guys and they immediately say 'you want to do a line'? I'm like 'yeah, sure.' And fuck, this is cool man, and . . . they're turning me on and I'm saying I'll get some coke, I'll buy some, and . . . turn you guys on. . . . I'd like to reciprocate but I don't have access to it. If you can get more, I'll buy some and turn you guys on. So right immediately they're like 'oh that's cool.'"

Later in an interview he gives me an example of how the core group of dealers used the drug once they were established. Art says to his friends,

"OK, I'm going to go to the library to study. Let's meet back here at ten. So it would be ten. And we never watched Letterman, but we'd say hey, do you want to watch Letterman? And that would be the sign, so we'd just get out like a half gram and hang out and watch Letterman. Not really to watch Letterman, but as an excuse. And we'd be like, OK, that's probably enough. We'd get to bed by two." Art is explaining the ritual involved, the "excuse," but also how the three friends collectively moderated their consumption and came together in a kind of bonding ritual at the end of the day.

This attempt at moderation didn't entirely work, but the three seemed to fare better than some of the others I interviewed. Art explains "There was one stretch, four or five months, when it was the heaviest consumption, I got the best fucking grades. And I think it's like . . . OK, I've done my studying, that's my work, once I'm done I can reward myself. I'm going to drink six beers and, with three of us, we'll do a gram and we'll drink . . . six beers each and we'll hang out for a little bit. It was like the reward for studying for five hours." Art never did drugs while studying; he used them as motivation to study.

Finally, despite Brad's reservations about the drug itself, he recognizes the social role of cocaine. He says, "Because for me, I mean, the first time I did it I was like 'Oh my god,' you know, 'I need to do this all the time' kind of thing. I can't see how I made it through a party without this before." Using the drug at parties seemed important to Brad, but less because of what it directly did to his brain than what it did to the party. "In a lot of ways I found it really boring to sit there and talk to some wasted person next to me at a party who would be like, 'Yeah, whassup,' kind of thing but . . . the coke . . . created this weird cocoon . . . where rather than having a diffuse social experience with a whole bunch of people at a party . . . you end up knitted into these small groups. . . . All the coke people would go together to some place, maybe someone's room or some car or some basement or whatever. And also people would pass out and it would only be the people high on coke that were up and we were able to have these more . . . intense exchanges. . . . Things felt more pressing, people were trying to get stuff out or say stuff in a way that didn't feel as . . . stupid. You know . . . with coke it felt more like people were just really . . . talking rapid fire. I was much more interested in this, it dovetailed more with my style, with my social style anyways, I think." Brad is referencing the excitability of the drug, its tendency to make people talkative, but what appeals to him is the use of this as a tool for intimacy.

In their living rooms, in bars, and at parties selling and doing drugs operate as a mechanism of sociality, a way of demonstrating social bonds, and a way of nurturing them. This did not happen in exactly the same way for all the dealers, but the general phenomenon is consistent. Partly this depends on the actual physical properties of cocaine, the fact that it is a stimulant and so only the people "high on coke were up" late at night wanting to talk. It does not last long, so it has to be re-administered frequently, which creates recurrent opportunities for sharing and bonding. And its effects tend to degrade over time, so people need ever more of it to experience the same effect, and this involves repeatedly contacting dealers. These are all reasons that cocaine is a very social drug. But at the same time the chemical properties of cocaine are not ends in themselves. They are bent to social purposes and these were the preeminent concerns of the people using it.

"ADDICTION"

While it is sometimes said that cocaine is not technically addictive, or that it is "psychologically" as opposed to "physically" addictive, the distinction does not seem to matter to the people I interviewed.[2] All of the dealers see cocaine as at least potentially problematic; most consider it dangerously addictive. This is generally blamed on the drug's chemistry—not the social techniques of its use—though there is some interesting variation and ambiguity.

For instance, we already heard Doug say of his cocaine days "If I've got that big pile of coke in front of me, I'm going to do it. Like alcohol now." For Doug the issue is that he has an addictive personality and both cocaine and alcohol are problems for him. He has adopted the Alcoholics Anonymous perspective that the first step to managing an addiction is admitting that you are powerless before the substance you desire. And while he already mentioned that he was "equally" addicted to cocaine and the money he made from it, quitting cocaine meant he also gave up the social world he built with it. He lamented, "Once you quit selling stuff all those people quit coming around and you realize you don't have a whole lot of friends. You thought you had a bunch. Once you quit doing drugs, they're not your friends anymore. . . . Selling drugs helps to develop a bigger circle. It's like I could go to the river, this one friend's got a boat . . . let's go to the river. Well, those trips to the river quit happening once I quit selling dope. He was only a friend because I was selling dope." That seemed pretty sad to me, and I said so. He replied, "It is, but that's the truth . . . as well as not making money all of a sudden." Quitting drugs was tough: Doug lost an important income stream, and many people he thought were his friends. Getting chemically free was part of the issue. But learning to live with less money and fewer people who seem to care about you was at least as difficult as quitting the substance itself.

Pete is by far the most harrowing spokesman for the horrors of cocaine. He told me many stories that illustrate this, but a couple make the point. One time a friend came over with "a briefcase full of cocaine to smoke." In his circle "freebasing" had become popular. Again, this is a method (in Pete's case) of mixing cocaine with water and baking soda and heating it to extract the cocaine "base." This can be smoked, and the technique gets large amounts of the drug to your brain very quickly. Smoking cocaine ought to have the same biochemical effects as inhaling it nasally, but since the drug travels to your brain faster and in much larger quantities, it is a distinctly different experience. Pete and his friend ingested something like thirty grams in one night (sixty times what Art and his friends did during Letterman) and the friend went into cardiac arrest. Pete resuscitated him, called an ambulance, and sent the friend to the hospital. Pete found out the next day that the friend had escaped from the hospital, acquired more cocaine, and went to smoke it with another mutual friend (whom I also interviewed, though he is not included in the book). For Pete, this was bad. He felt like he was going to be an accessory to his friend's death—sooner rather than later.

Of smoking cocaine Pete says, "It wasn't something I actually wanted to do, you know? And fuck, the first hit I'd run to the bathroom and puke and shit myself. And like weeks later [the same friend] would show up and I'd do it again. It's not a legitimately frickin' rational thing. It didn't actually make me feel that good. Emotionally I wasn't like 'I'm as fucking happy as I've ever been in my life.' But when he'd show up, I'd do it." At this point in the interview I tried a banal intervention: was it because of social pressure? Pete is emphatic: "no, it's because I wanted to, really bad. That's the fucked up part." In the interview I'm still confused. I asked, "Why did you want to do it if it didn't make you feel good?" Pete, exasperated with me, replied "yeah, that's the point I'm trying to make. I'd shit and puke and not feel good and then still want to do it next week."

So for Pete it seems smoking cocaine is simultaneously irresistible and awful. This is different than what you often hear from addicts—that their preferred drug is irresistible because it is wonderful. Pete didn't like the feeling that smoking cocaine gave him, never liked it, and yet he continued to do it with military determination. He blamed this on the substance of cocaine itself, not social pressure or anything else. In fact, as he is wont, he blamed it ultimately on his own lack of moral vigor.

In another story he recalls a time when he and the second of his two cocaine-smoking friends were strung out from doing huge amounts of the drug and were looking to buy more. Waiting for the dealer the two calmly discussed whether they should murder the connection and take the drugs. Hearing himself say such a thing was horrifying, even in the moment. "So at that point I'm thinking drugs are bad," he cracks grimly. As noted previously, he tried to get away from coke by moving (to Utah to ski, to Spain to study, and eventually to Hawaii to live). "California was making me crazy," he said. It seems "California" meant "cocaine."

So Pete goes from thinking cocaine is safe and desirable to unsafe and bad. Later, by the time Brad starts dealing in the 1990s, the idea that cocaine is bad has taken root. He says "for whatever reason I was more frightened of getting caught selling it than I was of getting caught selling anything else. . . . It's just so loaded, you know? There was something about being a coke dealer that really struck the fear of god in me in a way that being a pot dealer didn't, or even selling a party drug like ecstasy. I mean I think there was this idea that coke ruins people in a way that some of these other drugs maybe don't, you know that was circulating around me. I mean it was weird at first to be driving with that much pot, but it felt normal, more or less . . . I don't know it just felt less, I don't know what the word is. I just, I think I would have been . . . much easier for me to swallow being pinned to it in a more public way than it would to be pinned to this huge bag of coke."

In the interview I am trying to understand why cocaine was thought so much worse than the many other drugs Brad was selling, so I ask "Do you think that the crazy behavior was because the lack of sleep or do you think that was physiology of the stuff?" Brad thinks and says, "It felt like the physiology of the stuff, but it could have been from lack of sleep. Because I can remember nights where . . . it was weird, it was a whole different thing. Because we would stay up late drinking and then we would all get up at a regular time and then I would maybe take a nap later or go to bed early or something like that, but I can remember now that the times that we started doing coke you know we would go to bed at like 5 and I would sleep the next day until two in the afternoon or something like that . . . you know . . . when we were high on coke that whole night we would spend it doing a whole different kind of thing than if we were drunk. If we were drunk we would sort of sit around and play beer pong . . . but if we were high on coke we would be sort of riled up and doing stuff and moving around."

So Brad is concerned about the thing itself, the chemical. This is about 1999, and the general understanding of cocaine has undergone a transformation. At this point I say to Brad "you seem to have a very ambivalent relationship with coke from the beginning. I mean, you keep saying, 'I wanted to stop but I didn't,' 'I didn't sell it but it was ever-present,' you know, there's almost always a 'but' at the end of the story."

He responded "It was ambivalent. I mean I loved it, I loved doing it for a good stretch of time at first. But then I really felt possessed by it, in a way that . . . I felt compelled to do ecstasy and acid and mushrooms at first but I much more quickly maxed out on them. I almost want to use the word for 'getting full' or something. You know, I would get satiated, I would get to a point where I would be like, 'I really don't want that right now,' and in a couple months I would, you know, want it, but coke was never like that. . . . I would get to point where I would really want to stop but I would almost feel compelled, it felt like a compulsion, all of a sudden there it is again and I'm calling someone again or someone would suggest it and I would be like, 'Oh yeah.' Whereas it was much more clear with other drugs. I would have bad acid trips and someone would be like, 'Let's do acid again,' and I would be like, 'I don't do that anymore.' I eventually did LSD months and months later but it was much more of a clear line. But I also slid back into coke . . . I guess I slid back even when I would stop for a month or something . . . all of a sudden it would be there and I would be like, 'Yeah, I'll do that,' in a way that if acid or ecstasy had been provided I would be like, 'nah, nah, no, I'm not.'"

Brad concluded, "I was continuing the nosedive. And I was really constantly trying to stop myself, you know? And especially with coke. People really did seem to lose their willpower once they got a hold of coke. You know? They just really seemed to get obsessed with it."

CONCLUSION

Paul Gootenburg, has written that ". . . cocaine culture . . . is famously hedonistic, risky, and individualistic, whereas coca [the plant, in the form of leaves] is usually savored by Andean Indians to reinforce their shared traditional and community mores. Coca is bought and sold, but historically integrated in a bounded regional circuit reproducing a cultural belt of highland 'Andeanness'; cocaine, in its far briefer history, has become a rootless and ruthless global commodity."[3] It is easy to see the truth in this, and it is impossible to deny the ruthlessness of large-scale cocaine trafficking and the damage it has done to communities, nation states, and the relationships between them. However, this is not the whole story.

As we have seen, at lower levels of distribution, in the suburbs, cocaine has served many purposes. In the late 1970s and 1980s it was highly desired, considered to be low-risk, and very common. Selling it seemed both rational and almost ordinary. It may have been risky (though most dealers did not seem to think so), and it was certainly hedonistic, but individualistic? This is precisely backwards.

Suburban cocaine dealing is eminently social, the very opposite of individualistic, at least until people become "addicted" and thereby unreliable. The drug was sold by and to people who knew one another. Social connections were cultivated through economic transactions. Selling it, buying it, and taking it: family, friends, and fictive kin were brought together. People made "family" via the symbolic importance of cocaine, as we saw with Doug. They sometimes made friends, or distinguished friends from guests and customers by how they used cocaine with them. It was a key element of homosocial bonding, and a tool of sexual conquest (mostly, though not entirely, of women). One could even say, for dealers like Art, that cocaine reinforced "traditional and community mores," at least if you can accept that "traditions" and the "community" were very different in a California college dorm than among Andean farmers.

Of course it did not last. As Brad made clear, the way people thought about cocaine changed. By the new millennium cocaine was considered a different drug than it had been in the old days for Doug, Art, Wayne and Pete. Personal experience with the downsides of the chemical certainly had something to do with this, but it does not explain everything. The death of celebrities, the arrival of cheap, easily marketable "crack" cocaine and its subsequent "epidemic," also tarnished cocaine's reputation. The fact that cocaine came to be associated with black, urban poor communities instead of famous, rich white people accelerated the change of perception.

The odd thing is that people did still do the drug, as Brad told us. It just meant something very different than it had a couple of decades earlier. While beyond the scope of this book, it is evident that cocaine remains in circulation. Young people still seem to experiment with it, and somebody must still be selling it to them. However, cocaine *culture* as it existed in the early 1980s is decidedly over.[4] The youngest former dealer I interviewed, Simon, had this to say of coke dealers: "They become hollow, greedy, selfish people destroyed by substances." He considered cocaine to be violent and dangerous, among our most dangerous drugs, a long way from "what everyone aspired to do." If late twentieth century drug culture emerged at least partly as a political project, as an explicit "counter culture," by the 1980s drug dealing was utterly transformed. Drugs of all sorts—their social use and sale—transformed into an apolitical platform for group cohesion and identity formation, at best. At worst they destroy the social worlds they so effectively help to build.

NOTES

1. Kelley (2018) evocatively captures this sense of how sympathetically cocaine had been viewed in the 1970s, before it became associated with black people.

2. See Waldorf and Biernacki (1981) on the complexity of "addiction."

3. See Gootenberg (2009:18).

4. See Johnston et al. (2016) or the National Institute of Drug Abuse website: https://www.drugabuse.gov/.

Conclusion

In the Shadow of the Sixties: The Economic Foundations of Suburban Drug Culture

Drugs have been studied in many ways, but rarely from the vantage of economic anthropology. But the economics are vital, and conventional economics do not begin to tell the whole story. According to a 2014 PBS NewsHour program, "The United States spends almost $1,000 per person per year on pharmaceuticals. That's around 40 percent more than the next highest spender, Canada, and more than twice as much as . . . countries like France and Germany."[1] So our legal drug bill came to nearly-four billion dollars in 2014. Obviously, Americans love their medicine, and on the legal side of the ledger chemicals are transacted like any other commodity. For better or worse, they are *not* subject to the ambivalent economics of drug dealing.

However, in addition to legally commodified pharmaceuticals, we shell out an additional $100 billion every year on illicit substances—twenty-five times the legal bill[2]—and the total cost to society is at least twice that, or $200 billion a year.[3] *Every year*. Marijuana use had been stable (but is now climbing and it may rise further as criminalization recedes). And while from 2000 to 2010 spending on cocaine dropped nearly 50 percent, other illegal drugs have more than made up the difference, especially opioids.[4] Of course, alcohol and tobacco continue to be the most deadly recreational substances, by far, and the most expensive for the public purse, but illegal drugs remain a central concern of public health officials. The transaction of them is hardly universally benign, either. It is obvious to everyone that drug dealing can savagely undermine communities.

Perversely, illegal drugs also sustain communities. This book has attempted to show how this happens, to demonstrate that much (or even most) drug dealing operates through networks of kin and friends, how this mode got started in the suburbs in the 1960s, and, presumably, how it still works today. Our image of drug users—and drug dealers—emphasizes the role of poverty, violence, despair, and racism.[5] While this is sensible in some ways, what it leaves unexamined are white, middle-class users and dealers, especially those who avoid "addiction" and the criminal justice system. This is a large chunk of the American electorate, and the ignored source of the majority of our drug use and sales.[6] Drug dealing outside of depressed urban centers works very differently than the flagrant, street level sales we see in films, or what is presented in the majority of scholarly assessments.[7] We have a hard time imagining white suburbanites as drug dealers, and even some of the people interviewed for this book did not see themselves as dealers, at least initially. Even more rarely do we get to know the perspectives of "successful" dealers, people for whom there are few terrible consequences, folks who have found their way into (or retained their position in) the American mainstream regardless of their youthful misdeeds.

For the middle class it is hard to blame drug use on hopelessness and despair, factors usually cited as the root cause of drug abuse.[8] We could say they are reacting to the hollowness of late-capitalist society,[9] or that they are working against the decline of homosocial male intimacy lamented by scholars like John Ibson.[10] But all in all most of the people in this book seem to be reasonably healthy members of society, at least now, but they were hardly nihilists or outcasts even when they were dealing. Historically what seems to have happened is that networks of friends worked to distribute marijuana beginning in the 1960s and 1970s as part of the "counter culture." A set of norms and customary behaviors grew up around these transactions, a drug "subculture" grafted to drug transactions. This culture consolidated and expanded in the 1980s along with the rising popularity of cocaine, and for some of the people in this book this was the beginning and the end of their "career in dope." Still, an ever wider variety of drugs continued to move through the networks even as individuals retired and were replaced by other, younger dealers. The pattern of distribution varies from drug to drug, across communities, and over time. The popularity of specific drugs surges and wanes, but the basic principles of transaction seem durable.

It is helpful, I think, to make sense of the enduring, social use of drugs by considering them a kind of tool, as forms of technology—things made that we in turn use for some other purpose.[11] In this sense crack cocaine, as Bourgois shows us, is a tool that poor, urban men use (and sell) to generate respect.[12] It is a technology of the self. This is not unique to drugs. As Francesca Bray puts it, "most work that technologies do is to produce people: the makers are shaped by the making, and the users shaped by the using."[13] People employ drugs to generate states of mind (chemically, in individual brains), but these states of mind rely on cultural understandings to mean something to the users. And if users draw from their culture to make these meanings, they are at the same time remaking that culture. Culture and individuals exist in a dialectical relationship, each helps build the other.[14] Significantly, the dealing of the substances also builds networks of people: groups, friendships, relations. In a word, transactions make *society*—not just through drug use, but through the economic transactions that sustain the use. Drugs, in practice, are complex technologies complexly transacted.

The illegality of the drugs augments this generative social process, since it requires the people making deals to trust one another.[15] Each deal is a small gamble, a gambit that the other person can be trusted enough to participate in breaking the law together. Done repeatedly, drug dealing builds trust and helps to develop friendships. The social nature of drug use does this already—most people want to party together, not slink off to get high on their own—but the added impetus of illegality means that you can *only* procure the drugs by cultivating the contacts to get them. This recursive sociality increases the reliability of drug dealing partners and makes it very hard for law enforcement to infiltrate suburban networks.

The illegality of the drugs is also what makes it possible to profit, since 75–90 percent of money made on drugs accrues below the level of the importers.[16] But profit is a source of deep ambivalence for suburban dealers. We saw this repeatedly in the interviews. Codes of generosity are well established and fairly clear. Marijuana dealers are obligated to smoke with customers, and the price of the pot has something to do with the relationship one has with the dealer or grower. Prices drop as you buy more, but they also drop for people who are socially closer to the dealer. The same is often true for cocaine, with dealers more or less required to offer free drugs to customers if the sale is happening indoors in a private place. These demonstrations of friendship ought to be sincere, or seem that way. Some people also expect to share the drugs they buy with the dealer who sold it to them, at least occasionally. This "hanging out" and "partying" is very pronounced for social drugs like marijuana and cocaine, which have been our main focus, but even heroin dealers have "motives and customer interactions . . . too complex to be understood" purely in terms of "greed and profit."[17] Socializing is a large part of the reason people buy drugs in the first place; it is vital to the process of suburban dealing.

As we have seen, the combination of profit and generosity in the social context of drug deals represents a conundrum for codes of behavior. The culture is conflicted, we might say, though I think *ambivalent* is a better word. On one hand, successful dealing demands profit. Dealers cannot sell for less than they paid or they will not be in business long. And anyway, money is not only required to stay in business, it is also linked to power and masculinity. In contemporary American culture making money is a good in itself, not only a means to an end.[18] (We saw this most dramatically with Pete, but also with Wayne and others.) Even dealers who sell only to subsidize their own drug use, and to facilitate the socializing that is the point of the drugs, still have to grapple with the condition that they sell (to friends) for more than they paid (to other friends). And this is the issue: profiting from friends calls into question the authenticity of the friendship, and does so in a context where trusting friends is essential. In terms of both culture and economics, this is a muddle.

Behavioral economics and neuroscience offer some clues why this is so. The full implications of these fields for our topic are too extensive to treat here, but some basic points are worth noting: people think differently about market behavior than they do about morality or friendship. Matthew Lieberman, for instance, writes that "we think people are built to maximize their own pleasure and minimize their own pain. In reality, we are actually built to *overcome* our own pleasure and increase our own pain in the service of following society's norms."[19] In *The Moral Economy*, the economist Samuel Bowles compiles a wide range of evidence to make exactly this case. Even labeling an experimental condition "market treatment" inspires people to act more ruthlessly than they otherwise might, as does calling participants in a transaction "buyers and sellers" (instead of "responders" or something else more neutral).[20] This is even true across cultures. Compensating people economically for moral behavior can make them *less* moral, as in an experiment where a child given a toy to help an adult becomes less likely to lend a hand than a child who is simply asked. As it turns out, when we are called to calculate rewards for helping people, the part of us that derives inherent pleasure from being helpful is short-circuited. According to one researcher, "the competition inherent in markets . . . offers justifications for actions that, in isolation, would be unjustifiable."[21] In short, markets *make* people selfish as opposed to providing an arena in which people exercise "natural" selfishness. Thus, Adler calls conventional economics, which prides itself as the study of market relationships and rational decision making, "the science that *makes* us dismal."[22] Taking economics classes actually causes people to respond more selfishly. It seems selfishness, too, is learned and social.

Alan Sanfy did neural imaging to try and see why this might be so and with his coauthors concluded that, in fact, entirely different parts of the human brain are used for contemplating fairness and calculating advantage. They argue that there is a "neural locus" for our human "distaste for inequality and unfair treatment,"[23] which perhaps is why it is essential to quell any sense of unfairness in the context of a drug deal by leavening it with gifts, "hanging out," performing friendship. Humans are strangely prone to excite this inequality/unfairness aversion locus of our brain, and to forfeit benefits for ourselves in order to oppose what we perceive as unfairness to others. Humans obviously have the neural capacity to calculate their interests and pursue their desires, but we are also hard-wired with concern for others. We have two minds in one body. This "dual process theory" suggests that our "affective and deliberative processes" can work against each other; love and money can be at war within us.[24]

I think this speaks to the situation we find in suburban drug dealing. Dealers are called to calculate money and profit (market activities) in a home environment among friends (a context where this sort of calculation is abhorrent). The ambivalence this generates was clear in most of this book's interviews, though perhaps most strikingly with Pete, Wayne, and Arthur. I want to suggest that this ambivalence, the tension between self-interest and selflessness inherent to drug dealing, is critical to the dealing, and in turn *integral* to the long term reproduction of drug culture. It is not a random effect, but a functional part of what helps the culture endure and reproduce.

To make this point I will leave neuroscience and turn to classic work in French sociology, in particular a small book by Marcel Mauss called *Essai sur le don*, or, in English, *The Gift*. Mauss examines gifts in a variety of societies and he seeks to explain what is fundamental about them. This comes down to a three part regime: the obligation to give, to receive, and to reciprocate. Why this should be so, what inherent property of gifts creates this hold over people, is the subject of debate. Still, we all understand the visceral and contradictory power of gifts, at least if we have appeared at a dinner party without a bottle of wine or flowers for the host (you feel guilty), or if we have received a holiday present from someone we despise (awkward!), or if we have been stiffed on a tip after providing good service (enraging!).

Gifts are not necessarily nice. They need not be. Gifts can be given for many reasons: they can flatter but also humiliate, show affection or discharge a perceived obligation. Often they serve as reciprocity for a previous gift. Mauss was not trying to contrast evil commerce with virtuous gifts, as is sometimes supposed. Instead he was trying to illuminate just how odd commercial relations really are. What he means by "commercial relations" in this context is essentially making the best deal you can. This is what any economics textbook expects you to do and what every business school teaches you to accomplish. It is defined by getting the most you can out of a transaction. This is woven into the American psyche as a categorical imperative, or sometimes averred as "common sense" or "basic human nature," as when Adam Smith claims the human instinct to "truck, barter and trade" is what separates us from beasts. In other words, our cultural understanding of economic "interest" presumes "self-interest," usually in the short term.[25] We generally assume that self-interest can be separated from a broader field of social relations (which, in any case, only come down to other people's interests). Textbook economics are infused with such cultural assumptions—and vice versa.[26] But Mauss is far more enigmatic than this, and more searching, arguing that non-commercial "exchanges and contracts take place in the form of presents; in theory these are voluntary, in reality they are given and reciprocated obligatorily."[27] But, crucially, the "voluntary" is not obscured by the "obligatory," and "theory" is not obliterated by "reality."

Mauss urges us to transcend this binary and complicate our market values by seeking to "adopt as the principle of our life what has always been a principle of action and will always be so: to emerge from self, to give freely *and* obligatorily."[28] The argument turns on the "and."

When business happens among strangers, conventional economics makes some sense. I buy a donut from the chain store down the road and I do not worry about the cashier, the donut maker, the other customers, or the owner of the franchise. I hand over my money and I get my donut. This sort of transaction is bereft of real social engagement. The person at the counter has a uniform and a tag with a name. She greets me politely. I respond politely. We act *as if* we have a relationship. The fact that I get what I want—immediately, with exact change—and then I walk out suggests that the pleasantries were mere performance. The whole deal has been socially vacuous. We never had nor intended, and we do not now have, a relationship.

But this is weird. Even though it is a common experience in our society, it is very weird for humans to exchange things without some sort of relationship serving as the context for the deal. Living among strangers is a modern phenomenon and we are not very good at it. Under more typical social circumstances, and outside of the anonymous market, any transaction requires some knowledge of the other. Any exchange alters our knowledge of and connection to the other person. And this brings us into a far broader kind of economics, the one that Mauss wrote about, the one where people actually know one another and sometimes even care about that. Here, in the normal, non-market world, economic transactions are soaked in sociality.[29] This is not the aberration economists would have you think, and the context of drug dealing makes that apparent.

So, to make sense of the full range of economic transactions—including suburban drug deals—it helps to leave conventional economics behind and return to Mauss.[30] Many anthropologists have drawn lessons from this, and in what follows I am borrowing especially from the work of David Graeber. His reading of Mauss's model suggests three basic modes of transaction: communism, exchange, and hierarchy.[31] Communism sounds strange in this context, but it simply comes down to the way we do things for each other without consideration of a return. We do this every day when we "pass the salt" without asking someone at the table to pay for it, or "bum a cigarette" from a stranger, or offer a ride when we see an acquaintance walking in the direction we are driving. We give out candy at Halloween, donate turkeys at Thanksgiving, and buy small Christmas gifts for people we may never see again. These sorts of "gifts" are especially common in families, and may even be the basis of family life, but they are not rare even with strangers. We do not stop to calculate the return on these sorts of gifts. With our children, especially, we eschew our baseline American faith in self-interest without even realizing it. (Do any of us rationally believe our children will "pay us back" for all we have done for them?) Humans are fundamentally communists, in this sense at least, and no baby would survive if we were not.

By contrast, with gift *exchange* we do calculate, but not like we might in commercial relations. We expect the gifts we give to be more or less (but not exactly) reciprocated. The inexactitude is crucial, the lack of a specific debt. In these sorts of transactions, we are looking to balance the ledger . . . sort of. If we were to perfectly balance the exchanges we would dissolve the responsibility of one party to reciprocate voluntarily, and thus undermine the logic of the gift and the potential generation of a relationship, which, after all, has to be pursued of one's own free will for it to be authentic. This is the "and" in Mauss's formulation. My commercial exchange begat a sterile equilibrium insofar as I paid a specific amount and I got exactly the quantity of sugary fried dough I was promised. No vague obligation after the sale. No potential reciprocation. No relationship.

With gift exchange, by contrast, there must be a time lag, an intention beyond acquiring a commodity at the least possible cost in the shortest time possible. I buy this round, you buy the next. I host a dinner party, you invite me to a movie. I help you install a new water heater, you loan me your truck to go to the dump. I am not trying to maximize the number of beers, parties, or truck loans; I am building relations, friendships. We swap things or services to cultivate persons, to build ourselves as a person. Things move from individual to individual, but the objective fact of their movement tells us nothing of significance. The more we exchange in gift mode, the longer we do it with the same people, the less calculating we are. We are co-participating in the pleasure of sociality, not just acquiring things or services for ourselves. The point of the exchange *is* pleasure. Over the long term we may entirely stop calculating at all and we are back to baseline communism.

Throughout the process the important thing is that reciprocation is never exact and immediate because "equilibrium is the death of the gift."[32] If I buy you a beer and you buy me one at the same time, nobody has gifted anything and all we have produced is four beers between us and an awkward silence. Instead, in normal social life, you should thank me for the beer I bought you. You should drink it (with me, not walk away) and I will pretend there is no obligation to reciprocate. You should then buy me one (later) — or two, if you want, again there is no obligation. That's friendship, or at least the beginnings of it. The fact that either party can opt out at any point is what generates the goodwill. The obligation *must* be unspecified. You honored your sort-of-but-not-quite-binding obligation to me, and I noticed. You did not legally have to, but you did. Perhaps you like me? It will take more beer to find out. What Mauss calls gift exchange comes down to people fumbling towards relationships, the slow accretion of trust and goodwill that is, to put it in grandiose terms, the basis of civilization itself. This mode of transaction is foundational to drug dealing and the propagation of drug culture.

When I attempted to suggest to dealers that their gift exchanges were significant we saw some of them attempt to explain away gifts as self-interest. Wayne, in particular, first argued that giving away hillocks of cocaine was a calculated business strategy. Pete considered himself a failure for not having enough self-interest, for being too generous. And Doug flatly admitted that he had no idea why he gave away so much dope. He tried to rationalize it at first, but then gave up because giving was simply "what you were supposed to do"—as a human and a dealer. His "I don't know why I gave away so much dope" was the most revealing statement in this book, and for me one of the most moving. The reason he did not understand his own behavior is that in our culture we contrast gifts and sales, our own interests and the interests of others. We cannot really conceive of genuine interest in others, at least when we are drawing on economistic metaphors to explain ourselves to ourselves. Gifts mix us up. Gifts do not exist without interest, but they are aimed at the interests of others, and our interest in others.

Hierarchy is Graeber's final category. Here transactions are founded on unequal relationships. The demonstration and consolidation of hierarchy is the point of this sort of gift. If I buy my teenager a car (I am dreading this), it is a massive gift that I know will not be reciprocated. It is not gift *exchange*. I might be generous, on one level, I might be altruistic or even self-interestedly focused on being free from driving to soccer practice. But I am also making a statement that I am (still, I hope) in charge. My teen should understand that to accept such an offer is to acquiesce to a raft of obligations that come with it, mostly deference to me, including getting home at a curfew that I have set. Kings and fathers and other aspiring bigshots do this quite often. They show their power with gifts; they deliberately incur obligations through generosity. Here gifting can be competitive, even quasi-violent, with people giving away vast sums to increase status and demonstrate power.[33] Perhaps this is the origin of philanthropy, the urge that leads rich and powerful people to put their name on every park, bridge, and dorm room in this country. Even the lockers in my university gym are named via gifts.

The key observation is that these principles can operate at the same time, in the same context, through the same behavior. A purely objective account of things moving will miss what's important in the movement. A drug dealer splashing down a pile of cocaine can be simple communism (I have tons of this stuff, enjoy!). This might also be the start of a delayed, but equal exchange leading to friendship. (Think of Art's friends in college. His enterprise began with a desire to reciprocate.) And it can be a statement of wealth and power (look how cool I am, I can provide more drugs than you can ever reciprocate!). Such behavior might also be a strategic move, a calculated attempt by somebody like Wayne to increase his commercial profit. (I remain unconvinced that in his case it was, but it is possible in theory.) All three gifting modes, and commercial calculation, may be operative at once.

I want to emphasize that none of these "reasons" is in itself the singular *real* cause of the behavior.[34] As the economic anthropologists Richard Wilk and Lisa Cliggett put it, "it is because gifts contain all of these characteristics simultaneously—aspects of self-interest, elements of social integration, and possibilities for establishing or reaffirming moral order—that they are so powerful and persuasive. This is what makes [gifts] essential tools in all societies—they can simultaneously benefit an individual, create a social system, and communicate cultural values of what is important in the world."[35] Multiple motivations can be involved all at once. And this is where most analyses of drug dealing—and economics in general—have gone seriously wrong.

The origins of this book stretch all the way back to my undergraduate years in the American Studies Department at Cal State Fullerton. There I undertook an independent study with Mike Steiner that we called "Work in American Culture." Among the things Mike had me read was *Working*, by Studs Terkel (I also read his book on the *American Dream*, and Robert Schrank's *Ten Thousand Working Days*—I owe my teachers immensely for pointing me toward so much great scholarship). Unbeknownst to Mike, the silent backdrop to my study was the comparison of what it meant to work for money in the mainstream economy in contrast to what it meant to sell drugs among friends. Later, in graduate school, I happened to pick up a copy of *Freakonomics*. The authors used the research Venkatesh did on drug dealing on Chicago's South Side to bolster their overall case that conventional self-interest underpins virtually all human behavior.[36] I knew this was wrong (and in any case I don't think Venkatesh was saying that).[37] Bourgois had shown it was wrong with crack dealers,[38] Hoffer had shown it was wrong for heroin dealers,[39] and Bourgois and Schonburg had shown it was even wrong for homeless heroin addicts.[40] It is certainly wrong in the case of "dorm room dealers."[41] I wanted to show that it is especially wrong for suburban cocaine and marijuana dealers. I think it is wrong in general, or at least so radically partial that it prevents any coherent understanding of why people transact the things they do in the ways they do.

Few suburban dealers make money. For most of them, it's not what they are trying to accomplish, and it is certainly not *all* they are trying to accomplish. They want to have drugs because they want to take them—together, socially—and they want to be known as the type of person who has desirable things and, therefore, is desirable. Drugs follow cultural guidelines like everything else. There are rules to how you buy and sell, how you gift and share, and at the deepest levels some of these rules approach human universality. Gifts must be reciprocated, voluntarily *and* obligatorily. This is crucial to human social life. It should not surprise us that gifts and sharing underpin suburban selling. This, I think, is why the dealers in the book were so ambivalent when they discussed profit. Friends and money exist in different "regimes of value."[42] If dealers think about their behavior economically, they give me one sort of explanation for it ("I was making money because that is a sensible thing to do"). When I pushed them to think about the social context, and forced the observation that they were making money off of friends, they came to see that this was true, too.[43] Some, like Doug, were baffled. Wayne was defiant. Art got upset. Perhaps we would all do well to realize that our lives depend on such contradictions, such ambivalent economics. To quote Wilk and Cliggett again, "Perhaps successful behavior *always* has multiple motives; it is therefore difficult to interpret after the fact *because it is meant to be that way*. People want their acts to be ambiguous and hard to pin down; they may want to conceal their motives even from themselves."[44] My only quibble with this formulation is the difference between "ambiguous," by which the authors mean murky or hard to fathom, and "ambivalent," which I prefer because it points to a deeper, irresolvable contradiction.[45] Following Adam Phillips, I would say that "ambivalence does not . . . mean mixed feelings, it means opposing feelings" and (following Rycroft) it "refers to an underlying emotional attitude in which the contradictory attitudes derive from a common source and are interdependent."[46] The "common source" is our unity as individual persons. The "attitudes" are "interdependent" because they are inescapable and part of us; they spring from the human condition.[47] Read carefully I think that virtually all of the interviews reveal this, the way "impersonal trade and sociality are found in uneasy conjunction."[48] The conjunction is "uneasy" because we are called to behave in opposing fashions at the same time.

At the dawn of the twentieth century Emile Durkheim made the case for "the double existence that we lead simultaneously: one purely individual, which has its roots in our organism, the other social."[49] The issue for Durkheim is that "society has its own nature, and consequently altogether different demands than those that are involved in our nature as an individual."[50] He is talking about any society, not just our commercially oriented one, and he goes on (borrowing from Pascal) to describe the human condition as a "monster of contradictions."[51] So we, as people, are constituted by our societies as we constitute them. Society is not just a collection of separable individuals, but something like a macro-organism of a particular type.[52] In our type, we are, as Louis Dumont puts it "obliged to be free," because the independent individual is a functional necessity of the whole.[53] A complex, "organic" society demands the constitution of people as individuals. Still, society and individuals are interlocking processes, not stable things, and our shared sentiments and values help hold this together. Robertson puts this well when he encourages us to understand human life as "the *process* by which physique and meaning grow simultaneously, the interaction of an evolved body developing in a historical context."[54]

But the fact that society, culture, and individuals are processes interpenetrating one another does not mean they interact mechanistically. Incompatible rationales not only can be true at the same time, in the same context, they must be. We cannot dissolve the social into the self or the self into the social. We are always both.[55] As a species we have a "talent for friendship," and that is what drug dealing relies on and facilitates.[56] The ambivalent economics of dealing build the social foundation of our enduring American drug culture.

NOTES

1. Valerie Paris, "Why do Americans spend so much on pharmaceuticals," PBS, February 7, 2014, accessed on June 6, 2018, https://www.pbs.org/newshour/health/americans-spend-much-pharmaceuticals/.

2. Christopher Woody, "NARCONOMICS: 'The real drugs millionaires are right here in the United States," Business Insider, published March 16, 2016, accessed on June 7, 2018, http://www.businessinsider.com/where-drug-money-goes-2016-3/.

3. National Drug Intelligence Center, "National Drug Threat Assessment 2011, U.S. Department of Justice, published August 2011, accessed on June 7, 2018, https://www.justice.gov/archive/ndic/pubs44/44849/44849p.pdf.

4. Other scholars paint an even more dramatic picture. Dianne Coyle writes that "The worldwide market for illegal drugs is known to be huge, but how huge is a matter of guesswork, because neither sales quantities nor prices are known for certain. One widely accepted United Nations figure is $400 billion (bigger than the global oil industry), employing around 20 million people and serving 70 to 100 million customers. Perhaps half of the customers are in the United States, the biggest single market for drugs, as indeed for everything else" (2002:10). Paul Gootenburg notes that in 1967 only twenty-six pounds of cocaine were seized; in 1971 at least 436 pounds were seized; by 1979 100 tons were coming to the United States from Columbia (2009:306). In Gootenburg's 1999 edited volume Mary Roldán notes that by 1981 *Time* magazine estimated that "$30 billion dollars' worth of cocaine was being traded on United States streets" (1999:167). While the exact amount of cocaine in the American bloodstream is impossible to calculate, everyone agrees that there was a spectacular rise.

5. Bourgois puts it bluntly: "Substance abuse in the inner city is merely a symptom—and a vivid symbol—of deeper dynamics of social marginalization and alienation" (2003:2). See also Kleinmen et al. on "social suffering" (1997), Becker (1963), Bourgois and Schonberg (2009), Hannerz (2014 [1969]), and Venkatesh (2000).

6. For instance, 75 percent of marijuana profits, and 90 percent of the revenue from cocaine, is made inside the United States via the many hands it passes through between the importing cartels and the suburban user-dealers. Reuter and Kleiman observe that "Federal enforcement efforts have great difficulty in imposing significant costs on mass-market drugs. The sheer size of the markets forces a concentration on crops in the field, export-import transactions, and high-level domestic dealing. However, these components of the production-distribution process account for a modest share of the final retail price of the drugs; about one-quarter for marijuana and one-tenth for cocaine" (1986:290). See Vellinga for evidence of how different the upper echelons of the drug industry are from the local dynamics (2004), and Kleiman et al. (2012) for a succinct and dispassionate view of what to do about drug problems.

7. This is not to say we lack excellent studies of how urban dealing works. See Agar (1973), Bourgois (2003), Kelley (2018), Natarajan (2006), Page and Singer (2010), and Venkatesh (2000).

8. An alternative thesis that I will not pursue in this book is that the late-capitalist economy has generated forms of want and discontent that extend far beyond the economic. For instance, Braverman writes that "It is not that the pressures of poverty, unemployment, and want have been eliminated—far from it—but rather that these have been supplemented by a discontent which cannot be touched by providing more prosperity and jobs because these are the very things that produced this discontent in the first place" (2015 [1974]:14). From this vantage, drug use by the middle class whites might be considered a response to misery.

9. See Braverman (2015 [1974]).

10. See Ibson (2012).

11. Perhaps the cleverest recent formulation of this idea comes from Bruno Latour and the notion of *actant*. Latour writes, "We use *actant* to mean anything that acts and actor to mean what is made the source of an action. This is a semiotician's definition that is not limited to humans and has no relation whatsoever to the sociological definition of an actor by opposition to mere behavior. For a semiotician, the act of attributing 'inert force' to a hinge or the act of attributing it 'personality' are comparable in principle and should be studied symmetrically" (in Bijker and Law, 1992:177).

12. Lindegaard et al. say something similar, and they cite drug dealers as "motivated by . . . obtaining three kinds of status: belonging to a group, respect from peers, and wealth" (2014:85). The authors draw on "life course and rational choice perspectives (2014:85) to make their case. However, I would argue that such rationality is deployed in a cultural context that is constitutive of its results, and founded in ambivalence. It is culture that provides the choices, and they can be contradictory. Most of the time rationality is the means to achieve goals rather than the means of evaluating them.

13. See Bray (1997:16).

14. Robertson captures this dialectical notion of culture when he writes, "Culture is thus a complex illusion: it is never permanent, never finally accomplished, because its meanings have to be affirmed and reaffirmed in the lives of individuals. It has no objective reality because it cannot be encompassed by a single mind; its constituents have only a partial existence in the mind of any individual, and many understandings of each fragment of culture may pass through that individual's mind during his or her lifetime. The propagation of culture depends upon relations of reproduction—and vice versa" (1996:598).

15. See Moeller (2017) and Nordstrom (2007) on trust in the context of illegal behavior.

16. See Reuter and Kleiman (1986:290).

17. See Hoffer (2006:108).

18. This is an observation that is at least as old as Max Weber (*The Protestant Ethic and the Spirit of Capitalism*), and maybe even Toqueville's *Democracy in America*.

19. John Edward Terrell, "Evolution and the American Myth of the Individual," New York Times Opinionator, published November 30, 2014, accessed November 17, 2018. Emphasis added.

20. See Bowles (2016:91). See also Charness, Gary, and Gneezy (2008).

21. See Bowles (2016:95).

22. See Adler (2011), emphasis added. Some studies of drug dealing do find that "rational choice theory" explains behavior, but generally in "open air" or "flagrant" market exchanges (Bernasco and Jacques 2015).

23. See Bowles (2016:106).

24. This basic idea has a long history. Adam Smith, for instance, is famous for his argument about the "invisible hand," the idea that personal selfishness can lead to social good "as if by an invisible hand." But he counterbalanced his vision of "self-

love" with that of compassion, a theme he takes up in his *Theory of Moral Sentiments*—the rarely read counterpoint to *Wealth of Nations*.

25. Parry and Bloch summarize their celebrated collection of essays by writing, "Each of our case studies, we argue, reveals a strikingly similar concern with the relationship between a cycle of short-term exchange which is the legitimate domain of individual—often acquisitive—activity, and a cycle of long-term exchanges concerned with the reproduction of the social and cosmic order; and in each case the way in which the two are articulated turns out to be very similar. This suggests something very general about the relationship between the transient individual and the enduring social order which transcends the individual" (1989:2). My point is that American culture largely denies the "articulation" of the short-term self with the long-term social.

26. As noted above, Bauman writes that "The 'quantum' of economics is the optimizing individual. All of economics ultimately boils down to the behavior of such individuals" (2005:vii). Becker writes that "the economic approach provides a framework applicable to all human behavior—to all types of decisions and to people of all walks of life" (in Friedland and Robertson 1990:18).

27. See Mauss (1990:3).

28. See Mauss (1990:71, emphasis added). In French, *Qu'on adopte donc comme principe de notre vie ce qui a toujours été un principe et le sera toujours: sortir de soi, donner, librement et obligatoirement. . . .* Many have tried to resolve this *et*, though I think Mauss meant the formulation to be irresolvable. Pyyhtinen, for instance, writes "according to Mauss there are no voluntary and free gifts, but the gift is always marked by three obligations: the obligation to give, the obligation to receive and the obligation to reciprocate" (2014:11). This may be true, but the point is that one may always refuse these sorts of obligations. Mauss clearly says gifts are voluntary *and* are subject to a sense of obligation. To deny the voluntary element of a gift is to conceive of it as something other than a gift. It is a commandment, a tithe, a payment. Such payments are always specified. A gift is always unspecified in some respect (i.e. in type, size, timing, or something else) in order to underline the performative voluntariness.

29. Polanyi (1957, 1977).

30. Parry and Bloch note that for Aristotle exchange for profit was unnatural and harmful to the household (1989:2). Hirschman notes that from Plato to the Middle Ages European thinkers conceived of humans as torn between reason and passions. It was only in the modern era that the more sanitized (and calculable) notion of "interests" was born (2013). In this sense Durkheim, and disciples like Mauss, are returning us to something more like the ancient understanding—with the caveat that "passions" are not the enemy of reason.

31. See Graeber (2001:151–228).

32. This is from Godbout and Caillé, *The World of the Gift* (1998), as found in Epstein (2018:79).

33. This is the famed "agonistic giving" glossed as *potlatch* that Franz Boas finds among the native peoples of the Pacific Northwest.

34. Graeber writes, "Within human economies, motives are assumed to be complex. When a lord gives a gift to a retainer, there is no reason to doubt that it is inspired by a genuine desire to benefit that retainer, even if it is also a strategic move designed to ensure loyalty, and an act of magnificence meant to remind everyone else that he is great and the retainer small. There is no sense of contradiction here. Similarly, gifts between equals are usually fraught with many layers of love, envy, pride, spite, communal solidarity, or any of a dozen other things. Speculating on such matters is a major form of daily entertainment. What's missing, though is any sense that the most selfish ('self interested') motive is necessarily the real one . . . " (2011:238).

35. See Wilk and Cliggett. (2007: 174).

36. See Venkatesh (2000).

37. Venkatesh writes, "What had formed in the Robert Taylor Homes was a complex 'social economy,' that is, systematic patterns of exchange of goods and services

that had spatial, institutional, and cultural dimensions and so were more than simply 'adaptations,' that is, mechanistic behavioral responses to poverty. Throughout the community, the flowering underground economy affirmed social relationships, many of which had been in place before the 1970s, by creating patterns of obligation, reciprocity, and expectation among tenants. Conversely, the established networks and associations facilitated the introduction and consolidation of material and social exchange among individuals, households, and buildings" (2000:105).

38. Bourgois writes, "The appeal of the crack economy is not limited to a simple dollars and sense logic" (2003:91).

39. Hoffer writes, "Drug dealers' motives and customer interactions were too complex to be understood using this one-dimensional [i.e. self-interested] approach" (2006:108) and, more succinctly, "dealing heroin is not just about the money" (2006:xix).

40. Bourgois and Schonburg write, "a community of addicted bodies that is held together by a moral economy of sharing. . . . This gift giving envelops them in a web of mutual obligations and also establishes the boundaries of their community" (2009:6).

41. See Mohamed et al. (2010).

42. See Appadurai (1986). I am not the only one to forward such an argument. Gudeman, for instance, makes the case that "economy is built around the dialectical relation of two value realms, mutuality and trade, and contains a tension between two ways of making material life—for the self and for others" (2008:14). However, he goes on to say that "When markets expand, local constructions of economy are fragmented as calculated relationships replace mutuality" (2008:19). It seems to me that illegal drug sales have expanded to quite astonishing levels, but still depend very much on mutuality, and reinforce that mutuality.

43. In fairness to the economists, they do sometimes assert that "economics does not need to assume that individuals are selfish or greedy; their objectives may well include the happiness of friends or family, or even of people they haven't met in distant parts of the world" (Bauman 2005:4). The point is that such "objectives" have to be discrete, separable, and subject to *choice*. This is a methodological necessity of the mathematical treatment of behavior, but its disadvantage, in the case of gifts, is that it obscures the entangled and ambivalent nature of human existence. See Cohen (2014), Hill and Myatt (2010), Madrick (2014), and McCloskey (2002:25, 28) for critiques of "self-interest" from within the guild of economics. See Ng (2003) for work on the way short term interests fail to add up to better welfare or happiness. See Grossman for the ways in which economists have "modified their traditional model of consumer behaviour to incorporate the addictive aspects of illegal substances" (2005:15). What is intriguing to me is that they modify their understanding of rationality to accommodate addiction, but not to accommodate friendship. See Hoffer et al. for a study of drug "markets" that eschews many of the assumptions of economics (2009), and Mireille for a wide ranging economic assessment of the rationale, costs, and benefits of drug intervention (2001). Mireille makes the case for reasonable ways that economics can be deployed on social problems.

44. See Wilk and Cliggett (2007:194).

45. Elsewhere in the same volume they write, "The fundamental ambiguity of behavior is quite real; it reflects a compromise between diverse social and temporal priorities" (2007:194). Again, while this is sensible enough, I prefer the concept of ambivalence over ambiguity as I think it better captures the fundamental impossibility of a final resolution.

46. See Phillips (2015:16).

47. By contrast, Graeber argues that "there is no sense of contradiction" in the complex motives of the gift (2011:238), while I think there necessarily is. To me this has been clear from Mauss's original formulation, where, as quoted above, he urges us "to emerge from self, to give freely and obligatorily" (1990:71).

48. See Gudeman (2008:12).

49. See Durkheim (2005:44).

50. See Durkheim (2005:44).

51. See Durkheim (2005:38).

52. However, Guyer reminds anthropologists, who might be a little too willing to downplay the calculative rationality beloved of economists, that "If we in anthropology implicitly cede all of what used to be considered rationality to economics, this leaves us with a large problem of how to study that terrain, as people the world over search—with all the mental and physical resources available to them—for ways of making a living in a globalized economy. Theirs is not just an interpretive or expressive quest. They are building institutions as well: through imagination and the exercise of power, but also surely by calculative reasoning" (2000:1014).

53. See Dumont (1980:8).

54. See Robertson (1996:598), emphasis added. See also Goody (1958).

55. Keith Hart writes, "Against the contemporary move to replace markets with communist states, [Mauss] insists that the complex interplay between individual freedom and social obligation is synonymous with the human condition" and that "Mauss's chief ethical conclusion is that the attempt to create a free market for private contracts is utopian and just as unrealizable as its antithesis, a collective based solely on altruism. Human institutions everywhere are founded on the unity of individual and society, freedom and obligation, self-interest and concern for others" (2007:480, 481). So drug dealing is hardly an outlier. The way suburban dealing happens is consonant with the "human condition" and does not represent the "idiosyncrasies" that some economists believe it does.

56. See Terrell (2014).

Bibliography

Adler, Moshe. *Economics for the Rest of Us: Debunking the Science that Makes Life Dismal.* New York: New York Press, 2011.

Adler, Patricia A. *Wheeling and Dealing: An Ethnography of an Upper-Level Drug Dealing and Smuggling Community.* New York: Columbia University Press, 1985.

Agar, Michael. *Ripping and Running.* New York: Academic Press, 1973.

Alexander, Michelle. *The New Jim Crow: Mass Incarceration in the Age of Colorblindness.* New York: The New Press, 2012.

Allen, Douglas W. "Transaction Costs." In *Encyclopedia and Law Economics,* edited by Boudewijn Bouckaert and Gerrit De Geest, 893–922. Cheltenham: Edward Elgar, 1999.

Appadurai, Arjun. *The Social Life of Things: Commodities in Cultural Perspective.* Cambridge: Cambridge University Press, 1986.

Bauman, Yoram. *Quantum Microeconomics.* Retrieved from: http://www.smallparty.org/yoram/quantum, v. 3.2, 2005.

Becker, Howard S. *Outsiders: Studies in the Sociology of Deviance.* New York: Free Press, 1963.

Becker, Howard S. *Telling About Society.* Chicago: University of Chicago Press, 2007.

Beckert, Jens and Frank Wehinger. "In the Shadow: Illegal Markets and Economic Sociology." *Socio-Economic Review* 11, no. 1 (2013): 5–30. doi: 10.1093.

Bernasco, Wim and Scott Jacques. "Where Do Dealers Solicit Customers and Sell Them Drugs? A Micro-Level Multiple Level Study." *Journal of Contemporary Criminal Justice* 31, no. 4 (2015): 376–408. doi: 10.1177/1043986215608535.

Biernacki, Patrick and Dan Waldorf. "Snowball Sampling: Problems and Techniques of Chain Referral Sampling." *Sociological Methods and Research* 10, no. 2 (1981):141–163. doi: 10.1177/004912418101000205.

Bijker, Wiebe E. and John Law, eds., *Shaping Technology/Building Society: Studies in Sociotechnical Change.* Cambridge, MA: MIT Press, 1992:225–58.

Bloch, Maurice. "Durkheimian Anthropology and Religion: Going in and Out of Each Other's Bodies." *HAU: Journal of Ethnography* 5, no, 3 (2015): 285–99. doi: 10.14318.

Block, Fred and Margaret R. Somers. *The Power of Market Fundamentalism: Karl Polanyi's Critique.* Cambridge: Harvard University Press, 2014.

Boeri, Miriam W., David Gibson, and Liam Harby. "Cold Cook Methods: An Ethnographic Exploration on the Myths of Methamphetamine Production and Policy Implications." *The International Journal on Drug Policy* 20, no. 5 (2009): 438–43. doi: 10.1016.

Bonnie, Richard J. and Charles H. Whitebread. "The Forbidden Fruit and the Tree of Knowledge: An Inquiry into the Legal History of American Marijuana Prohibition." *Virginia Law Review* 56, no. 6 (1970): 972–1169. doi: 10.2307/1071903.

Bourdieu, Pierre. *La Distinction: Critique sociale du jugement.* Paris: Les Editions de Minuit, 1979.

Bourgois, Philippe I. *In Search of Respect: Selling Crack in El Barrio.* Cambridge: Cambridge University Press, 2003.

Bourgois, Philippe and Jeffrey Schonberg. *Righteous Dopefiend.* Berkeley: University of California Press, 2009.

Bowles, Samuel. *The Moral Economy. Why Good Incentives Are No Substitute for Good Citizens.* New Haven: Yale University Press, 2016.

Braverman, Harry. *Labor and Monopoly Capital: The Degradation of Work in the Twentieth Century*. New York: Monthly Review Press, 2015 [1974].

Bray, Francesca. *Technology and Gender: Fabrics of Power in Late Imperial China*. Berkeley: University of California Press, 1997.

Browne, Katherine E. and Barbara Lynne Milgram. *Economics and Mortality: Anthropological Approaches*. Lanham: Altamira Press, 2009.

Carey, Matthew. *Mistrust: An Ethnographic Theory*. Chicago: Hau Books, 2017.

Carling, Jørgen. "Scripting Remittances: Making Sense of Money Transfers in Transnational Relationships." *The International Migration Review* 48, no. 1 (2014): 218–62. doi: 10.1111/imre.12143.

Caulkins, Johnathan P. and Peter Reuter. "Illicit Drug Markets and Economic Irregularities." *Socio-Economic Planning Sciences* 40, no. 1 (2006): 1–14. doi:10.1177/1057567717746215.

Cepeda, Alice and Avelardo Valdez. "Behaviors Among Young Mexican American Gang-Associated Females: Sexual Relations, Partying, Substance Use, and Crime." *Journal of Adolescent Research* 18, no. 1 (2003): 90–106. doi: 10.1177/0743558402238278.

Charness, Gary and Uri Gneezy. "What's in a Name? Anonymity and Social Distance in Dictator and Ultimatum Games." *Journal of Economic Behavior & Organization* 68, no. 1 (2008): 29–35. doi: 10.2139.

Chibnik, Michael. *Anthropology, Economics, and Choice*. Austin: University of Texas Press, 2011.

Clark, Ethan L. *Cannabis Sativa for Health and Hemp*. Hauppauge: Nova Science Publishers, Inc., 2011.

Clarke, Robert and Mark Merlin. *Cannabis: Evolution and Ethnobotany*. Berkeley: University of California Press, 2013.

Cleckner, P. J. "Dope is to Get High: A Preliminary Analysis of Intracultural Variation in Drug Categories among Heavy Users and Dealers." *Addictive Diseases* 2, no. 4 (1976): 537–52.

Cohen, Daniel. *Homo Economicus: The (Lost) Prophet of Modern Times*. Malden: Polity Press, 2014.

Conley, Dalton. *Being Black, Living in the Red: Race, Wealth, and Social Policy in America*. Berkeley: University of California Press, 1999.

Conley, Dalton. *Honky*. Berkeley: University of California Press, 2000.

Coyle, Dianne. *Sex, Drugs and Economics: An Unconventional Introduction to Economics*. New York: Texere Publishing, 2002.

Crawford, David. "Suburban Drug Dealing: A Case Study in Ambivalent Economics." *Research in Economic Anthropology*, 36 (2016): 197–219. doi: 10.1108/S0190-128120160000036008.

Crawford, David. *Moroccan Households in the World Economy: Labor and Inequality in a Berber Village*. Baton Rouge: Louisiana State University Press, 2008.

Curtis, Ric and Travis Wendel. "Toward the Development of a Typology of Illegal Drug Markets." In *Crime Prevention Studies Volume 11*, edited by Mangai Natarajan and Mike Hough, 121–52. Boulder: Lynne Rienner Publishers, 2000.

Derrida, Jacques. *Given Time*. Chicago: University of Chicago Press, 1992.

Desai, Meghnad. *Marx's Revenge: The Resurgence of Capitalism and the Death of Statist Socialism*. New York: Verso Books, 2002.

Dorn, Nicholas, Karim Murji, and Nigel South. *Traffickers: Drug Markets and Law Enforcement*. London: Routledge, 1992.

Dressler, William, Kathryn Oths, and Clarence Gravlee. "Race and Ethnicity in Public Health Research: Models to Explain Public Health Discrepancies." *Annual Review of Anthropology* 34, no. 1 (2005): 231–52. doi: 10.1146

Du Bois, W. E. B. *The Souls of Black Folk*. Chicago: A.C. McClurg, 1903.

Dunlap, Eloise, Bruce D. Johnson, and Ali Manwar. "A Successful Female Crack Dealer: Case Study in Deviant Behavior." *Deviant Behavior* 15, no. 1 (1994): 1–25. doi: 10.1080/01639625.

Dumont, Louis. *Homo Hierarchicus*. Chicago: University of Chicago Press, 1980.

Durkheim, Emile. "The Dualism of Human Nature and its Social Conditions." *Durkheimian Studies/Études Durkheimiennes* 11 (2005): 35–45. http://www.jstor.org/stable/23866721.

Epstein, Robert. *Chaucer's Gifts*. Cardiff: University of Wales Press, 2018.

Etzioni, Amitai. *The Moral Dimension: Toward a New Economics*. New York: Free Press, 1988.

European Monitoring Centre for Drugs and Drug Addiction. "Cannabis drug profile." EMCDDA.europa.eu. http://www.emcdda.europa.eu/publications/drug-profiles/cannabis (accessed June 19, 2018).

Fairlie, Robert W. "Drug Dealing and Legitimate Self-Employment." *Journal of Labor and Economics* 20, no. 3 (2002): 538–37. doi: 10.1086/339610.

Fitzgerald, John Lawrence. "Mapping the Experience of Drug Dealing Risk Environments: An Ethnographic Case Study." *The International Journal on Drug Policy* 20 (3) (2009): 261–69. http://www.ncbi.nlm.nih.gov/pubmed/19171472.

Foster, James. "Documented Deaths by Caffeine." CaffeineInformer.com. Accessed July 6, 2018. https://www.caffeineinformer.com/a-real-life-death-by-caffeine.

Frank, Arthur W. "Why Study People's Stories? The Dialogical Ethics of Narrative Analysis." *International Journal of Qualitative Methods* 1 (1) (2002):109–17. http://ejournals.library.ualberta.ca/index.php/IJQM/article/view/4616.

Franzen, Axel and Sonja Pointner. "Anonymity in the Dictator Game Revisited." *Journal of Economic Behavior & Organization* 81, no. 1 (2012): 74–81. doi: 10.1016/j.jebo.2011.09.005.

Friedland, Roger and A. F. Robertson. *Beyond the Marketplace: Rethinking Economy and Society*. New York: Aldine de Gruyter, 1990.

Friedman, Samuel R., Peter L. Flom, Benny J. Kottiri, Alan Neaigus, Milagros Sandoval, Richard Curtis, Bruce D. Johnson, and Don C. Des Jarlais. "Drug Dealing and Attitudes and Norms about Drug Dealing Among Young Adults and Their Peers in a High-Risk Community." *International Journal of Drug Policy* 14, no. 3 (2003): 261–68. doi: 10.1016/S0955-3959(03)00068-9.

Frith, Kirk and Gerard McElwee. "An Emergent Entrepreneur? A Story of a Drug-Dealer in a Restricted Entrepreneurial Environment." *Society and Business Review* 2, no. 3 (2007): 270–86. doi: 10.1108/17465680710825460.

Geertz, Clifford. "The Cerebral Savage: On the Work of Claude Levi-Strauss." *Encounter*, 28, no. 4 (1967): 25–32.

Goel, Sharad, and Matthew J. Salganik. "Assessing Respondent-Driven Sampling." *Proceedings of the National Academy of Sciences of the United States of America* 107, no. 15 (2010): 6734–747. doi: 10.1073/pnas.1000261107.

Godbout, Jacques and Alan Caillé. *The World of the Gift*. London: McGill-Queens University Press, 1998.

Goody, Jack. *The Developmental Cycle in Domestic Groups*. Cambridge: Cambridge University Press, 1958.

Gootenberg, Paul. *Andean Cocaine: The Making of a Global Drug*. Chapel Hill: University of North Carolina Press, 2009.

Gootenberg, Paul. *Cocaine: Global Histories*. New York: Routledge, 1999.

Graeber, David. *Toward an Anthropological Theory of Value: The False Coin of our Own Dreams*. New York: Palgrave Macmillan, 2001.

Graeber, David. *Fragments of an Anarchist Anthropology*. Chicago: Prickly Paradigm Press, 2004.

Graeber, David. *Debt: The First 5,000 Years*. New York: Melville House, 2011.

Grossman, Michael. "Individual Behaviours and Substance Use: The Role of Price." *Advances in Health Economics and Health Services Research* 16 (2005): 15–39. doi: 10.3386/w10948.

Gudeman, Stephen. *Economy's Tension: The Dialectics of Community and Market*. Oxford: Berghahn Books, 2008.

Gupta, Vanita. "The 40-Year War on Drugs: It's Not Fair, and It's Not Working." American Civil Liberties Union of Washington State. June 1, 2011. Accessed September 11, 2015. https://www.aclu.org/blog/smart-justice/sentencing-reform/40-year-war-drugs-its-not-fair-and-its-not-working.

Guyer, Jane I. "Rationality or Reasoning? Comment on Heath Pearson's "Homo Economicus Goes Native, 1859–1945." *History of Political Economy* 32, no. 4 (2000): 1011–15. Doi: 10.1215/00182702-32-4-1011.

Hagerman, Margaret A. *White Kids: Growing Up with Privilege in a Racially Divided America*. New York: NYU Press, 2018.

Hammerstein, Peter and Edward H. Hagen. "The Second Wave of Evolutionary Economics in Biology." *Trends in Ecology & Evolution* 20, no. 11 (2005): 604–609. doi: 10.1016/j.tree.2005.07.012.

Hann, Chris and Keith Hart. *Economic Anthropology*. Cambridge: Polity, 2011.

Hannerz, Ulf. *Soulside: Inquiries into Ghetto Culture and Community*. Chicago: University of Chicago Press, 2014 [1969].

Hart, Keith. *The Hit Man's Dilemma*. Chicago: Prickly Paradigm Press, 2005.

Hart, Keith. "Marcel Mauss: In Pursuit of the Whole. A Review Essay." *Comparative Studies in Society and History* 49, no. 2 (2007): 473–85. doi: 10.1017/S0010417507000564.

Hart, Keith, Jean-Louis Laville, and Antonio David Cattani. *The Human Economy: A Citizen's Guide*. New York: Polity Press, 2011.

Henslin, James. *Social Problems: A Down-to-Earth Approach, Eighth Edition*. New York: Pearson, 2008.

Hill, Roderick and Anthony Myatt. *The Economics Anti-Textbook: A Critical Thinker's Guide to Microeconomics*. Black Point: Fernwood Publishers, 2010.

Hirschman, Albert O. *The Passions and the Interests: Political Arguments for Capitalism before its Triumph*. Princeton: Princeton University Press, 2013.

Hoffer, Lee D. *Junkie Business: The Evolution and Operation of a Heroin Dealing Network*. Belmont: Wadsworth Publishing, 2006.

Hoffer, Lee D., Georgiy Bobashev, and Robert J. Morris. "Researching a Local Heroin Market as a Complex Adaptive System." *American Journal of Community Psychology* 44, nos. 3–4 (2009): 273–86. doi: 10.1007/s10464-009-9268-2.

Jacobson, Mireille. "Drug Deals: Prices, Policies, and use Rates" PhD diss., Harvard University, 2001, UMI Dissertations Publishing.

Ibson, John. *Picturing Men: A Century of Male Relationships in Everyday American Photography*. Chicago: University of Chicago Press, 2012.

Jacques, Scott and Andrea Allen. "Drug Market Violence: Virtual Anarchy, Police Pressure, Predation, and Retaliation." *Criminal Justice Review* 40, no. 1 (2014): 87–99. doi: 10.1177/0734016814553266.

Jacques, Scott and Richard Wright. *Code of the Suburb: Inside the World of Young Middle-Class Drug Dealers*. Chicago: University of Chicago Press, 2015.

Johnston, Lloyd D., Patrick M. O'Malley, Richard A. Miech, Jerald G. Bachman, John E. Schulenburg. "Monitoring the Future National Survey Results on Drug Use 1975–2015." Ann Arbor: The Institute for Social Research, 2016. http://www.monitoringthefuture.org/pubs/monographs/mtf-overview2015.pdf.

Kant, Immanuel. *Prolegomena to any Future Metaphysics and the Letter to Marcus Herz, February 1772*. Translated by James W. Wellington. Indianapolis: Hackett Publishing Company, Inc., 2010.

Karch, Steven B. *A Brief History of Cocaine*. Boca Raton: CRC Press, 2005.

Kelley, Pam. *Money Rock: A Family's History of Cocaine, Race, and Ambition on the New South*. New York: The New Press, 2018.

Kelly, Brian C. and Jeffrey T. Parsons. "Predictors and Comparisons of Cocaine use in Club Subcultures." *American Journal of Alcohol Abuse* 34 (6): 774–81, 2009. doi:10.1080/00952990802455451.

Kleiman, Mark. "Modeling Drug Markets: Overview," John F. Kennedy School of Government, Program in Criminal Justice Policy and Management, Harvard University, Cambridge, MA, 1991.

Kleiman, Mark A. R., Jonathan P. Caulkins, Angela Hawken, and Beau Kilmer. "Eight Questions for Drug Policy Research." *Issues in Science and Technology* 28, no. 4 (2012). https://issues.org/kleiman-2/

Kleinman, Arthur, Veena Das, and Margaret Lock, eds. *Social Suffering.* Berkeley: University of California Press, 1997.

Kropotkin, Peter. *Mutual Aid: A Factor of Evolution.* Newburyport: Dover Publications, 1902.

Langer, John. "Drug Entrepreneurs and Dealing Culture." *Social Problems* 24, no. 3 (1977): 377–86. doi: 10.2307/800090

Levine, Harry Gene and Craig Reinarman. *Crack in America: Demon Drugs and Social Justice.* Berkeley: University of California Press, 1997.

Levitt, Steven D. and Stephen J. Dubner. *Freakonomics: A Rogue Economist Explores the Hidden Side of Everything.* London: Allen Lane, 2005.

Liebow, Elliot. *Tally's Corner: A Study of Negro Streetcorner Men.* Boston: Little, Brown, and Co., 1967.

Lindegaard, Marie Rosenkrantz, and Scott Jacques. "Agency as a Cause of Crime." *Deviant Behavior* 35, no. 2 (2014): 85–100. doi: 10.1080/01639625.2013.822205.

Lucas, Robert E. B., and Oded Stark. "Motivations to Remit: Evidence from Botswana." *Journal of Political Economy* 93, no. 5 (1985): 901–18. doi: 10.1086/261341.

Lui, Meizhu, Barbara Robles, Betsy Leonder-Wright, Rose Brewer, and Rebecca Adamson. *The Color of Wealth.* New York: The New Press, 2006.

Madrick, Jeff. *Seven Bad Ideas: How Mainstream Economists have Damaged America and the World.* New York: Alfred A. Knopf, 2014.

Maher, Lisa. "Don't Leave Us this Way: Ethnography and Injecting Drug use in the Age of AIDS." *International Journal of Drug Policy* 13, no. 4 (2002): 311–25. doi: 10.1016/S0955-3959(02)00118-4.

Maher, Lisa. *The Illicit Drugs Reporting System Trial: Ethnographic Monitoring Component.* Sydney: National Drug and Alcohol Research Centre, 1996.

Mauss, Marcel. *The Gift: The Form and Reason for Exchange in Archaic Societies.* New York: W. W. Norton, 1990.

McCloskey, Deirdre. *The Secret Sins of Economics.* Chicago: Prickly Paradigm Press, 2002.

Merlin, M. D. "Archaeological Evidence for the Tradition of Psychoactive Plant use in the Old World." *Economic Botany* 57, no. 3 (2003): 295–323.

Mills, C. Wright. *The Sociological Imagination.* Oxford: Oxford University Press, 1959.

Mitchell, Timothy. "The Work of Economics: How a Discipline Makes Its World." *European Journal of Sociology/Archives Européennes De Sociologie/Europäisches Archiv Für Soziologie,* vol. 46, no. 2, 2005, pp. 297–320. *JSTOR,* www.jstor.org/stable/23999581.

Moeller, Kim. "Drug Market Criminology: Combining Economic and Criminological Research on Illicit Drug Markets." *International Criminal Justice Review.* 28 (2010) 1–15. 105756771774621.10.1177/1057567717746215.

Mohamed, A. Rafik and Erik D. Fritsvold. *Dorm Room Dealers: Drugs and the Privileges of Race and Class.* Boulder: Lynne Rienner Publishers, 2010.

Morningstar, Patricia J. and Dale D. Chitwood. "How Women and Men Get Cocaine: Sex-Role Stereotypes and Acquisitions Patterns." *Journal of Psychoactive Drugs* 19, no. 2 (1987): 135–42. Doi: 10.1080/02791072.1987.10472397.

Murphy, Sheigla, Dan Waldorf, and Craig Reinarman. "Drifting into dealing: Becoming a Cocaine Seller." *Qualitative Sociology* 13, no. 4 (1990): 321–43. doi: 10.1007/BF00989408.

Musto, David. "America's First Cocaine Epidemic." *The Wilson Quarterly* 13, no. 3 (1989): 59–64. http://www.jstor.org/stable/40257908.

Natarajan, Mangai. "Understanding the Structure of a Large Heroin Distribution Network: A Quantitative Analysis of Qualitative Data." *Journal of Quantitative Criminology* 22, no. 2 (2006): 171–92. Doi: 10.1007/s10940-006-9007-x.

National Drug Intelligence Center. "National Drug Threat Assessment 2011." U.S. Department of Justice. Published August 2011 and accessed on June 7, 2018. https://www.justice.gov/archive/ndic/pubs44/44849/44849p.pdf.

National Institute on Drug Abuse. DrugAbuse.gov. https://www.drugabuse.gov/.

Newton, David E., Ph.D. *Marijuana: A Reference Handbook*. Santa Barbara: ABC-CLIO, 2013.

Ng, Yew-Kwang. "From Preference to Happiness: Towards a More Complete Welfare Economics." *Social Choice and Welfare* 20, no. 2 (2003): 307–50. doi: 10.1007/s003550200184.

Nordstrom, Carolyn. *Global Outlaws: Crime, Money, and Power in the Contemporary World*. Berkeley: University of California Press, 2007.

Page, J. Bryan and Merrill Singer. *Comprehending Drug Use: Ethnographic Research at the Social Margins*. New Brunswick: Rutgers University Press, 2010.

Paris, Valerie. "Why do Americans spend so much on pharmaceuticals?" PBS. Published February 7, 2014 and accessed on June 6, 2018. https://www.pbs.org/newshour/health/americans-spend-much-pharmaceuticals.

Parry, Jonathan and Maurice Bloch. *Money and the Morality of Exchange*. Cambridge: Cambridge University Press, 1989.

Pendergrast, Mark. *For God, Country and Coca-Cola: The Definitive History of the Great American Soft Drink and the Company that Makes It*. New York: Basic Books, 2000.

Phillips, Adam. "Against Self-Criticism." *London Review of Books* 37, no. 5 (2015): 13–16, https://www.lrb.co.uk/v37/n05/adam-phillips/against-self-criticism.

Polanyi, Karl. *The Great Transformation*. Boston: Beacon Press, 1957.

Polanyi, Karl. *The Livelihood of Man*. New York: Academic Press, 1977.

Pyyhtinen, Olli. *The Gift and its Paradoxes*. Surrey: Ashgate Publishing, 2014.

Reding, Nick. *Methland: The Death and Life of an American Small Town*. New York: Bloomsbury Press, 2010.

Reuter, Peter. *Disorganized Crime: The Economics of the Visible Hand*. Cambridge: MIT Press, 1983.

Reuter, Peter and Mark A. R. Kleiman. "Risks and Prices: An Economic Analysis of Drug Enforcement." *Crime and Justice* 7 (1986): 289–340. doi: 10.1086/449116.

Robertson, A. F. "The Development of Meaning: Ontogeny and Culture." *Journal of the Royal Anthropological Institute* 2, no. 2 (1996): 591–610. doi: 10.2307/3034298.

Rosenfeld, Sophia. "Free to Choose: How Americans have become tyrannized by the culture's overinvestment in choice." *The Nation*. June 3, 2014. Accessed November 21, 2018. https://www.thenation.com/article/free-choose/.

Royster, Deirdre. *Race and the Invisible Hand: How White Networks Exclude Black Men From Blue-Collar Jobs*. Berkeley: University of California Press, 2003.

Rubin, Vera. *World Anthropology: Cannabis and Culture*. Munchen: Walter de Gruyter, 2011.

Schaffer Library of Drug Policy. "A Fiscal Analysis of Marijuana Decriminalization." DrugLibrary.org. Accessed on June 4, 2018. http://druglibrary.org/schaffer/hemp/moscone/chap1.htm.

Singer, Merrill. *Something Dangerous: Emergent and Changing Illicit Drug use and Community Health*. Long Grove: Waveland Press, 2006.

Singer, Merrill. *Introduction to Syndemics: A Critical Systems Approach to Public and Community Health*. New York: Wiley, 2009.

Salganik, Matthew J. and Douglas D. Heckathorn. "Sampling and Estimation in Hidden Populations using Respondent-Driven Sampling." *Sociological Methodology* 34 (1) (2004): 193–240. http://www.jstor.org/stable/3649374.

Sales, Paloma and Sheigla Murphy. "San Francisco's Freelancing Ecstasy Dealers: Towards a Sociological Understanding of Drug Markets." *Journal of Drug Issues* (2007): 919–50.

Schwyzer, Hugo. "Turns Out Women Have Really, Really Strong Sex Drives: Can Men Handle It?" The Atlantic. Published on June 6, 2013 and accessed on June 6, 2018.

https://www.theatlantic.com/sexes/archive/2013/06/turns-out-women-have-really-really-strong-sex-drives-can-men-handle-it/276598/.

Sterk, Claire. *Fast Lives: Women Who use Crack Cocaine.* Philadelphia: Temple University Press, 1999.

St. Pierre, Allen. "Whack and Stack: 2010 Marijuana Cultivation Eradication in America." *Norml* (blog). June 27, 2011. Accessed July 6, 2018. http://blog.norml.org/2011/06/27/whack-and-stack-2010-marijuana-cultivation-eradication-in-america/.

Substance Abuse and Mental Health Services Administration. "SAMHSA's National Help Line." Samhsa.gov. https://www.samhsa.gov/find-help/national-helpline.

Terkel, Studs. *Working.* New York: Ballantine, 1972.

Terkel, Studs. *American Dreams, Lost and Found.* New York: Pantheon Books, 1980.

Terrell, John Edward. *A Talent for Friendship: Rediscovery of a Remarkable Trait.* Oxford: Oxford University Press, 2014.

Terrell, John Edward. "Evolution and the American Myth of the Individual." New York Times Opinionator. Published November 30, 2014 and accessed on November 17, 2018. https://opinionator.blogs.nytimes.com/2014/11/30/evolution-and-the-american-myth-of-the-individual/?module=BlogPost-ReadMore&version=Blog%20Main&action=Click&contentCollection=The%20Stone&pgtype=Blogs&region=Body#more-155102.

Veblen, Thorstein. *The Theory of the Leisure Class.* New York: Open Road Media, 2016.

Vellinga, Menno, ed. *The Political Economy of the Drug Industry: Latin America and the International System.* Gainesville: University of Florida Press, 2004.

Venkatesh, Sudhir Alladi. *American Project: The Rise and Fall of a Modern Ghetto.* Cambridge: Harvard University Press, 2000.

Visweswaran, Kamala. "Race and the Culture of Anthropology." *American Anthropologist* 100, no. 1 (1998): 70–83. doi: 10.1525/aa.1998.100.1.70.

Waldorf, Dan. *Careers in Dope.* Englewood Cliffs: Prentice Hall, 1973.

Waldorf, Dan and Patrick Biernacki. "The Natural Recovery from Opiate Addiction—Some Preliminary Findings." *Journal of Drug Issues* 11, no. 1 (1981): 61–74. doi: 10.1177/002204268101100104.

Waldorf, Dan, Craig Reinarman, and Sheigla Murphy. *Cocaine Changes: The Experience of Using and Quitting.* Philadelphia: Temple University Press, 1992.

Weber, Max. *From Max Weber,* tr. and ed. by H. H. Gerth, and C. Wright Mills. New York: Free Press, 1946.

Wherry, Frederick F. *The Culture of Markets.* Hoboken: Wiley, 2013.

Wilk, Richard R. and Lisa C. Cliggett. *Economies and Cultures: Foundations of Economic Anthropology.* Boulder: Westview Press, 2007.

Winant, Howard and Michael Omi. *Racial Formation in the United States: From the 1960s to the 1990s.* New York: Routledge, 1994.

Woody, Christopher. "NARCONOMICS: 'The real drugs millionaires are right here in the United States.'" Business Insider. Published March 16, 2016 and accessed on June 7, 2018. http://www.businessinsider.com/where-drug-money-goes-2016-3/.

Index

alcohol, 6, 7, 9, 24, 38, 94, 112; as deadly recreational substance, 117; as gateway drug, 48
Alcoholics Anonymous, 112
alkaloids, 7–8
Altamont, x
America, at war with itself, x
American Dream (Terkel), 125
American Enterprise Institute, 70
American Studies Department, Cal State Fullerton, 125
amphetamines, xv, 21
Andean Indians, 6–7, 8, 115
Appadurai, Arjun, 130n42
Arthur (interviewee), xx, 46, 47, 49, 51; cocaine collective of, 46, 47, 50, 51, 52, 65, 101, 105; as drug dealer to friends, 46, 50–51, 60n2; as drug user, 47, 47–48, 49; family support for, 52; grandparents of, 47; Letterman as code, 111, 113; as parent, 103; parents of, 47, 52, 53; quitting selling of cocaine, 101; Shawn as dealer and friend, 48–49, 49–50; from Southern California, xix, 47; Tyler as dealer and friend, 48–49, 49–50; wholesale connections of, 50

behavioral economics, 120
Bernhardt, Sarah, 7
blacks, xxivn45, xxvin62
Blow, 13
Bolivia, 6
border, with Mexico, 87
Brad (interviewee), xix, xx, 40–42, 107–108; arrest of, 38, 41; as athlete, 28, 29, 30, 31, 33, 35–36, 36; cocaine and, 38–40, 101–102, 105, 114–115; college and, 28, 35–36; Ecstasy sale

by, 36, 37, 39; Elliot as friend of, 34–35, 36, 37, 38, 39, 42, 108; as *entrepôt*, 27; experience of, 36, 37–38, 38–39, 114; family finances of, 29–30, 35; father loss of, 28–29

hallucinogens sale by, 36; as hippie, 36–37; in jail, 34; LSD sale by, 37, 101; MDMA sale by, 37; mother of, 28–29, 34; from New Jersey, 27; personal disintegration of, 39; pot and, 28, 29, 30–32; as pot dealer, 32, 33–34, 101; pot suppliers and, 34–35; psychedelic mushrooms sale by, 36, 37–38, 38–39, 114; quitting drugs, 42; sense of responsibility of, 28–29; as suburban drug dealer, 28

Bray, Francesca, 118
Breaking Bad, xvii
the Bronx, New York, 14

caffeine, 7, 9
cannabidiol (CBD), 3
cannabinoids, 3, 4, 86
cannabinol (CBN), 3
cannabis, ix, xv, xviii–xix, 2–3, 4; as agricultural heritage of North America, 4; Amnesia Haze as, 96; chemistry of, 1; consumption of, 2; culture of, 1; decriminalization of, 2, 4, 12n16; early popularity of, xi; from friends, 9; illegality of, 4; Kush, 85, 96; laws, 85; legalization of, 2, 4, 12n16, 85–89, 93; sale by container, 31; sale by weight, 31; social acceptability of, 87, 93. *See also* marijuana
Cannabis afghani, 2
Cannabis Cup (1998), 79

141

and, xiv

upper level dealing, 13
urban drug dealing, xii, 45, 67; crack
    cocaine and, xv, 116, 118; flagrant
    drug dealing and, xiv, 13, 19;
    prosecutions for, x; as retail, 13

Valium, 38
vaporizer, 4
vasoconstrictor, 6
Venkatesh, Sudhir Alladi, 125, 129n37
Verne, Jules, 7
Victoria (queen), 7
Vin Mariani, xi, 6–7
violence, drug dealing and, ix,
    xvi–xvii, xxiin3, xxvn54, 19

war on drugs, communities of color
    and, xxiin9
Watergate, x
Wayne (interviewee), xix, xx, 46, 52–53,
    57–58, 59; arrest of, 55, 58–59; as
    cocaine dealer, 46, 54, 60n6, 105;
    drug dealing, risk of, 55; as drug
    user, 46, 54; family support for, 55;
    on fatherhood, 101; father of, 54; on
    friends, 58; generosity of, 53, 56;
    mother of, 54; partying by, 54, 55,
56, 63, 101; quitting drugs, 58–59,
    101; risk evaluation by, 55–56; sex
    and, 63–64, 110
wealth, as aphrodisiac for women, 62
wealth disparities, xxiin10
weed, 4, 21, 87, 94. *See also* cannabis;
    marijuana; pot
Weeds, xvii
white policing, in poor communities,
    xxiiin22
white privilege, x, xxiin9
Wilk, Richard, 125, 126
wine tonic, 6–7
Woody (interviewee), xx, 64, 68–69, 94;
    as cocaine dealer, 65–67, 91–94, 102;
    from Colorado, xix, 64; friends
    pricing and, 66; on getting older,
    92–93; on his generation, 93; on
    parenting, 92–93, 99; partying by,
    65, 66, 67, 92; on quitting selling of
    cocaine, 91–94; on risk, 92; sex,
    cocaine and, 67–68; socializing and,
    67, 68
"Work in American Culture"
    (Crawford and Steiner), 125
Working (Terkel), 125
World of Warcraft, 98–99

Xanax, 38

About the Author

David Crawford received his BA in American Studies from Cal State Fullerton, and a PhD in Anthropology from the University of California, Santa Barbara. He is the author of two other books and the editor of one. He teaches at Fairfield University in Connecticut.

www.ingramcontent.com/pod-product-compliance
Lightning Source LLC
Chambersburg PA
CBHW022320280326
41932CB00010B/1164